AGRARIAN SOCIETY OF THE PUNJAB

Agrarian Society of the Punjab

(1849–1901)

HIMADRI BANERJEE

MANOHAR

2026

First published 1982
POD reprint 2026

ISBN 978-93-88540-71-1

Published by
Ajay Kumar Jain *for*
Manohar Publishers & Distributors
4753/23 Ansari Road, Daryaganj
New Delhi 110 002

Printed and bound in India

To the Memory
of
My Father

Contents

Abbreviations

Official Positions

AC Assistant Commissioner
CC Chief Commissioner
CR Commissoner of the Punjab Superintendent of a division
DC Deputy Commissioner of a district
DCS Deputy Commissioner of Settlement
DJ Divisional Judge
DLRA Director of Land Records and Agriculture, Punjab
EAC Extra Assistant Commissioner
FC Financial Commissioner, Punjab
IGI Inspector General of Irrigation, Punjab
JAC Judicial Assistant Commissioner
Jr. Secy. Junior Secretary
LG Lieutenant Governor of the Punjab
Offg. Officiating
SC Settlement Collector
SLC Settlement Commissioner, Punjab
SO Settlement Officer
Sr. Secy. Senior Secretary

India Government Records

Foreign (Secret) Secret Consultation, Foreign Department

Rev and Agr	Revenue and Agriculture Department Proceedings
(A)	Revenue and Agriculture Department, Agriculture Branch
(AH)	Revenue and Agriculture Department, Agriculture and Horticulture Branch
(F)	Revenue and Agriculture Department, Famine Branch
(LR)	Revenue and Agriculture Department, Land Revenue Branch
(R)	Revenue and Agriculture Department, Revenue Branch
Home (J)	Home Department, Judicial Branch
Home (Public)	Home Department, Public Branch
KW	Keep-With to Proceedings

Punjab Government Records

PGR Rev and Agr	Revenue and Agriculture Department Proceedings, Punjab Government
(R)	Revenue and Agriculture Department, Revenue Branch
(Irrigation)	Revenue and Agriculture Department, Irrigation Branch

Official Documents and Other Publications

Agricultural Indebtedness	*Report on Agricultural Indebtedness and Land Alienation to Money-lenders in Parts of the Rawalpindi Division*
A.R.	*Assessment Report*
D.G.	*District Gazetteer*
ERR	*Extracts from the Revenue* (or *Land Revenue) Administration Reports* (of local officers bound with the Provincial Revenue or Land Revenue Report)

FC Selections	*Selections from the Records of the Office of the Financial Commissioner, Punjab*, New Series
India Selections (*F*)	*Selections from the Records of the Government of India, Foreign Department*
India Selections (P.W.D.)	*Selections from the Records of the Government of India, Public Works Department*
LAR	*Annual Report on the Punjab Alienation of Land Act XIII of 1900*
P.A.R.	*General Report on the Administration of the Punjab and its Dependencies*
Parl. Papers	*Parliamentary Papers*
P.P.B.E.C.	*Report of the Punjab Provincial Banking Enquiry Committee, 1929-30*
Public Selections	*Selections from the Public Correspondence of the Punjab Administration*
Punjab Selections	*Selections from the Records of the Government of the Punjab and its Dependencies*, New Series
Punjab Famine Report, 1878-79	*Punjab Report in Reply to Inquiries issued by the Famine Commission, 1878-79*
RR	*Annual Report on the Revenue* (or *Land Revenue*) *Administration of the Punjab*
S.M.	*Punjab Settlement Manual*
S.R.	*Settlement Report*

Preface

This book is a revised version of my Ph.D. thesis. In this work I had the opportunity to utilise only the official records and reports available in India. The Punjab Government records preserved in the India Office Library, London and the Punjab Board of Revenue, Lahore remained beyond my reach.

In course of my research I have been fortunate enough to receive help from various sources. I am most indebted to Dr. Binay Bhusan Chaudhuri for introducing me to the study of agrarian history and for providing me with the indispensable stimulus and encouragement throughout the period. I must also thank Dr. A.C. Banerjee, Dr. S. Sen, Dr. A. Dasgupta and Dr. B. De for showing a keen interest in my research. Equally helpful was the assistance provided by Dr. Ganda Singh and Dr. Fauja Singh at Patiala. At the National Archives Shri S. Sarkar provided assistance on a generous scale. Dr. B.S. Nijjar, Director of the Punjab State Archives and Mr. H.R. Saggi, Librarian were always very helpful and sympathetic. The Indian Council of Historical Research extended necessary financial assistance for research work at Patiala.

I owe a special debt to the Librarian and staff of the West Bengal Secretariat Library, Calcutta for locating many valuable official records for my research. In the final stage of my research I also received many valuable suggestions from Dr. Indu Banga, Dr. Kenneth Jones, Dr. Tom Kessinger and Dr. Barbara Ramusack. I am greatly indebted to Dr. B. Bapui who have read the entire manuscript in draft and given me his valuable suggestions. Shri Ramesh C. Jain of Manohar Publications was always very accommodating and I am also thankful to him.

Himadri Banerjee

Introduction

The present work is an attempt at a study of some of the major influences to which the agrarian society of the Punjab was exposed during the second half of the 19th century. The starting point of this enquiry is the beginning of British rule in the Punjab in 1849 and it ends in 1901, the year of the introduction of the Land Alienation Act (Act XIII of 1900). This study covers nearly the whole of the British Punjab as it stood prior to the creation of the North-Western Frontier Province at the beginning of the present century. Only the two north-eastern hill districts, namely, Kangra and Simla, have been left out in view of their distinct topographical and climatic conditions which mark them out from the rest of the province. The numerous Native States also lie outside its purview, since the British land laws did not apply there and the impact of the socio-economic changes experienced by the districts directly under British rule was felt only partially in those places.

The exact nature of the impact of British rule on the Indian economy has long been a fascinating subject of debate among scholars. Quite a few of them think that potential elements of growth in the pre-British Indian economy have been frustrated by British colonial exploitations. They therefore regard British rule as nothing but a period of growing economic impoverishment. Factors like new forms of landholding, insecurity of tenure, over-assessment and the high rental demand 'opened up a golden age for the money-lender'. Another important feature of the new order of the things was the cultivation of certain commercial crops which often led to the growth of universal indebtedness among the members of the rural proprietary body and of their gradual expropriation from the ancestral holdings. Thus the old social framework of agriculture witnessed, these scholars concluded, a gradual breakdown under British rule while the Indian economy was characterised by a long spell of stagnation.

Such an argument has been questioned by many scholars. Dr. Morris D. Morris, for example, while propounding the rival view contended that no such general decline characterised the Indian economy during British rule. He questioned the conventional doctrine that the pre-British economy was ready for an industrial and general growth and the conclusion he reached was that 'the British did not take over a society that was ripe for an industrial revolution and then frustrate the development'. It is argued that given the lack of political stability, low agricultural and non-agricultural productivity and an insignificant commerce, per capita income was relatively low in the Indian subcontinent in the centuries before about say 1800. About the general behaviour of the Indian economy in the 19th century on the other hand the 'tentative conclusion' of Prof. Morris is that during this period the per capita output grew and the growth may have been substantial.

In view of these conflicting opinions among scholars, it would be worthwhile to take up the Punjab during the second half of the 19th century as a test case. Actually in this province the British administration got a unique opportunity of introducing certain administrative experiments which were hardly possible in many of the old regulated provinces like Bengal. During these years the Punjab with its enterprising peasantry in the prosperous canal colonies was considered to be a model of British administrative efficiency. 'At the heart of the Punjab political tradition', it is argued. 'lay the desire to create and preserve a stable rural base'. As the champion of the hereditary proprietary village communities against the conflicting claims of the intermediaries, whom they regarded as 'useless drones on the soil', the British settlement officers were often looked upon as the *ma baap* by the peasantry. In some cases this attitude survived the disquieting indebtedness and expropriation of the peasant proprietors towards the close of the century. The Land Alienation Act of 1901 was simply 'a renewal of the ideological and emotional commitments' of British officialdom to the Indian peasantry.

This period naturally forms an interesting subject of research in India and abroad .In course of the past two decades a number of books have been published. . Norman Dr G. Barrier's *The Punjab Alienation of Land Bill of 1900* (Durham, N.C., 1965) is a notable contribution to our understanding of the agrarian history of the Punjab. However, the choice of his theme—the formulation and enforcement of the Punjab Land Alienation Act—precluded a detailed discussion of the major determinants of the agrarian economy of this period. In his study, he deals chiefly with the various aspects of the problem of growing rural indebtedness and transfers of land in the second half of the 19th century.

Another important contribution in this field of research was made by Dr. P.H.M.van den Dungen. His book, *The Punjab Tradition* (London, 1972) provides a wealth of new data on the changing phases of official opinion on the problem of growing rural indebtedness and transfers of land in the Punjab from 1869 to 1909. Dr. Dungen's main contention was that different local officers, even at the district level, played a very significant role in formulating the general official policy on land transfers and the final enactment on indebtedness was the result of the response of the Government of India to arguments mainly emanating from the local officers. According to him, the Punjab officials since the time of Sir John Lawrence sought to promote rural peace and the loyalty of the peasant proprietors to British rule. Since he entirely concentrated on the evolution of an official policy, various agrarian changes that had little or no bearing on this main field of investigation, inevitably fell outside the purview of his study.

Dr. Tom G. Kessinger's study on the village of *Vilyatpur 1848-1968* (University of California Press, 1974) is another significant contribution. Dr. Kessinger has narrated, mainly on the basis of extant village revenue records which have largely been ignored by the historians of the Punjab society, the story of socio-economic transformation of a Jullundur *Doab* village during the period from 1848 to 1968. According to him, there was a general improvement in the behaviour of the rural economy during these years. The position of the Sahotas (a subcaste of the Jats) who enjoyed a position of pre-eminence in 1848 by virtue of their ownership of village lands, underwent a significant change over the years. With the opening out of the markets, the village economy was linked with the outside world and there were changes in the techniques of cultivation, crop pattern and land utilisation. There was also a definite increase in the per capita output and investment in agriculture. New job opportunities resulted in a good deal of mobility among the *sepidars*. They were no longer ready to accept the unchallenged leadership of the Sahotas in the village. Dr. Kessinger's findings do not understandably apply to the whole of the Punjab of our period. There were a good deal of regional variations in the agrarian economy of the Punjab which were not clearly evident from the writings of Dr. Kessinger. Actually the populous and prosperous Jullundur *Doab* villages do not represent the behaviour of the agrarian economy across the Indus. The frontier districts, more particularly the Daman and Marwat villages, generally presented an altogether different rural scene. Here the nature was not always very bountiful and villages of the ordinary type were few and far between. Society in such a place was generally subservient to tribal custom and mobility of labour was universally discouraged by the Pathan landlords of this tract.

The present work is an attempt to fill some of the gaps in the existing studies on the agrarain society of the Punjab. Here an attempt has been made to study the rural changes at two levels: in the first place, to study and analyse some significant trends in the agrarian economy of the Punjab during the second half of the 19th century and secondly, to explain the changes in the social framework of agriculture. These two aspects of the agrarian society are no doubt interrelated and often indistinguishable from one another. The present study makes this distinction simply for the sake of convenience.

The present work starts with a general description of the agrarian society at the time of the annexation of the Punjab. The story is narrated in the first chapter with a special reference to its regional variations like annual rainfall, crop pattern, distribution and composition of the proprietary body. It also deals with the numerous occupational groups who rendered manifold services in connection with the usual agricultural operations almost throughout the year.

Early Brititsh records make it clear that the agrarian society of the Punjab as the British found it did contain some potential elements of growth. But it would require a lot of investments in the way of capital and human efforts to make them yield the expected results. Government initiative in canal construction to effect a permanent solution of the irrigation problem of the Indo-Gangetic plain made a promising start in this direction. The second chapter is a study of its impact on the production organization and peasant economy of the Punjab, leading among other things to a new form of colonial settlement in the *bar* lands. But while concentrating on the beneficial aspects of canal irrigation, the present work takes care to give sufficient coverage to the critics of the canal system. Here clarification of the relevant views of the different authorities has also been attempted.

This period also witnessed a growing commercialization of agriculture in the province. This development has also received the attention of scholars over the years. Many of them concluded that this was merely another form of subsistence agriculture functioning under certain distinct historical conditions. It was their impression that its benefits did not reach the proprietors because of their universal indebtedness to the rural *sahukars*. This view has been subjected to a close look in the third chapter and a detailed and careful reading of the available source materials has been attempted towards a better understanding of the problem. This chapter, while analysing the circumstances leading to the growth of commercialization of agriculture, deals with the cultivation of three important crops, namely, wheat, cotton and sugar-cane and its impact on the rural economy of the province.

British land revenue administration and the development of the settlement policy form the subject matter of the next chapter. During Sikh rule the state demand was mostly collected in kind while the British Government now claimed it in cash. It was also accompanied by a gradual increase in the quantum of state demand from time to time. There were changes in the structure of revenue administration which deeply affected the position of the landholders. While analysing these developments the much debated question of the quantum of land revenue and its close relations with the rural debt problem have also been taken up in this chapter.

Notable changes also occurred in the rural credit relations of this period. The bulk of this credit came from the *sahukars* who played a decisive role in the rural economy of the province through the financing cultivation and marketisation of agricultural products. Their control over rural credit gave them a decisive role in the production organization and in very many places such a control was reinforced by the acquisition of the proprietary right. This affected certain aspects of the agrarian relations. A general decline of agriculture in the province is often related to this development. The new group of landlords, it is argued, were often no better than a mere parasitic element with little interest in the cultivation of their purchased holdings, so that the emergence of this group led to a general depression in the agrarian economy. Such an argument is open to question and there is evidence, as summarised in the fifth chapter of the present work, which shows that transfers of holdings did not necessarily mean a change for the worse, with regard to the effective cultivation of land.

There were also some striking developments in the landlord-tenant relations during the period under review. In a number of submontane and south-eastern districts rent enhancement led to a protracted legal battle over their respective rights on land while in the extreme west along the frontiers, tenants could hardly air their grievances because of the dominant position of the landlords in the agrarian economy. But in a few central districts across the Chenab, tenants were in a position of extraordinary advantage; they were masters of the situation and frequently dictated terms to their proprietors. These regional variations in the landlord-tenant relations suggest a considerable modification of their customary relations prevailing at the time of the annexation. This period also witnessed two successive pieces of tenancy legislation designed to bring this relation within a legal framework. All these developments have been taken up in the sixth chapter of the present work.

Certain significant changes occurred at another level of agrarian relationship—the relationship of the peasant proprietors with their village servants. They constituted a considerable section of the rural population, rendered invaluable service almost throughout the year and their wages were determined by customary rules. But it is often argued that they suffered miserably under British rule and their wages also considerably declined by the end of the last century. This view, however, scarcely holds good for the entire Punjab and the last chapter of the present works deals with the changing status and economic condition of the village servants.

1

Agrarian Society at the Outset of British Rule

The annexation of the Punjab began a 'full enquiry into the rights and liabilities of all persons having an interest in the soil'[1] and the reports of the early settlement officers contain a mass of information about them. They reveal that apart from a small group of intermediaries in some particular regions between the state and the peasant owners, there were three broad layers in the agrarian society of the Punjab: peasant proprietors, tenants, and artisans and menials.

At the outset of British rule in the Punjab, the 'great mass of landed property' was held by the small peasant proprietors, cultivating all or part of holdings.[2] They derived their rights over the land from their (or from their ancestors') contributions to the foundation of new villages by clearing and colonizing the waste. Such were the *morigads*[3] who claimed to have planted the first stake on the soil. From these *morigads* land usually passed to their heirs in successive generations, descending from father to all his sons of the same mother in equal proportions. Land passed to other members or nearest relatives, only in the absence of male heirs. Those who inherited and cultivated land were generally known as the zamindars. This form of colonization and inheritance of land was common among the Jats[4] and Gujars of the south-eastern and central districts of the province.[5] In many of the south-eastern districts, the members of the proprietary body were 'often united by real or assumed ties of kinship' and their rights and duties over village lands were generally measured by ancestral shares. But in the central districts, the administration of the Sikhs 'had created a state of things in which the land in each man's possession had to be recognized as the measure of his liabilities, and also of his right in any common property or profits.[6]

Rights over land in the Punjab also developed by virtue of conquest.[7] In the frontier districts like Hazara and Bannu many warlike tribes (for example, the Biloches and the Pathans) occupied land as conquerors. They claimed and established their rights over conquered areas which they termed *ilaqa* while they regarded themselves as *waris*. These conquering tribes were very jealous of their rights and never allowed others to claim this important status. Occasionally strangers were allowed to settle and cultivate certain shares of their village lands, but 'this right was never confused with the *wirasat*[8] which belonged only to the conquering and superior families'.[9]

At the outset of British rule, however, the position of these traditional landowning families was not always a very happy one. Many settlement officers reported that they fared very badly at the hands of the Sikh revenue officials and in a number of districts they were frequently deprived of their 'old privileges and superiorities'.[10] This miserable plight of the traditional landlords was a legacy of a hundred years' of Sikh rule in the Punjab and the early settlement reports also did not fail to mention some of the causes of it.

The dominant ambition of the Sikh Government was the collection of the maximum possible amount of revenue from the land. This, the Sikhs were intelligent enough to grasp, needed the rapid colonization of the vast, uninhabited and unreclaimed tracts and the steady extension of cultivation. In the context of an abundance of land and scarcity of labour,any cultivator (it was immaterial whether he was a proprietor of land or a mere cultivator having no proprietary right over land) who undertook the pioneering task of breaking the waste lands, bringing them under the plough or introducing any permanent improvement in the techniques of cultivation, naturally earned the universal admiration and support of the Sikh revenue officials. It greatly strengthened their position over their operational holdings. Further the revenue demand of the Sikhs was generally so heavy that it became almost 'the paramount consideration' of many proprietors 'to have it distributed on the greatest number of shoulders'.[11] And so far as its payment was concerned, the Sikhs had no 'respect for the antecedent status of the occupants of the soil'. Those who paid the revenue were strongly protected by them; but those who failed were shown no mercy.[12] They virtually treated every landholder as equal, a mere 'revenue-producing machine'.[13] In many cases, the hereditary owners of lands and other cultivators were placed 'on the same miserable plain'. If any proprietor failed to pay his revenue, 'the Government took it from the cultivator, who from that time was looked upon as the owner of the land'.[14] Consequently, in many districts the rights of the older proprietors were overridden to such an extent that their position virtually became 'nothing more than an empty name'.[15] This process of change, however, went to very different lengths in different districts of the province and deserves special attention.

To begin with, in the arid south-western districts of Multan and Muzaffargarh, a vast tract of land was originally held by a motley group like the descendants of former pastoral tribes, holy men, broken down *jagirdars* and other officials.[16] When Sawan Mall[17] was deputed to settle the land revenue of this region, he was fully convinced that these men were incapable of extending cultivation over the waste lands. So he encouraged 'strangers and Hindu capitalists to sink wells, dig canals, and cultivate the lands of the nominal owners'. At the same time he did secure to the latter a share of the produce often known as *hakk zamindari* in this part of the province. Beyond the payment of that fee, these cultivators were made perfectly independent of the old proprietors and were not thenceforth liable to ejectment, even if their lands remained uncultivated.[18] In a number of central Punjab districts an equally important change occurred. Thus from Gujrat the settlement officer reported that the members of the village proprietary body (who were generally the descendants of different warlike tribes) were often so harshly treated by the Sikhs that their position became 'symbols more of misery than of benefit'. Perhaps anticipating that these traditional landowners of this tract, with their local influence and power, might create difficulties in the consolidation of their rule, the Sikhs tried to set aside their rights by settling lands in favour of the actual tillers of the soil. The *waris* descended from the original founder of the village and the ordinary cultivator, whose father or grandfather had settled in it, were thus often placed on a common footing. '*Malikana* dues were unknown. Ancestral shares were forgotten or had fallen entirely into disuse. *Malba* was levied from both alike upon the extent of cultivating possession, so (were) the revenue, cesses, burdens of every kind'.[19] Similarly in some of the north-western districts they fared no better at the hands of the Sikhs. In Hazara, for example, the rights of the *waris* survived only in villages where the Sikhs gave them *jagirs* or in parts of the country where it did not suit them to interfere directly.[20]

In as much as the Sikh rule weakened the hold of the traditional proprietary families on land, it also strengthened the position of the actual tillers of the soil on their respective holdings in the same proportion. With the Sikhs 'each class was estimated at its cultivating power';[21] consequently, whenever the choice lay between an idle and extravagant proprietor and an industrious cultivator, they generally did not hesitate to support the latter. In their drive to extend cultivation over the waste lands,[22] they even overlooked the usurpation of proprietary right by these enterprising band of cultivators in different districts of the province.[23] Thus many of the cultivators of 'industrious races' gradually acquired the rights of the older proprietors 'whose lands they had originally been content to cultivate'.[24] This policy of the Sikhs often gave rise to 'quasi-proprietary tenures, known by various names' in different parts of the Sikh empire.[25] Thus in the districts of Gujrat, Jhelum and Rawalpindi this tenure was generally known as *malik kabza* which indicated that the holder's ownership was limited to the land actually in his possession and he had no right over the village waste. He, however, could let, sell or mortgage this piece of land as he pleased and he was also responsible for the payment of its revenue.[26] Similarly, *chakdars*, *taraddadkars* and *sildars* also enjoyed full ownership over their holdings, but were only subjected to the payment of certain fees to their original owners.[27] 'The proprietary right of the holders of these tenures was underlined by the fact that they could get their lands cultivated by tenants'.[28]

This significant change in the rural landed property right thus brought in its train an interesting form of double ownership in certain districts of the province. These tenures were generally recorded in the cis-Sutlej and south-western districts; there it was frequently found that the proprietary right over land was often 'split up among two or more individuals'. The original owners of lands were entitled to certain quit rents while the incoming cultivators enjoyed almost all the rights and privileges associated with the proprietary right. This form of double tenure was caused by the declining influence of the traditional landowning families (usually regarded as *ala maliks* or superior proprietors by the settlement officers) over the *chakdars* and other cultivators (generally described as *adna maliks* or inferior proprietors in the British settlement records) under the Sikhs.[29]

Besides these rural proprietors, there were also tenants closely associated with the village agrarian production organization. Many of them were descendants of those whose ancestors helped the village proprietary body in the foundation of new villages. Many again were related to the proprietors by ties of kinship and assisted them in repelling the attacks of common foes.[30] The persistent pressure from the Government to maintain the land in a high state of cultivation or else to make room for others who could do it, compelled the village proprietors to induce these tenants to settle in their villages and share the heavy burden of land revenue. In addition to the land revenue, the tenants also paid cesses, *kamiana* and other proprietary dues in different districts of the province.[31] Sometimes the proprietors also received some petty services, such as supply of wood and grass from them.[32] 'So long as the tenants paid the revenue to the state and charges due to the village or the proprietor, they were not ejected from their lands'[33] Many of them were again allowed to transmit their cultivating possession to their descendants.[34]

The village proprietors also did not usually challenge these rights because land was then plentiful and cultivators were scarce; anybody who broke the waste and shared the revenue of the state thus conferred a privilege on the proprietary body. They were 'in a general way obliged to consult their wishes and interests'.[35] Their rights might have been occasionally violated by individual proprietors, but this did not necessarily lead to their arbitrary eviction from their lands they had cultivated over the years. Such evictions, though recognized in customary rules, were condemned by 'the sense of the country'.[36] In cases when such evictions actually occurred, these were 'ordinarily provoked by infractions of tribal usage or of personal obligations to a superior, by feuds and quarrels, or by the intrigues of a tenant with the rivals or enemies of his lord'.[37] Otherwise the zamindars were not ordinarily keen on exercising this right, because 'there was never any occasion to do so: so little was land coveted at that period'.[38]

Another vital aspect of the agrarian society of the Punjab at the outset of British rule was the services rendered by the *kamins* to the zamindars. They assisted the zamindars almost throughout the year: the tarkhan or carpenter fabricated the plough and kept it in good repair; the lohar or blacksmith usually made the iron plough; the kumhar or potter supplied all the earthen vessels for the use of the persian wheels. These *kamin* groups also included menials like chamars and churas. They were mostly 'of aboriginal and vagrant stocks',[39] who, after abandoning their vagrant habits, gradually settled down in the rural tracts to work as village menials. The chamars made the leather holders, whips, ropes and bands, required by the zamindars while the churas were the sweepers of the village.

These village servants, however, did not always enjoy a very respectable status in the agrarian society. Some of them were considered untouchables and outcastes, for instance, the churas and chamars. At the bottom of the *kamin* community stood the churas who used to eat carrion and carry nightsoil. Just above them were the chamars who took all the hides of dead cattle and flesh of cloven-footed animals which were not touched by the lohars and tarkhans. Their low social or ritual status in fact derived from such degrading occupations. They were allowed to reside only in the outlying areas of the village, not inhabited by zamindars. But the kumhars, tarkhans and lohars enjoyed a slightly higher status. They were sometimes regarded as higher *kamins*.[40]

These *kamins* received their wages in kind at harvest from the common heap of produce. Their wages were generally determined by the utility of their services rendered to the community and bore no relations to their status in the rural society. Thus *kamins* enjoying the highest remuneration included artisans and menials like the tarkhans, lohars and chamars whose services were regarded as essential in connection with agricultural operations. But the kumhars received a somewhat lower rate of wages though their status was slightly higher than that of a chamar. They were, however, better paid in well-cultivated tracts, for there they were regularly employed to supply earthen jars for the persian wheels. Elsewhere, particularly in dry areas, they were not always regarded as regular *kamins* and accordingly their rates and wages were much lower.[41] These payments to village artisans and menials indicated their right to a fixed portion of agricultural surplus at the time of harvest. Usually they were not deprived of their shares by the zamindars. But occasionally they faced extreme difficulties in recovering their rightful dues and were compelled to render forced labour. Leaving aside these exceptional cases of hardships, they were generally found working in close co-operation with the village zamindars.

Zamindars again received their necessary credit from the village *Sahukars*.[42] It is commonly believed that the Punjab was not their original homeland. They had gradually spread in the province from the south and south-east. They first settled into towns; from such centres they then started shops in the village and gradually diffused themselves among the members of the agrarian society.[43] These *sahukars* were divided into innumerable groups and there was scarcely a village without them.

Zamindars borrowed from the *sahukars* to meet their 'four necessary purposes'—food, cattle purchase, seed and land revenue payment. They also took loans to defray expenses on occasions of marriages or of other rituals, kept a running account with them and tried to repay their debts when the harvest was over. These *sahukars* did not usually demand an exorbitant rate of interest because of the wide prevalence of the *damdupat* principle, according to which the interest on a loan accumulated only to the extent of the capital and never beyond it. The common rate of interest was one per cent. 'To charge more than one per cent was considered a mark of unsound business'.[44] But even then, if the *sahukars* tried to exact a higher rate of interest, the *kardars* immediately intervened.[45] The Government sought to maintain cultivation at the highest level so as to raise from land as much revenue as possible. But a *sahukar's* exploitations might cause desertion of zamindars from their cultivable holdings, eventually leading to a decline in cultivation and a loss of revenue. Consequently, the *kardars* intervened with a view to preventing these developments.

During Sikh rule the village *sahukar*, when he lent money, received payment out of the surplus of the first good yield and did not usually attempt to exact usurious interest. He was then considered to be the 'humble accountant' and 'servant of the dominant class—the agricultural community'.[64] In most cases, their relationship with the zamindars was one of mutual dependence and they shared their prosperity and adversity. But in the frontier districts, these *sahukars* were almost universally hated and many of the contemporary proverbs bear ample testimony to this fact.[47] In Bannu and Muzaffargarh they were even forbidden to wear a turban and had to work under extremely difficult conditions. They were the object of 'unmentionable indignities'. They were commonly regarded as *kirars*, a word almost synonymous with coward. Here they were often brutally manhandled and even murdered. Herbert Edwardes, Assistant to the Resident at Lahore, mentioned a few such occurrences in his diaries.[48] The fact was that they were mostly Hindus and their harsh trade transactions with the poor Muslim cultivators of the western Punjab made them an object of universal hatred.

It is, however, extremely difficult to gauge their indebtedness at the hands of these *sahukars*. It is commonly assumed that in many parts of the province such indebtedness prevailed on a large-scale. In the Gurdaspur district, as a result of the Sikh practice of collecting revenue before the crop was cut, as one settlement officer wrote, the zamindar was forced to borrow from the *sahukars*, at 25 per cent annual interest.[49] Similarly on the eve of the annexation, in Shahpur there were few proprietors who had no credit relations with the *sahukars* of the district.[50] In Marwat also zamindars took loans from their creditors in order to meet the land revenue demand of the Government. This indebtedness in a number of cases gave rise to sale and mortgage of land in different parts of the province.[51]

In spite of their indebtedness and consequent transfers of lands, we do not come across any large-scale eviction of the zamindars by the money-lenders. In those days, it was universally believed that a 'man might be starved, but he could not be enslaved' by a money-lender; what prevented the large-scale eviction and appropriation of the zamindars' holdings was the prevalence of factors like the effective enforcement of the pre-emption laws, abundance of cultivable waste, non-availability of markets and the existence of low prices of agricultural produce in the rural society of the province. Besides the Sikh revenue officials greatly discouraged this process, fearing that it might lead to a decline in cultivation and an eventual loss of revenue to the state.[52]

While the *sahukars* were thus discouraged from evicting their indebted clients, they had enough security for the recovery of their debts. An important factor in this was the universal social approval of debt payment.[53] It was widely believed that with all his assets, 'the debts of grandfather also descended to the father and from him to his son', the interest affording to money-lenders 'a comfortable subsistence'. Though discouraged from evicting the owners from their lands, they, however, found that the state eagerly supported their cause against a person trying to evade the repayment of his debt.

The behaviour of the agrarian economy understandably varied from region to region. These variations were due to both geographic and demographic factors. In the submontane districts like Hoshiarpur, Gurdaspur, Ambala and Sialkot, agriculture had already attained a substantial level of development. Regular rainfall and steady growth of population encouraged agriculturists, belonging to sturdy races like the Jats and Arains, to extend cultivation and at the outset of British rule there was practically very little land left to be brought under the plough.[54]

But the south-eastern districts like Hissar, Rohtak and Karnal presented a different picture largely because of the abundance of cultivable waste and scarcity of population. Zamindars had larger holdings and there was a general cry for cultivators to bring these wastes under the plough. The situation was made worse by the frequent failures of rain and insecurity of harvest. Occasionally zamindars were rewarded with a bumper harvest, but 'good years were few and bad years were many'. Above all, there was frequent anarchy leading to desertion of cultivators from their ancestral holdings.[55]

Agriculture was not prosperous in the central Punjab *bar* lands. The *bar* was 'a rich maiden soil covered with grass and underwood' and generally 'thinly populated by widely scattered villages of herdsmen and thieves' who generally tended their own cattle.[56] Occasionally, some parts of the *bar* were cultivated by the indigenous nomads, popularly known as the Janglis with the aid of their primitive agricultural implements. Actually irregular rainfall coupled with an extreme temperature prevented enterprising rural folk from settling there and bringing these lands under the plough. According to one estimate nearly one-third of this tract still remained uncultivated on the eve of British rule.[57]

In the south-west, in districts like Multan and Montgomery, prosperous villages were occasionally visible. In this tract, due to precarious rainfall, cultivation was only possible on the lands protected by wells or by other means of artificial irrigation. But during Sawan Mall's administration a systematic attempt was made to bring more lands under the plough by encouraging enterprising cultivators to settle and invest in the construction of wells. He also caused canals to be dug and thus made life and property secure.[58] These canals provided irrigation to the kharif crops during the inundation periods of the rivers Chenab and Sutlej. Thus cultivation increased and agriculture often became a remunerative occupation. It was then estimated that 'in Multan alone about one-half of the fields' were under the tillage, 'abundantly watered' by means of persian wheels.

But agricultural prosperity reached a high water-mark in a number of central Punjab districts. This was largely due to the dry climate, regular rainfall, fertile lands enriched by the flood deposits and the enterprising nature of the proprietary body. Here prosperous agrarian communities under the leadership of the Jat zamindars produced different varieties of crops and they were universally regarded as the finest specimen of the Punjab peasant proprietors. Their chief products were wheat and other kinds of grain, indigo, sugar, opium, cotton, hemp and oil seeds while their gardens yielded guavas, dates, mangoes, limes, lemons, peaches, apricots, figs and 'a great variety of fruits unknown even by name to Europeans'.[59]

Of the different central Punjab districts, some deserve our special attention. On the eve of British rule Jullundur was in a high state of cultivation and there was practically no waste brushwood or forest whatsoever.[60] Similarly exhaustively cultivated were rural tracts around Gujrat[31] and Shahpur.[62] In Lahore also a remarkable increase in cultivation occurred. However, in the 'Rechna Doab portion of the District, the land though in many places of fair quality, was little cultivated.'[63]

Agriculture was thus not equally prosperous throughout the province. This partly accounted for the wide variations in the economic conditions of rural proprietors from region to region. To begin with, in Jullundur and Amritsar the zamindars were comparatively better off than in the dry rainless parts of the western Punjab. In many of the *manjha* villages, amidst dry climate combined with normal rainfall, the Jat zamindars tried their best to get the maximum return from their ancestral lands. On the other hand, in the absence of permanent and reliable means of irrigation, regular cultivation in the west largely depended much on the precarious rainfall and the periodic river floods. In the south-eastern districts like Karnal and Gurgaon too their economic condition was often equally bad. Zamindars of this tract fought a relentless battle against famine, drought and scarcity throughout the year. This struggle against physical forces was frequently reflected in the character of a Jat[64] who constituted the predominant element of the proprietary body. Their relentless zeal in cultivation was only occasionally rewarded, for here not more than one good year could be expected in a cycle of five;[65] and probably two would be bad. Besides the Jats, the Meos and the Rajputs were two other important proprietary communities of this tract; but unlike the Jats they were not of an enterprising nature and consequently economically less solvent.

But the submontane districts of Sialkot, Hoshiarpur and Gurdaspur presented a somewhat different picture. In this tract zamindars were almost wholly dependent on the bounty of nature; annual rainfall of thirty to forty inches coupled with fertile lands nearly ruled out famines and rich crops could be grown widely. Consequently, zamindars were comparatively well off. But one thing frequently stood in their way to prosperity—increasing pressure of population of land, often leading to fragmentation of ancestral holdings. As small holdings invariably meant small incomes, they often had to borrow from the money-lenders. In some parts of these districts, indebtedness gradually developed. In Gurdaspur, for example, borrowing for the purpose of paying land revenue was quite common while in Sialkot their indebtedness had already assumed a dangerous proportion on the eve of British rule.[66]

No account of the agrarian economy would be complete without a reference to the trade in the agricultural produce of this period.[67] Wheat and maize, produced nearly everywhere in the province, constituted two important articles of trade;[68] they were often exported to foreign markets of Kabul and central Asia. Of other articles of trade mention should also be made of pepper, sugar, dried ginger and turmeric,[69] sent down the Indus by country boats. The province also had a brisk internal trade and the Mughal roads served as an important line of communication.

In these trade transactions Amritsar was commonly regarded as the busiest commercial centre.[70] It was centrally situated and was linked up with the major wheat-producing districts by the Mughal roads. Merchants from Kashmir and Afghanistan as well as from other parts of the province itself assembled there; the Povindah[71] traders from the west, the Banias from the east, the Khojas from the central districts frequently thronged the grain market there, particularly during the *Diwali*. It is, however, extremely difficult to make an accurate estimate of the internal and external trade, as no registers were regularly kept at the different trading marts of the province. According to one estimate[72] it amounted to £ 122,010 in 1843 and it increased to £ 441,000 in 1847.

But during the closing years of Sikh rule, a number of circumtances greatly retarded the development of this trade. The anarchy following the death of Ranjit Singh severely restricted the quick movement of agricultural product from one part of the province to another. The high rate of customs duties levied by the different Sikh chiefs and the Lahore administration also adversely affected this trade by raising the prices of different commodities.[73] In many cases traders in order to evade these payments, took the southern routes along Multan[74] and sought to bypass the major trading centres like Amritsar and Jullundur. Naturally the trade of this province suffered.

This trade was also affected by the absence of effective means of communications. In view of the fact that the overland means of communications were mostly bullock carts or camels, an inevitable consequence of the bad state of most roads was the extremely slow movement of commodities from one part of the province to another. The old Mughal roads (due to lack of maintenance) had nearly disappeared, surviving as narrow tracts through the woods and jungles and were always infested with robbers'. These roads 'would become impassable during the rains on account of mud, so much so that the camels would sink up to their haunches in mud, while the oxen would be unable to extricate the carts which would get jammed in the mud'. The situation is best summed up in the following words of Lieutenant Colonel Steinbach[75] (who sometimes served Ranjit Singh in the capacity of a military personnel):[76]

> Since the demise of the Old Lion . . . trade has declined, owing to the distracted and insecure state of the country; the robberies upon the high road, vexatious exactions in the shape of duties and tolls, interruptions to manufactures, the absorption of capital in military armaments and civil contests, the withdrawal of large monetary resources from circulation and their removal to places of security, have all had their effect in checking and cramping mercantile operations.

NOTES

1. *S.M.*, 18.
2. *P.A.R.*, *1872-73*, 11. See also *Lahore S.R.*, *1873*, 35; *Rawalpindi D.G.*, *1883-84*, 69; *Jullundur D.G.*, *1883-84*, 28-31.
3. *Ferozepore D.G.*, *1883-84*, 55; *Sirsa S.R.*, *1884*, 322-3.
4. The Jats were so much the principal agricultural community in the Punjab that words like the Jats and the zamindars were almost used synonymously in many of the south-eastern and central districts. Thus from Ludhiana, Davidson, the settlement officer, reported: 'On approaching a village, and asking what people live in it, if any other race but Jats live in it, the name of the race will be given in reply.

But if the population are Jats, the reply will be zamindars live there. "Zemindar log buste;" in fact the word zemindar is here only applied to the Jats.' *Ludhiana S.R., 1859*, 29. See also Sir George Campbell, *Memoirs of My Indian Career*, I (Macmillan & Co., London, 1893), 59; *Rohtak S.R., 1880*, 53.

5. B.H. Baden-Powell, *The Land Systems of British India*, II (Clarendon Press, Oxford, 1892, hereafter *Land Systems*), 611.
6. *S.M.*, 69.
7. Baden-Powell, *Land Systems*, II, 634.
8. The word *wirasat* is Arabic and indicates inheritance only. But in reality this right of the *waris* arose not out of 'law but on political power in its rudest sense'. *Hazara S.R., 1876*, 109.
9. Baden-Powell, *Land Systems*, II, 635. This zealous attempt of resisting the entry of any outsiders to their rank continued even after the establishment of British rule and the contemporary official reports also did not fail to make mention of it. For details, see *P.A.R., 1872-73*, 11-2.
10. *S.M.*, 57.
11. *Rawalpindi S.R., 1865*, 170.
12. *Hazara S.R., 1876*, 125.
13. Baden-Powell, *Land Systems*, II, 635.
14. Reply from C.P. Elliot, Offg. DC Ludhiana, *Parl. Papers, 1870*, LIII, 461.
15. *S.M.*, 54.
16. *Ibid.*, 78.
17. Diwan Sawan Mall was the youngest of the three sons of Hoshnak Rai, a Chopra Khatri of Akalgarh. He was born in 1788 and in 1820 he was appointed the Accountant of Multan. In 1821 he was made Governor of a half of the province of Multan and of the whole province in 1829. He retained his post till his death in 1844. His benevolent rule contributed much to the economic prosperity of Multan. 'By his energetic, firm and just government of the province Sawan Mall succeeded in raising the province to a state of prosperity it had never attained'. For details, see Alexander Burnes, 'Political, Geographical and Commercial Reports and Papers [1835-37]', *The Panjab Past and Present*, XII-I, April 1978, 80-1; Joseph D. Cunningham, *A History of the Sikhs* (S. Chand & Co., New Delhi, 1966), 269; *Multan D.G., 1901-02*, 59-60; *Gujranwala D.G., 1893-94*, 29; Mohan Lal, *Travels in the Punjab, Afghanistan, and Turkistan* (Languages Department, Punjab, Patiala, 1971), 401.
18. H.R. James, Muzaffargarh S.R., 1850, *Public Selections*, I (Lahore, 1852), 14-5.
19. Hector Mackenzie's report on Gujrat quoted in *S.M.*, 57. Prof. Tom G. Kessinger's recent study on Vilyatpur also suggested that in some parts of Jullundur district the Jats 'virtually replaced the Muslim Rajputs as the district's main revenue payers' even during Sikh rule. Similarly Prof. Indu Banga pointed out that in Amritsar district the

Rajputs were 'completely ousted' by the Jats, Kambohs and Arains. For details, see Tom G. Kessinger, *Vilyatpur 1848-1968: Social and Economic Change in a North Indian Village* (University of California Press, 1974), 29; Indu Banga, *Agrarian System of the Sikhs* (Manohar Book Service, New Delhi, 1978), 170.

20. Actually Captain Hector Mackenzie's settlement report on Gujrat clearly revealed that in the wilder tracts along the Indus, the Sikhs granted some significant concessions to the *maliks* of the warlike tribes because they enjoyed 'a position of authority in the tribe or community'. Incidentally, these *maliks* also held important official positions like *muqaddams*. Where the land revenue was collected in kind, the Sikhs often gave them *inams*; sometimes they also exempted a certain portion of their land from assessment. In return these *maliks* collected the revenue and managed the affairs of their villages. This practice of collecting land revenue through the *maliks* continued even afterwards. For details, see *S.M.*, 57-8.
21. Memorandum by P.S. Melvill, Offg. CR Amritsar division. *Parl. Papers, 1870*, LIII, 524.
22. The Lahore administration specifically instructed the *kardars* to 'provide for the proper cultivation of the land'; actually their 'energies were entirely directed towards extending the agricultural resources' and 'to maintain cultivation at the highest possible level'. The following instruction towards the *kardars* deserves special attention: 'Treat the subjects well. Work in extending cultivation. . . . Every harvest and every year let cultivation and the revenue increase'. For details, see *Muzaffargarh S.R., 1882*, 52; Sita Ram Kohli, 'Land Revenue Administration under Maharaja Ranjit Singh', *The Panjab Past and Present*, V-II, October 1971, 448.
23. *Sialkot S.R., 1865*, 98.
24. *P.A.R., 1849-50 and 1850-51*, 101.
25. Banga, *op. cit.*, 176.
26. *S.M.*, 67.
27. *Ibid.*, 79-85.
28. Banga, *op. cit.*, 178.
29. *S.M.*, 67-8, 80-2.
30. Memorandum by H.C. Fanshawe, Offg. Jr. Secy. Punjab, Rev and Agr (R) May 1885, 20A.
31. Banga, *op. cit.*, 182.
32. *Hazara S.R., 1876*, 110.
33. Banga, *op. cit.*, 181.
34. For details, see Chapter VI.
35. Reply from J.M. Macnabb, DC Sialkot, *Parl. Papers, 1870*, LIII, 458.
36. Memorandum by Colonel E. Lake, FC Punjab, *Ibid.*, 437.
37. *Hazara S.R., 1876*, 124-5.
38. Reply from Major W.R. Elliot, DC Karnal, *Parl. Papers, 1870*, LIII, 462.

39. Denzil Ibbetson, *Panjab Castes, Being a reprint of the Chapter on 'the Races, Castes and Tribes of the People' in the Report on the Census of the Panjab published in 1883 by the late Sir Denzil Ibbetson, K.C.S.I.* (Languages Department, Punjab, Patiala, 1970), 266-7.
40. *Ibid.*, 270.
41. For details, see Chapter VII.
42. The extent of their dependence on *sahukars* is thus indicated by a contemporary proverb:

    'Guru bin gat nahin,
    Shah bin pat nahin.'

    [Without the Guru, there is be no salvation;
    without the money-lender, there is no reputation.]
43. S.S. Thorburn, *Musalmans and Money-lenders in the Punjab* (William Blackwood & Sons, Edinburgh, 1886, hereafter *M.M.*), 36.
44. *Hazara S.R., 1876*, 85. The following proverb further illustrates this point: '*Mota biaj shahumaran khowe*' i.e.. Too great interest ruins the money-lender. See also Major J. Clarke, 'Some Accounts of the Agricultural Condition and Operations of Perguna Goojranwala', *Public Selections*, II (Lahore, 1854), 133-8.
45. Malcolm Lyall Darling, *The Punjab Peasant in Prosperity and Debt* (Manohar Book Service, New Delhi, 1977, hereafter *Punjab Peasant*), 170.
46. Thorburn, *M.M.*, 37-8.
47. For example, one proverb says:

    'Kan, kirar, kuta da,
    Visah na kije sute da.'

    [Even if they sleep, do not trust a crow, a *kirar* and a dog.]
48. Thus Herbert Edwardes wrote in his diary: 'In Bunnoo the position of the Hindoos was peculiarly degraded . . . entirely dependent on the individual Mullicks. . . . Once when I was encamped in the Sooraunee tuppehs, two half-buried human bodies were discovered, whose wounds bore evidence to the violence of their death. I was afraid they were some of my own men, and instant inquiry was made in camp; when some Bunnoochees came forward to explain that they were "only two Hindoos, who had gone out without a guard to collect some debts".' Major Herbert B. Edwardes, *A Year on the Punjab Frontier in 1848-49* (Languages Department, Punjab, Patiala, 1971), 81-2.
49. *Gurdaspur S.R., 1859*, 21.
50. *Punjab Government Records*, VI, *Lahore Political Diaries, 1847-1849, Political Diaries of Lieutenant Reynell G. Taylor, Mr. P.S. Mewill, Pandit Kanahya Lal, Mr. P.A. Vans Agnew, Lieutenant J. Nicholson, Mr. L. Bowring and A.H. Cocks.* (Allahabad, n.d.), 9 February 1848, 416.
51. For details, see Chapter V.
52. It is interesting to note that during the first few years following the annexation of the Punjab, the Punjab Board of Administration largely

continued this protective policy of the Sikhs in matters of land transfers. For details, see *P.A.R., 1849-50 and 1850-51*, 78.

53. *Hazara S.R., 1876*, 85.
54. The following statistical return prepared at the time of the first provincial census (1855) will further illustrate this point:

District	Area in acres	Cultivated area in acres	Culturable area in acres	Population per square mile
1	2	3	4	5
Ambala	11,72,567	6,81,321	1,04,990	426.83
Hoshiarpur	14,10,245	6,90,216	75,242	383.63
Gurdaspur	10,72,194	7,30,274	1,06,448	470.01
Sialkot	8,64,214	5,51,052	1,17,712	475.27
Punjab	5,22,40,170	1,27,51,161	54,60,301	155.80

Source: *India Selections* (*F*), No. XI, Report on the Census taken on the 1st January 1855 of the Population of the Punjab Territories, 31.

55. Thus the condition of Kythal on the eve of British rule was described by the settlement officer: 'Many villages were altogether deserted, the owners taking refuge in large villages which were able to defend themselves both against their rulers and their fellow-subjects'. A similar condition also prevailed in Thaneswar (Karnal). For details, see Darling, *Punjab Peasant*, 219.
56. The Resident at Lahore, 25 May 1847, Foreign (Secret) Consultation, No. 136. 26 June 1847.
57. *Ibid.*
58. Thorburn, *M.M.*, 11.
59. Lieut.-Colonel Steinbach, *The Punjaub* (Languages Department, Punjab, Patiala, 1970), 46.
60. *Jullundur S.R., 1852, Parl. Papers, 1854*, LXIX, 254.
61. *Punjab Government Records*, IV, *Lahore Political Diaries, 1846-1849, Journal and Diaries of the Assistants to the Agent, Governor-General North-West Frontier and Resident at Lahore* (Allahabad, 1911), 16, 17 and 18 March 1848, 135; Sahamat Ali, *The Sikhs and Afghans* (Languages Department, Punjab, Patiala, 1970), 62.
62. *Punjab Government Records*, V, *Lahore Political Diaries, 1847-1849 Political Diaries of Lieut. H.B. Edwardes, Assistant to the Resident at Lahore* (Allahabad, 1911), 20 November 1847, 141.
63. *Lahore S.R., 1860*, 9.
64. Darling, *Punjab Peasant*, 84.
65. *Ibid.*
66. *Ibid.*, 169.
67. For details, see W.H. McLeod, 'Trade and Investment in Sixteenth and Seventeenth Century Punjab: The Testimony of the Sikh Devotional Literature', Harbans Singh and N. Gerald Barrier, eds., *Essays in Honour of Dr Ganda Singh* (Punjabi University, Patiala, 1976), 89-91; M. Elphinstone, *An Account of the Kingdom of Caubul*, I (Oxford University Press, Karachi, 1972), 383-4.

68. *P.A.R., 1849-50 and 1850-51*, 7.
69. F.C. Arora, *Commerce by River in the Punjab or a Survey of the Activities of the Marine Department of the Government of the Punjab 1861-62 to 1871-72* (Punjab Government Record Office Publications, Monograph No. 9, Lahore, 1930), xxvi.
70. Thus Ganesh Das, author of *Charbag-i-Punjab*, described Amritsar in the early 1850s: 'Today there is no other city in the whole of the Punjab which is as large as Amritsar. Merchants from all countries have come to Amritsar and settled here. Many *khatris* of Lahore have adopted Amritsar as their home'. J.S. Grewal and Indu Banga, tr. & eds., *Early Ninteenth Century Punjab* (Guru Nanak Dev University, Amritsar, 1975) 133. See also Major H.M.L. Lawrence, *Adventures of an Officer in the Punjab*, I (Languages Department, Punjab, Patiala, 1970), 214; H.L.O. Garrett., tr. & ed., *The Punjab—A Hundred Years Ago, as described by V. Jacquemont (1831) & A. Soltykoff (1842)* (Languages Department, Punjab, Patiala, 1971), 26-9.
71. For details, see David Ross, *The Land of the Five Rivers and Sindh* (Languages Department, Punjab, Patiala, 1970), 89-90; Edwardes, *op. cit.*, 382-6.
72. Arora, *op. cit.*, 25.
73. This will be further evident from the following price table of different goods per maund in Afghanistan and Lahore:

Goods brought from Afghanistan	Price in Afghanistan	Price per maund in Lahore
1	2	3
	Rs. a. p.	Rs.
Munjeet (Red dye from Mookkur near Khilat-i-Ghilzie)	9 0 0 a maund	20
Almonds (Khilat-i-Ghilzie)	6 0 0 ditto	17
Zeerub (Kandahar)	8 0 0 ditto	10
Raisins (Ditto)	2 4 0 ditto	7
Abjosh (A kind of raisin much used in medicinal preparations and brought from Kandahar also)	2 0 0 ditto	10
Figs (Kandahar)	1 4 0 ditto	7

Source: *Punjab Government Records*, V, *Lahore Political Diaries, 1847-1849, Political Diaries of Lieut. H.B. Edwardes, Assistant to the Resident at Lahore*, 5 May 1847, 112.

74. Memorandum on the Trade and Customs of the Punjab, Foreign (Secret) Consultation, No. 98, 23 September 1848.
75. For his career, see C. Grey, *European Adventures of Northern India, 1785 to 1849* (Languages Department, Punjab, Patiala, 1970), 325-6.
76. Steinbach, *op. cit.*, 49.

2

Colonization

During the second half of the 19th century there was a striking expansion of the total cultivated area of the Punjab. In the central Punjab districts a vast tract of waste land was brought under the plough, particularly after the completion of various irrigational schemes in the 1880s and 1890s. The extreme western and south-western districts also saw a rapid agricultural development. This remarkable increase in the size of cultivation was accompanied by certain significant changes in the crop pattern and standard of living, especially in the newly developing canal colonies of the province.

But on the eve of the annexation, a considerable portion of the province virtually consisted of arid waste. It was then estimated[1] that 'probably not a fourth of the culturable area was under cultivation'. The Sikhs were, however, aware of the fact that the absence of regular water supply generally obstructed any major increase of cultivation in the arid regions of the province. Accordingly steps were taken to excavate a number of inundation canals from rivers like the Chenab and Indus.[2] Well-irrigation was not neglected either. In this connection the name of Diwan Sawan Mall deserves our special attention. His benevolent rule in the districts of Multan and Muzaffargarh paved the way for the emergence of a healthy agricultural settlement[3] in the midst of wilderness. A similar attempt for the construction of wells was made 'in the tracts known as the Doaba (Jullundur and Hoshiarpur districts), Riarki (district of Gurdaspur and Tehsils of Amritsar and Ajnala) and Darap (Sialkot district and part of Gujranwala district)'.

Even after the establishment of British rule, wells continued to provide a part of the necessary water supply. In the districts of Gujranwala,[4] Sialkot,[5] Hoshiarpur[6] and Jullundur,[7] there was practically no irrigation except from wells. In other parts of the province too well-irrigation played a very significant part in the rural economy and in the last decade of the century an increase in the number of wells occurred even in Dera Ghazi Khan (30 per cent), Montgomery (24.1 per cent), Jhang (22.1 per cent) and Muzaffargarh (19.8 per cent).[8] Thus taken as a whole, the total number of wells in use in the province increased from 1,46,000 in 1849 to 3,17,000 in 1900-01.

Irrigation from wells had a far reaching impact on the rural society. With the development of well-irrigation, emphasis tended to shift from extensive to intensive cultivation around well lands.[9] It also brought about a significant change in the crop pattern during the period under review. It not only whipped up the cultivation of cash crops like pepper, cotton, tobacco and vegetables but also *chari* to feed the well-bullocks. Again in some parts of the province, it stimulated the process of consolidation of holdings by means of mutual exchanges among the zamindars.[10]

It is, however, interesting to note that the bulk of the credit for constructing these wells came from the money-lenders and it was largely an outcome of the Government policy. Usually the official assistance was in the form of a loan, hedged in with a number of formalities. Their repayments were also enforced with extreme rigidity. The amount granted was often inadequate while its rate of interest was very high. Perhaps the Government could have served the cause of irrigation better by a softer attitude. But bureaucratic lukewarmness stood in its way.[11] The increasing popularity of well-irrigation in the Punjab was, therefore, largely the result of private enterprise and not one of official endeavour.[12]

But in matters of irrigation from canals, the Punjab Government took the lead and maintained it almost throughout this period.[13] Its first fruit was the Bari Doab Canal which was expected to irrigate the *doab* lying between the Beas and Ravi. In undertaking this project the provincial government was guided by certain specific political and economic considerations.[14] One of the motives behind immediately beginning the construction work of the Bari Doab Canal was the problem of giving employment to the disbanded Sikh soldiers. It was also expected that this canal would preserve 'from uncertainty of season' the *manjha* whose inhabitants were the 'flowers of the nation'.[15] With this end in view, excavation started in 1850 and it was fully completed in 1860-61. In that year 89,756 acres were irrigated while by the close of the century it was found commanding 8,61,301 acres.[16]

In 1869 another important irrigation project was launched, namely, the Sarhind Canal. It was planned to take off from the left bank of the Sutlej so as to irrigate portions of the British districts of Ludhiana and Ferozepore, and the Native States of Patiala, Jind and Nabha, to the west of the Ghaggar.[17] The project originated from the local demand for water in the rainless tract of the province.[18] Preliminary investigations relating to its constructions had been made as early as 1836,[19] but it was not fully ready for irrigation until 1887. In 1901 this canal irrigated 9,61,927 acres and it did bring 'comparative affluence to a large population previously leading a hand-to-mouth existence, and in famine years fed multitudes of starving refugees' from Bikaner and Sirsa.[20]

Besides undertaking new projects, the Punjab Government also turned attention to the reopening and improving of some of the old canals. The Western Jumna Canal was the first work of its kind; it then irrigated only small portions of the districts of Karnal and Delhi. But imperfect construction and bad alignment of canals led to swamps and water-logging. These difficulties prompted the Government to take some positive steps to improve the situation. One such project 'contemplates the formation of additional branches to the canal for the irrigation of a large tract of country, where there is usually a deficiency of rain, and the inhabitants of which were described as industrious and very anxious for water'. Accordingly one main line extending from Indri to Manak was contemplated; further three more new main or arterial drains were opened. They not only contributed much to reducing water-logging in this tract but also increased the area commanded by irrigation.[21] With this successful realignment of the Western Jumna Canal, the three major eastern rivers

(Jumna, Ravi and Sutlej) were harnessed to irrigate some parts of the thickly populated south-eastern and central districts.

Early in the 1880s the Government also sought to divert the rivers of the Chenab, Jhelum and Indus, one after another over their respective *doabs*, thus reclaiming some 15,000 square miles of the country.[22] Except for the low-lying portions nearest the rivers, these were so far practically a desert waste. Accordingly the Government took the initiative and its first outcome were the Lower Sohag and Para Canals. These two purely inundation canals taking off from the Sutlej irrigated a moderate area just east of the city of Montgomery. They were 'constructed mainly for the purpose of bringing under cultivation a very large area of Government waste lands, which had previously been unculturable for want of water'.[23] In the early 1890s it irrigated 32,509 acres while in 1901 it actually commanded 86,163 acres.[24]

The next important landmark was the construction of the Sidhnai Canal in the Multan district. It was opened in the kharif season of 1886-87[25] for irrigating the western part of the Ravi-Sutlej watershed. Prior to the introduction of the Sidhnai Canal in this tract, 8,000 acres under the plough were in scattered plots where wells had been sunk and 'where old villages were struggling for existence'. But with the introduction of this canal new wastes were broken up and in 1900-01 nearly 1,69,780 acres were irrigated by it.[26]

Almost simultaneously the Swat River Canal brought perennial water in the north-western corner of the Peshawar valley (1885). Here the existing source of meagre water supply often caused bitter feuds among the villagers. This scheme was devised partly to redress this difficulty and partly to provide water for the high table-land lying between the Swat-Kabul rivers.[27] The area irrigated in the first year (1885-86) was 44,092 acres, which rose to 74,373 acres the very next year,[28] and to 1,66,031 acres in 1900-01.[29]

Soon the Government decided to irrigate and colonize the *Rechna Doab* lying between the Chenab and Ravi by taking waters from the Chenab. Here the lands were mostly of an excellent quality and they were entirely 'at the disposal of the Government'. But precarious rainfall rendered cultivation extremely difficult without the aid of artificial irrigation.[30]

The tract was also predominantly inhabited by pastoral and nomadic tribes doing a little occasional cultivation along the river beds in favourable season. The objects which the Punjab Government had in view in colonizing these lands had been various—one of which was 'to relieve the pressure of population in those districts where agriculture had already reached the limit which the land available for agriculture could support'.[31]

In 1862 the necessity for this irrigation project was first recognized.[23] But in 1890 it was finally decided to utilise the whole of the supply of the Chenab. It was then estimated that some 62 per cent of the total area would be 'irrigated annually by the canal,—18 per cent in the kharif and 44 per cent in the rabi'. In 1892 a perennial canal to irrigate the upper portion of the Chenab watershed was opened. It was the largest project of its kind which the Punjab Government had executed up to that time in the province. In 1901 the area commanded by this canal amounted to 1,830,525 acres.[33]

Besides constructing major perennial canals, the Government also took a keen interest in the management of various minor inundation canals. They consisted almost entirely of old works which had been repaired, restored and extended by the Government since the annexation of the Punjab. The districts irrigated by these canals had excellent soils, though their exploitation depended much on rain or irrigation. Usually these inundation canals supplied waters to the western districts during kharif season. Of the numerous such inundation canals, one deserves special attention—the Muzaffargarh inundation canal system. This canal system included a series of small canals taking their water from the Indus and Chenab in the fork of these two rivers. From 1849 to 1857 the Government could scarcely aid the people in maintaining these canals. It was only after irrigation had fallen off considerably that the Punjab Government decided to interfere and finally took it up under its direct supervision in 1880. This canal system largely secured the area of crops under its command and in 1900-01 irrigated nearly 2,93,853 acres.[34]

Canal irrigation thus increased remarkably during the period under review. This led to a significant increase in the size of cultivation. In Lahore it started even in the late 1850s with the completion of the first regular settlement. It was then estimated that the total cultivated area was approximately 6,61,000 acres or nearly 37½ per cent of the total area. With the opening of the Bari Doab Canal it increased to 8,25,684 acres (nearly 25 per cent) including 52,267 acres irrigated (1864). In the succeeding decades, this development continued and the settlement officer reported that this steady increase of cultivation was 'due almost entirely to canal extension' in the Lahore *manjha*.[53] According to settlement statistics of this period (1888-93) 'slightly over one-half the district area' was then under tillage.[36] In the northern part of the Ferozepore district (particularly in Ferozepore and Zira tahsils[37]) between 1854 (first regular settlement) and 1884 (revised settlement) the increase of cultivation was also 'very large',[38] while in its Lower Rohi circles it was comparatively less. Taken as a whole here the total increase amounted to 40 per cent.[39] In Pargana Muktsar and Ilaka Mamdot even more striking development took place during the same period.[40] In Gujrat also cultivation increased. In the 1890s it was estimated that in the 'whole district 71 per cent of area is now under cultivation, as compared with 50 per cent at revised settlement' (1874).[41] But throughout this period, this increase was not uniformly distributed over all the tahsils of this district.[42] Almost a similar state of affairs prevailed in the three tahsils of the Shahpur district in the 1890s.[43] In Jhelum also cultivation increased quite remarkably (41 per cent) and the settlement officer held the view that the district 'had nearly reached the end of its tether'.[44] In the Amritsar district, however, there was very little increase of its cultivated area[45] during this period. But in districts like Sialkot,[46] Jullunder,[47] Hoshiarpur[48] and Gurdaspur[49] whatever increase in their cultivated area occurred, was mostly of a very limited nature and took place on the inferior and marginal lands. Here, however, the destructive action of the *chohs* contributed much to the decline of cultivation on the rich lands of these districts.[50]

New cultivation was again fast increasing in the south-eastern districts of Karnal, Rohtak and Hissar. In spite of waterlogging in some parts of Karnal district, it reported an increase of nearly 6 per cent in its cultivation during the first forty years following the establishment of British rule. In the next forty years (particularly after the opening of the Sirsa Branch Canal) the settlement officer recorded an increase of 13 per cent of cultivation in the *khadir* and 15 per cent in the *bangar* regions.[51] In some villages zamindars even enchroached on the 'land reserved for grazing and other common purposes'.[52] In Rohtak district cultivation increased and it amounted to nearly 32 per cent (1879).[53] In this increased cultivation, 'so great an area of jungle' was brought under the plough that it became 'necessary to sow a larger area than formerly with fodder crops for the cattle'. It was also found that cultivation in Gohana and Sampala tahsils had 'almost reached its utmost limit' while in Jhajjar tahsil it amounted to 22 per cent.[54] In the Sirsa region of the Hissar district, quite a considerable area was brought under the plough. In the 1840s only 20 per cent of the total area was cultivated; but in the early 1880s the district officer reported an increase of nearly 35 per cent of the area under cultivation.[55]

In the frontier districts like Dera Ghazi Khan, Peshawar and Bannu across the Indus, one notices everywhere signs of agricultural activity. Dera Ghazi Khan deserves our special attention,[56] for it alone had an increase of 103.4 per cent of its cultivation during the first quarter of British rule. In Bannu and Peshawar districts also cultivation increased. In the Marwat tahsil (Bannu) it varied from 40 to 50 per cent[57] while in the Nawshera tahsil (Peshawar) it amounted to nearly 25 per cent and took place mainly on the 'poorest and almost useless *barani* soils'.[58] A large-scale increase of cultivation was also reported from the south-western districts of Multan[59] and Muzaffargarh.[60]

Perhaps one of the most far-reaching developments in cultivation took place in the central Punjab Chenab Colony during the closing years of the century. For the better implementation of the colonization scheme, this tract was broadly divided into three circles: the Rakh Branch circle, the Jhang Branch circle and the Gugera Branch circle. In 1892 the first phase of colonization started in the Rakh Branch with the distribution of 2,30,761 acres of lands.[61] In the Jhang Branch, however, it began in 1896 with the allotment of only 82,654 acres while in 1899 the Gugera Branch was opened with 3,25,751 acres of lands for distribution in the first instalment.

Subsequently more lands were distributed in these three circles and in 1901 it was estimated that nearly 1,580,546 acres were granted to the colonists.[62]

These canals also led to a radical change in the crop pattern of the province. They stimulated the cultivation of certain valuable crops like wheat, cotton and sugar-cane and replaced the pre-canal staples like *jowar* and *Bajra*.[63] Wheat was always regarded to be the most important crop of the province. In 1868-69 only 1 per cent of the wheat area was protected by the canals. But with the spread of irrigation, there developed 'a decided tendency to grow more wheat on irrigated lands', especially in seasons when the scarcity of rainfall prevented its extension on the unirrigated lands.[64] Thus in course of the next quarter of a century, the protected area of wheat increased by nearly 151 per cent.[65] In the Chenab Canal Colony it was considered to be the most popular crop and nearly 80.32 per cent of its total rabi area was under wheat alone in one particular year. In Jhang, in particular (a district included in the Chenab Canal Colony), an 'enormous increase' took place in the wheat acreage 'since the opening of the Chenab Canal'.[66] Like wheat, cultivation of cotton considerably increased during this period. In 1877-78 it was estimated that nearly two-thirds of cotton crop was protected by irrigation[67] while in the early 1920s the irrigated area produced about four-fifths of the same crop.[68] Similarly the acreage under sugar-cane considerably increased 'on irrigated lands in those districts in which the canals and other sources of artificial irrigation have most largely developed'[69] and in 1921 it was found that nearly half of sugar-cane grown in the Punjab was irrigated by the canals.[70] While bringing more lands under certain valuable crops, canal irrigation did not fail to increase the average yield per acre in various districts of the province. According to one estimate of this century, productivity of an acre of irrigated land was larger by 20 to 300 per cent than that of an acre of unirrigated land.[71] The benefits from irrigation were also evident from the rising prices of irrigated lands and the flourishing export trade in agricultural produce from the canal colonies of the province.

During the period under review, canal irrigation also encouraged a 'continual movement' of peasant population in search of lands protected by canals. Generally speaking, this process may be said to have started in the early 1860s when the Bari Doab Canal began irrigating the land lying between the Ravi and the Beas. In the Lahore *manjha*, zamindars were attracted from all the more congested parts of Amritsar, Gurdaspur and Sialkot and the settlement officer did not fail to record a keen competition 'for tenancies on canal-irrigated land'.[72] A rapid increase of population occurred also in Gujrat district, particularly during the period from 1868 to 1881 and it was generally ascribed to the 'notoriously good' health of this district.[73] Similarly with the opening of the Sarhind Canal, Ferozepore witnessed a steady immigration of population from the adjoining districts and the Native States. In 1881 it was found that the total immigration to Ferozepore was nearly 70 per cent in excess of its emigration.[74] In the closing years of the century, this increase continued and it was particularly striking in the Fazilka tahsil.[75] A similar phenomenon was visible in the frontier districts like Peshawar and Dera Ghazi Khan.[76]

In most of the south-eastern districts also, rural inhabitants were migrating to more secure regions, free from the effects of droughts and famines. Here insecurity of harvests generally prompted them to emigrate from dry tracts (where cultivation almost entirely depended on a capricious rainfall, often below five inches) to fertile areas.[77] This movement received an additional encouragement with the increase of the canal irrigated area from the Western Jumna Canal. Of all the south-eastern districts, Hissar deserves our special attention. It stood between the fertile districts of Karnal and Rohtak on the east and the far less fertile Native States of Patiala, Jind and Rajputana on three other sides and included a part of the sparsely populated Sirsa region. With the introduction of British land revenue settlement, it encouraged immigration from the neighbouring regions. From 1868 Sirsa alone witnessed an increase of 20 per cent of its population while the rate of increase for the whole province during the same period was only 7 per cent. Sir Denzil Ibbetson, the Census Superintendent, concluded that the 'dry climate of the greater part of the district seems to be very healthy' and a 'considerable part of the increase of population must be due to immigration' 'from all directions'.[78] Even afterwards this region continued to witness a steady demographic growth and it mainly took place in Hissar and Hansi tahsils watered by the Western Jumna Canal. Another eastern district, namely Rohtak, also had a large-scale immigration in its northern tahsils resulting in an increase of nearly 25 per cent of its population [79] and this was once again largely due to the introduction of canal irrigation and the 'fine soil' of the district.

In Multan also, with the completion of the Sidhnai Canal, a large-scale immigration of population was recorded. Prior to it, Multan was 'a scantily peopled district' and only the Salt Range and the Jhelum Valley had 'a steady demographic rise'. But with the opening of the Sidhnai Canal, a sizable area was available for colonization, which led to a widespread migration. In this colony, immigrants were generally expected to be recruited from the crowded districts like Amritsar and Gurdaspur belonging to the 'best agricultural tribes' such as the Jats and the Arains.[80] But in reality they did not all come from these districts as envisaged by the Punjab Government prior to the commencement of this project. The colonists mostly came from Jhang.[81]

But the largest scale of permanent migration within the province took place from the densely populated central and submontane districts[82] towards the Chenab Canal Colony during the closing years of the last century. In these districts problems like fragmentation and subdivision of holdings, increasing volume of indebtedness, limited availability of culturable waste, repeated outbreaks of malaria—all tended to make the peasants' life unbearably hard there. Already in the context of existing technology, cultivation had reached the near optimum point. Consequently, zamindars were in search of an outlet. The Punjab Government was equally aware of their difficulties.

It was, therefore, decided that the largest number of colonists should be recruited chiefly from 'the congested districts' of Ambala, Amritsar, Ludhiana, Hoshiarpur, Jullundur, Gurdaspur and Sialkot,[83] so as to give them some relief.[84] Further, they should also represent enterprising 'healthy rural communities of the best type' available in the province. Accordingly 35.98 per cent of the total allotted area in the Chenab Canal was given to the Jat zamindars who constituted the 'flowers of the Punjab peasantry'. They came to the Chenab Colony with 13 or 14 years' experience of canal irrigation on the Bari Doab Canal. This 'placed them at an immediate advantage' in 'the economical use of water'.[85] Next came the Arains, traditionally famous for their hard working and frugal habits in the districts of Jullundur and Hoshiarpur. They were given nearly 10.7 per cent of the total allotted area[86] and in point of efficiency they were next only to the Sikh Jats. The Kambohs of Amritsar and Jullundur, universally acclaimed for their efficient cultivation, were given 3.01 per cent of the total allotted area in this tract.[87] Thus here the immigrant colonists generally represented the best agriculturists available in the province and in this way there was a 'shift of resources, in terms of labour and possibly capital in some degree, from the densely populated parts of province'[88] to the Chenab Colony where these resources could be more effectively used.

The Chenab Canal Colony marks an important landmark in the agrarian history of the Punjab during the second half of the last century.[89] It brought into existence a new type of healthier village settlement, the like of which hardly existed in the province.[90] This quick success of the colonization scheme was no doubt largely due to the small peasant colonists coming from the central and submontane districts who held nearly 80 per cent of the colony lands in Lyallpur.[91] They received on lease a few *killas* to 2 squares of lands on condition of permanent residence and cultivation of their holdings. Here they also enjoyed compact holdings in contrast to small and scattered fragments in other parts of the province. Further, they generally represented 'a higher than average proportion of the population in the working age group of 15-40' with some initial capital to start cultivation in the *bar* lands. Finally, they also found the soil 'for the most part of good quality', commonly known as the *maira*, capable of producing all types of valuable crops.[92]

But two other categories of the colonists, namely, the 'yeoman' and 'capitalist' grantees failed completely. In the cases of the 'yeomen' grantees, it was intended to attract the pick of the peasant proprietors—'men who by their wealth, energy or ability had raised themselves above their fellows without ceasing to belong to the agricultural community, and whose credit and resources, it was hoped, would prove of value in the development of an infant colony'. But this hope was not fulfilled because of their habitual absenteeism. Similarly the 'capitalist' grantees also had no good record to their credit. Here they were expected to act as natural leaders of the new society. They were also to attract strong men who were to furnish a basis from which newer agricultural improvements might be introduced in future. But they failed to infuse any such sense of leadership in this tract. They often 'quarrelled with their sub-tenants' and refused to spend 'any large amount of money on the development' of their grants.[93]

In spite of this failure of the 'yeomen' and 'capitalists', peasant grantees toiled hard to make the Chenab Canal Colony a grand success in the present century.[94] During the early stages of colonization, they, however, faced various difficulties.[95] But they gradually withstood them and proved their worth as first rate cultivators in the province. Annual colony reports clearly pointed out that an all-round development took place in the colony tract over the years.[96] Their unremitting zeal also did not fail to impress the indigenous nomad Janglis. Before the opening out of these canals they were mostly of pastoral habits, owning cattle and only doing a little occasional cultivation. Their general disinclination to hold or cultivate permanently any plot of land now gradually disappeared. Many of them 'acquired much knowledge about agriculture from the colonists' and thus within ten to twelve years started 'diverting their energies to the peaceful pursuits of farming'.[97]

These canals thus brought about a significant change in the rural economy of the Punjab during the period under review. Initially, however, these changes had been achieved largely at the expense of the indigenous inhabitants of the river valleys. They were almost treated as unwelcome outsiders[98] in their own home lands and they were immediately not even allowed to participate in this new agrarian enterprise. Their misery was further aggravated with the diversion of water from the Sutlej, Ravi and Chenab. It did affect agrarian operations along the downward streams of these rivers. It was soon revealed that with the diversion of a considerable amount of water from these rivers, smooth functioning of the numerous inundation canals at their downward streams was universally affected. It also led to a widespread failure of the *sailab* cultivation in the districts of Montgomery, Jhang and Gujranwala, though in Montgomery the damage done to the indigenous population was particularly of a serious nature.[99] It so greatly ruined the prosperity of many riverain estates that a considerable number of 'previously well-to-do peasant and yeoman families were reduced to want'.[100] Many of them even migrated to the canal colonies. But those who remained in their old homes, they 'have seen their tenants leave them, their rents decreased, and their income from their lands rapidly diminish'.

It is interesting to note that it took place at a time when the Chenab Colony brought in its train a good deal of prosperity for the immigrant colonists.[101] This inequal distribution of rural prosperity could have partly been avoided if the official policy was not dictated by 'purely business principles'. Actually, with a view to achieving a large and quick financial success in the form of an increased land revenue receipts from the colonists, the Punjab Government thought it proper to colonize these lands by enterprising settlers coming from other parts of the province. Thus in the case of the Chenab Colony, it 'sacrificed, or at least postponed, local Muhammadan interests for large and quick returns'.[102] And the Government was well aware of the fact that, unless the interests of these people were safeguarded, construction of a canal in sparsely populated districts like Jhang could have disastrous results.[103] But it did not take any immediate step for the alleviation of their misery. Subsequently, however, some compensations were made to the owners of land on the Ravi and Chenab for the injury done to them by the perennial canals; many of them were given lands on the Chenab Canal; these grants, however, could be made only to small percentage of the sufferers and most of them practically remained uncompensated.

If such had been the fate of the zamindars of the central and south-western Punjab due to canal irrigation, their fellow brothers also faced similar difficulties in a number of south-eastern and central districts almost during the same period. Here the *reh*[104] or saline efflorescence caused by over-irrigation and wrong alignment of canals contributed much to the sufferings of the zamindars. As early as 1845-46 this evil was detected in some of the villages irrigated by the Western Jumna Canal. In course of a decade in the districts of Rohtak, Delhi and Karnal, about 60 or one-tenth of the total number of canal villages were greatly affected by the *reh*.[105] An enquiry in 1867 clearly pointed out that in canal irrigated villages like Balsee or Wysuree (Rohtak district) the *reh* was present; here 'the aspect of the inhabitants was sickly to a degree, the child yellow, with the painfully grotesque appearance'.[106] It was then also revealed that the villages 'enjoying the great advantages' of irrigation were almost invariably those where malaria[107] and other debilitating diseases (goitre, spleen disease, etc.) had assumed a very virulent form. Similarly in the Chenab Canal Colony the problem of water-logging was not entirely unknown. But as late as 1897 the Punjab Government was confident that this colony could never become water-logged because sufficient steps were already taken so that the natural flow of rain water was not affected which usually aggravated this problem in Karnal and Delhi. In spite of this confident assertion of the Punjab Government, *reh* developed in this tract at the beginning of the present century and the settlement officer of the Gujranwala district did not fail to take note of it in the Hafizabad tahsil.[108] Subsequently, it spread to other regions and the districts of Lyallpur, Jhang and Montgomery were not completely free from it. It was estimated in 1927 that nearly 7,00,000 acres were already affected by water-logging and there was every likelihood of its expansion to about 1,00,000 acres more.[109] But still the mad craze for acquiring a few acres of canal irrigated lands scarcely diminished. Zamindars demanded *nahari* lands because the canals not only extended an adequate degree of security against drought and famine, but assured an increased yield which the *barani* lands could not always do.[110]

NOTES

1. Early British records clearly point out that cultivation was chiefly centred on a strip of country running parallel to the base of the northern hills and about fifty to eighty miles broad. This tract included mainly the submontane districts and the Jullundur *Doab* where regular rainfall, fertility of the soil, a temperate climate and above all the habitation of the enterprising Jats brought about a rapid increase of cultivation even before the establishment of British rule. But across the Chenab, there was virtually no cultivation except that commonly known in these areas as the *sailab*. It was 'a country of rolling sand dunes patched with grass, and of hard, unfruitful plains glistening with salt'. Some of the cis-Sutlej districts also (for example, Ferozepore) were 'nothing but a dreary and desert plain' with 'an almost continual duststorm' as the 'normal state of atmosphere'. Similarly, the extreme south-eastern districts (Hissar and Sirsa in particular which frequently witnessed the ravages of famines) recorded no major agricultural enterprise to their credit. This region was 'a sort of No-man's land, uninhabited save by a few marauding Bhattis and other nomad tribes'. For details, see J. Lawrence, Late Offg. Resident at Lahore, 31 March 1848, Foreign (Secret) Consultation, No. 60, 28 April 1848; *P.A.R., 1849-50 and 1850-51*, 171; *Ferozepore S.R., 1859*, 2; *Report on the Census of the Punjab*, I, *1881*, 98; Lepel H. Griffin, *The Rajas of the Punjab* (Languages Department, Punjab, Patiala, 1970), 164-5; F.C. Arora, *op. cit.*, xxvi; Darling, *Punjab Peasant*, 46, 112.
2. According to an estimate of the present century nearly 3, 75,000 to 4,00,000 acres were then under canal irrigation. Gurdit Singh, 'Irrigation in the Punjab during the Maharaja's Time', Teja Singh and Ganda Singh, eds., *Maharaja Ranjit Singh First Death Centenary Memorial* (Languages Department, Punjab, Patiala, 1970), 148.
3. *Muzaffargarh S.R. 1882*, 51-2, 83-4, 87, 91.
4. In Gujranwala at the settlement survey of 1866-67 it was found that wells provided the necessary water supply for nearly 75 per cent of the total cultivation. *Gujranwala D.G., 1883-84*, 49-50.
5. According to one estimate nearly 47 per cent of the cultivated area of this district remained under well-irrigation. *Sialkot D.G., 1883-84*, 64.
6. Towards the close of the last century well-irrigation became so popular that during the period between 1889-90 and 1899-1900 there took place an increase of 57 per cent for masonry wells and 109 per cent for temporary (*kachcha*) wells. *Report of the Indian Irrigation Commission, 1901-03, II* (Calcutta, 1903, hereafter *R.I.I.C.*), 30.
7. In Jullundur 33 per cent of the cultivated area was under well-irrigation (1878). Here the popularity of well-irrigation may be judged from the fact that the irrigated area between the regular (1851) and revised settlements (1885) increased at an average rate of 2,000 acres annually and from 1885 to 1901-02 at the rate of 4,500 acres annually.

Jullundur D.G., 1883-84, 43; *Ibid., 1904,* 202; *Jullundur S.R., 1892,* 106.

8. Incidentally these districts also reported an actual decrease in the well-irrigated area during these years. *R.I.I C.*, II, 31.
9. Usually the area commanded by a well was never large and in some cases it amounted to an acre. Owing to the smallness of the area commanded by each well and the strenuous labour and the high cost involved in irrigation, zamindars confined their irrigation to a small area to ensure the maturity of crops. *Hoshiarpur S.R., 1916,* 4.
10. In Jullundur, for example, in the 1880s this process of consolidation of holdings was practised under 'great difficulties' but in the present century it became 'a widespread tendency'. *Jullundur S.R , 1892,* 107; CR Jullundur division's review, 23 November 1917. *Ibid., 1918,* 3.
11. Evidence of Rao Bahadur Chaudhuri Lal Chand, *Royal Commission on Agriculture in India,* VIII, *Evidence taken in the Punjnb* (Calcutta, 1927), 108.
12. A similar opinion was expressed by J. Wilson, the Settlement Commissioner, Punjab, in 1901: '... during the last eight years ... the actual amount advanced for well construction cannot have much exceeded one lakh a year, against the sixteen lakhs a year spent by the people on construction of wells ... during the last ten years only 3,132 new wells were made and 289 old ones repaired with the aid of advances under the Land Improvement Act, while ... the landowners in that period constructed or brought into use 53,000 masonry wells, or 15 times as many as were aided by the State'. Note by J. Wilson on the future irrigation policy in the Punjab, 22 October 1901, *R.I.I.C.*, Appendix, 35.
13. Even before the annexation of the Punjab, the British Government was well aware of the potentialities of the province for canal irrigation. But during the first few years following the annexation, it generally followed a policy of 'non-interference' in this field. This policy was soon abandoned in favour of direct intervention. This change was the product of various factors some of which deserve special attention. To begin with, construction of canals—both perennial and inundation—involved huge expenses which the Government alone could undertake. Secondly, it was also destined to be a very good source of official income. Actually it was with an eye on the probable 'earnings of the canals' that the Punjab Government thought it prudent to take the initiative in this matter. Thirdly, these canals were to pass through arid waste lands mostly under official disposal. On its part the Government did not want to alienate its rights over them to any private individuals. It was widely believed that if the canals were not constructed under state supervision it could have given rise to many confusions and petty rivalries among zamindars for acquiring these lands. Finally, during Sikh rule numerous inundation canals were often at work in some of the south-western districts of the province. Their annual repair, clearance, stoppage of breaches, preservation of banks,

were mostly done by the unpaid labour of the zamindars and their dependents, under the general supervision of the Government officials. Occasional grants were even made for extending and improving these canals. In some cases also the Government regularly shared the cost of maintenance with the irrigators and exercised control through *kardars* and other village officials. The British Government thought it prudent to continue this official initiative in matters of canal irrigation. For official attitude on canal irrigation, see Memorandum by J.B. Lyall, FC Punjab, 2 August 1882, para 8, Rev and Agr (R) November 1883, 29A; Review of Irrigation in India in 1899-1900, Rev and Agr (LR) August 1901, 53B; *P.A.R., 1849-50 and 1850-51*, 133.

14. Robert B. Buckley, *The Irrigation Works of India and their Financial Results* (W.H. Allen & Co., London, 1880), 144-5.
15. *P.A.R., 1849-50 and 1850-51*, 139-40.
16. Note by Colonel J.W. Outley, IGI Punjab, on the 'Canal Rates' of the perennial canals of the Punjab, 16 June 1896, Rev and Agr (LR) August 1896, 44A.
17. For its water distribution, see Paul W. Paustian, *Canal Irrigation in the Punjab* (Columbia University Press, New York, 1930), 45.
18. This region was predominantly inhabited by the enterprising Sikh Jats. 'The primary object of the canal', wrote Wace, the Settlement Commissioner, 'is to place tracts with a scanty rainfall, in a position as secure and favourable as tracts with a good rainfall'. Major E.G. Wace, SLC Punjab's No. 1088, 12 October 1881, *FC Selections*, New Series, No. 8, No. 34, No. LXII, Papers Relating to Canals, 489.
19. *Sarhind Canal Opened by H.E. The Marquis of Ripon*, 2.
20. S.S. Thorburn, *The Punjab in Peace and War* (Languages Department, Punjab, Patiala, 1970, hereafter *P.P.W.*), 268.
21. In 1820 it irrigated only 155 acres while in 1900-1901 it commanded 5,67,125 acres, *Karnal D.G., 1892*, 316; *R.I.I.C.*, II, 5.
22. Thorburn, *P.P.W.*, 270.
23. Report on the Lower Sohag and Para Canal Project, P.W.D., Irrigation Branch, Punjab, Rev and Agr (LR) March 1897, 1A. See also Memorandum recorded by the FC Punjab regarding the Sohag Para Settlements, PGR Rev and Agr (R) February 1893, 7-9A: Extension of the Lower Sohag and Para Canals, PGR Rev and Agr (Irrigation) June 1901, 17-26A.
24. *R.I.I.C.*, II, 5.
25. *Revenue Report of the Irrigation Department, Punjab, 1886-1887*, Rev and Agr (R) February 1888, 16-17B.
26. *R.I.I.C.*, II, 5.
27. Buckley, *op. cit.*, 167; *Charsada A.R., 1894*, 19.
28. Note by Colonel J.W. Outley, IGI Punjab, on the 'Canal Rates' of the perennial canals of the Punjab, 16 June 1896, Rev and Agr (LR) August 1896, 44A.
29. *R.I.I.C.*, II, 5.

30. Report on the colonization of the government waste lands situated in the Rechna Doab and commanded by the Chenab Canal, Rev and Agr (LR) September 1897, 60A.
31. The Punjab Government had another important motive in colonizing this tract: To colonize the area in question with well-to-do yeomen of the best class of agriculturists, who will cultivate their own holdings with the aid of families and of the usual menials, but as much as possible without the aid of tenants and will constitute healthy agricultural communities of the best Punjab type'. Chander Prabha, 'District-wise Rates of Growth of Agricultural Outputs in East and West Punjab During the Pre-Partition and Post-Partition Periods', *The Indian Economic and Social History Review* (hereafter *IESHR*) VI, No. 4, December 1969, 334-8.
32. Note by Colonel Home, IGI Punjab, on the project for the extension and completion of the Chenab Canal, 22 March 1892, Rev and Agr (LR) December 1892, 17A, KW 11.
33. *R.I.I.C.*, II, 5.
34. *Ibid.*, 10.
35. *Lahore A.R.*, *1891*, 13.
36. It was also revealed that 'of the total increase of cultivation' (amounting to 33 per cent since the first regular settlement) 'more than five-sixths' was due to 'the extension of the Bari Doab Canal' which irrigated 'one-third of the entire *manjha* tract'. According to the settlement officer the newly broken up lands in the Lahore *manjha* were considered as good as the old ones. *Lohore S.R.*, *1894*, 3, 20-1; *Kasur A.R.*, *1891*, 22.
37.

Name of tahsils	Increase of cultivation in per cent
1	2
Ferozepore	52
Zira	44

Source : E.G. Wace, SLC Punjab's No. 268, 15 May 1884, Rev and Agr (A) August 1884, 10-12A. See also *Zira A.R.*, *1888*, 22.

38. *Ferozepore S.R.*, *1891*, 7.
39. *Ibid.*, 9.
40. *Ilaka Mamdot and Pargana Muktsar A.R.*, *1875*, 43; *Pargana Muktsar and Ilaka Mamdot S.R.*, *1878*, 13; *Ibid.*, *1892*, 4.
41. *Gujrat S.R.*, *1893*, 23.
42. In 1874 (revision of settlement) Gujrat district reported an increase of nearly 1,05,335 (nearly 30 per cent) acres since 1866-67 (regular settlement) in which Phalia tahsil alone contributed 43,792 acres. Subsequently in the 1890s Gujrat tahsil recorded an increase of only 15 per cent while in the Phalia tahsil it amounted to nearly 72 per cent. This, according to the settlement officer, was due to the comparative 'secluded' and 'underdeveloped condition' of this tahsil in the 1850s.

But from the 1860s steady development of well-irrigation encouraged the breaking up of the 'easily culturable lands' which hitherto remained beyond the plough. For details, see *Gujrat S.R., 1874*, 139; *Ibid., 1893* 23; CR Rawalpindi division's review, *Phalia A.R., 1891*, 8.

43. Here the increase of cultivation in the different tahsils since the regular settlement had been 131 per cent in Bhera, 173 per cent in Shahpur and 89 per cent in Khusab tahsils. The more rapid increase in the first two tahsils was largely due to the extension of irrigation from the inundation canals. *Shahpur S.R., 1894*, 5.

44. *Jhelum S.R., 1902*, 4.

45. In the early 1860s nearly 70 per cent of the total area was under cultivation and in Amritsar and Tarn Taran tahsils only 15.9 per cent and 14.3 per cent respectively remained beyond the plough. This district was so widely cultivated that at the revision of settlement (1888-93) the settlement officer was able to report an increase of only 8 per cent of its cultivated area since the completion of the first regular settlement. He also reported that this increase was of 'little importance, being made up of chiefly of minute additions, of poor quality, to existing *barani* and *nahari* lands'. In Tarn Taran also a similar condition prevailed towards the close of the century. Even at the settlement of 1910-14, it was found that these two tahsils were 'so closely cultivated' that they had 'no likelihood of further expansion in them'. *Amritsar S.R., 1873*, 4, 6-7; *Ibid., 1914*, 3; CR Lahore Division's review, *Tarn Taran A.R., 1891*, 4; *Amritsar A.R., 1892*, 6.

46. In 1868 only 15.20 per cent of the total cultivated area still remained uncultivated in the Sialkot district. In the 1890s the settlement officer found that 'the newly broken soil' was 'markedly inferior to the old soil'. This extension took place generally at the cost of the grazing grounds for cattle. *Report on the Census of the Punjab, 1868*, 14; *Sialkot S.R., 1895*, 36, 40, 42, 44.

47. Even before the annexation, Jullundur was universally regarded to be 'an extensively cultivated district' of the province. Subsequently in the late 1860s it was found that there remained only 6.57 per cent of the culturable waste to be brought under the plough. The district officer pointed out that there was virtually 'not much margin for an increase of rural population, except by increased yield being obtained from the soil by means of a higher system of cultivation'. Accordingly in Jullundur the area under double-cropping steadily increased over the years and a recent study on Vilyatpur (a village in the Jullundur district) also pointed out that even in 1848 almost one-third of the cultivable land was double-cropped. This area with some minor fluctuations tended to increase during the second half of the century. *Report on the Census of the Punjab, 1868*, 14; Kessinger, *op. cit.*, 119.

48. The first regular settlement (1852) found that cultivation in the richer and more favoured soils had already reached its utmost limit and any further increase of cultivation could take place only on poorer soils of the hills. Actually in the following decades, cultivation increased on the

'poor lands' of the hill circles. Otherwise the district, reported Montgomery, the settlement officer of the 1880s, did not register much progress' 'as regards extension of cultivation' during the thirty years following the 1850s. In some cases, zamindars, however, introduced the method of double-cropping by shortening the fallow period. *Hoshiarpur S.R., 1885*, 141; T.G. Walker, Sr. Secy. FC Punjab's No. 241, 29 March 1888, Rev and Agr (R) August 1888, 30-32A; *Una S.R., 1915*, 6.

49. Similarly in Gurdaspur there was an increase of only 5 per cent of cultivation between 1865-72 and 1890-91. In the early 1890s it was revealed that 'the whole district' was 'closely cultivated' and there was 'little room for extension of the area of cultivation' which had 'practically remained stationary since last settlement'. So the method of double-cropping was becoming extremely popular in all its tahsils. In Pathankot, for example, the settlement officer wrote in the early 1890s, 'it stands at 119 per cent as against 108 in Gurdaspur and 110 in Batala. In the Andhar and Pathanti this rises as high as 138 and 143 per cent respectively'. *Gurdaspur S.R., 1892*, Statement II; *Ibid., 1912*, 3; *Gurdaspur D.G., 1914*, 94; *Pathankot A.R., 1890*, 33.

50. In the districts of Ambala, Jullundur and Hoshiarpur destructive hill torrents from the Siwalik range caused an immense harm. This injury was in the form of soil erosion or drifts of sand and boulders and locally known as the *chohs*. In explaining its origin, Fanshawe, a senior official from the Punjab, pointed out that prior to 1852 the waste lands of the Siwalik, which were at that time well protected by trees and bushes, were controlled by the Government servants; but after the first regular settlement of the Hoshiarpur district (1852) these lands were divided up among the villagers adjoining the hills. Subsequently these burshwood and trees were destroyed by them resulting in a gradual denudation of forests along the foothills. Consequently, the *chohs* started pouring down from the hills sandy deposits to the plains at almost every mile, 'till at last not only the whole area of the rich plains of Hoshiarpur is affected, but the mischief extends to Rahun in the Jullundur District beyond'. In the Hoshiarpur district no less than 1,000 villages were affected; it also ravaged nearly 70 villages in Jullundur and was not entirely unknown in the Rupar, Kharar, Jagadhri and Naraingarh tahsils of the Ambala district. Actually in Hoshiarpur the damage was of a very serious nature. In his report (1879) the Conservator of Forest pointed out that in one tahsil 35,000 acres of rich lands were covered with sand by the *choh*; these lands, if reclaimed, the same officer added, 'might be on our [British] rent rolls bringing in a yearly revenue of at least Rs. 50,000'. The *chohs* continued to cause enormous damage till the closing years of the last century. In 1889 it was estimated that in course of last ten or twelve years, on account of the action of the *chohs* in Hoshiarpur and Jullundur, 16,650 acres of lands were covered into *choh* bed or had totally lost their productive power, while 23,260 acres in addition had

also been damaged. 'People of this tract have lost at a low estimate over 20 lakhs of rupees in the market value of their land'. According to another estimate (1901), Hoshiarpur district in the last decade of the century lost nearly 7,000 acres of rich lands with an annual loss in land revenue of Rs. 32,000. This increased devastation even led to a decrease of roughly 2.2 per cent of the district population. Comparing the cultivated area of the years of kharif and rabi of 1890-91 and that of 1900-01, the district officer commented: 'The destructive action of the *chohs* has thrown much good land out of cultivation, while the new cultivation has no doubt been of an inferior quality. This process has in all probability operated in the direction of a decrease in population by emigration'. For details, see Extract from an abstract of proceedings of a meeting of the Legislative Council of the Punjab held at Simla, 16 August 1899, Legislative Department, October 1900, 4-6A; The Punjab Land Preservation (*Chohs*) Bill, Legislative Department November, 1899, 4A; *Punjab Selections*, New Series, No. XV, The Chohs of Hoshiarpur, 2-19; *Hoshiarpur S.R., 1885*, 18; *Census of India, 1901*, XVII, Part I, 62.

51. *Karnal S.R., 1912*, 33.
52. Remarks by P.D. Agnew, DC Karnal, *ERR 1892-93*, 6.
53. *Rohtak S.R., 1880*, 126.
54. *Jhajjar A.R., 1879*, xiii.
55. *Report on the Census of the Punjab, 1881*, I, 98.
56. During the first few years following the establishment of British rule, it was found that nearly nine-tenths of the culturable area remained waste. But with the development of canal irrigation, cultivation increased from 3,25,479 acres (1859-60) to 1,034,697 acres (1897). It is, however, extremely difficult to measure separately the size of this increased cultivation in all the four tahsils of this district in view of their frequently changing size. All that can be said is that in the Sangarh tahsil 'the increase', in the opinion of the settlement officer, 'has been large' while in the Jampur tahsil it 'amounted to 20 per cent'. *Dera Ghazi Khan S.R., 1876*, 115, 120, Statement VIII; *Ibid., 1898*, Appendix G.
57. *Bannu S.R., 1879*, 184-5.
58, *Peshawar S.R., 1898*, 64.
59. In Multan cultivation increased by nearly 16 per cent during the period from 1857-60 to 1873. In course of the next twenty-five years another 33 per cent increase was recorded by the settlement officer. *Multan S.R., 1901*, 8-11.
60. *Muzaffargarh S.R., 1904*, 9.
61. In the early 1890s a few acres of lands were granted to some Mazhabi pensioners of the army. They were not enterprising colonists, many of them even mortgaged their holdings to money-lenders. For details, see *Annual Report for the Chenab, Jhang, Chunian and Jhelum Colonies, 1904-5*, 1-2; *Chenab Colony S.R., 1915*, 7.
62. *Chenab Colony S.R., 1915, 12.*

63. *Gujranwala S.R., 1894*, 4. This will also be evident from the following table.

Changes in wheat, *bajra* and *jowar* acreages from 1873 to 1901.

Name of the crop	Acres	
	1873	1901
1	2	3
Wheat	5,820,861	8,485,990
Bajra	2,490,078	1,347,076
Jowar	2,002,252	851,196

Source : Agricultural Statistics of India, Appendix, Part II, Rev and Agr (A) January 1882, 72-76B; Summary of Remarks on the kharif crops of the Punjab, 1901, Rev and Agr (A) February 1902, 3B.

64. Report on fluctuations in prices of wheat and the trade in that cereal in the Punjab, Rev and Agr (A) December 1895, 7-9A.
65. In 1893-94, 1,096,748 acres of wheat were under irrigation. *Revenue Report of the Irrigation Department, Punjab, 1893-94*, Rev and Agr (LR) May 1895, 6B.
66. Final Report on the wheat crop of the Punjab for 1898-99, *RR 1898-99*, Appendix B, vii.
67. *Report on the cotton cultivation of the Punjab, 1877-78*, 4.
68. W. Roberts and O.T. Faulkner, *A Text Book of Punjab Agriculture* (Civil and Military Gazette Press, Lahore, 1921), 120.
69. Note by E.B. Steedman, DLRA Punjab, 3 March 1899, Rev and Agr (R) June 1899, 6-8A.
70. *Report of the Indian Sugar Committee* (Simla, 1921), 68.
71. Average yield of wheat, cotton and sugar-cane in pounds in irrigated and unirrigated lands in three important districts of the province.

District	Wheat (1906-1907)	Increase in per cent	Cotton (1906-1907)	Increase in per cent	Sugar-cane (1906-07)	Increase in per cent
1	2	3	4	5	6	7
Lahore						
Unirrigated	720		240		1000	
Irrigated	1080	50	440	83	1700	70
Delhi						
Unirrigated	600		280		1440	
Irrigated	900	50	480	70	2000	38
Shahpur						
Unirrigated	800		260		400	
Irrigated	960	20	520	100	1600	300

Source: *Report on the Season and Crops of the Punjab, 1906-07*, Statement V. See also George Blyn, *Agricultural Trends in India, 1891-1947 Output, Availability and Productivity* (Philadelphia, 1966),

167-8, 201.

72. *Report on the Census of the Punjab, 1881*, I, 84: *Lahore S.R., 1894*, 24.
73. *Gujrat S.R., 1874*, 7.
74. *Report on the Census of the Punjab, 1881*, I, 84.
75. *Ibid., 1901*, XVII, Part I, Subsidiary Table VII.
76. *Ibid., 1891*, XIX, Part I, Abstract 11; *Ibid., 1901*, XVII, Part I, 69-70; *Dera Ghazi Khan S.R., 1876*, 17.
77. *Census of India, 1901*, XVII, Part I, 71.
78. *Ibid., 1881*, I, 98.
79. *Rohtak S.R., 1880*, 120.
80. C.M. Rivaz, CR Lahore division's No. 554, 17 July 1888, Rev and Agr (R) July 1890, 14A.
81. The total number of immigrants from the five districts of the Punjab from 1891 to 1901.

District of origin	1891	1901
1	2	3
Amritsar	2,226	3,854
Sialkot	1,528	2,451
Lahore	3,677	1,616
Jhang	24,751	25,439

Source ; *Census Reports* for the respective years.

82. Density of population per square mile in the submontane and central districts from 1881 to 1901.

District	1881	1891	1901
1	2	3	4
Amritsar	561	623	643
Jullundur	552	634	641
Sialkot	524	572	555
Gurdaspur	436	500	498
Ambala	442	459	434
Ludhiana	426	447	464
Hoshiarpur	401	450	440
Punjab	152	167	178

Source : Same as above.

83. Collector's report for the lease of government waste lands (Punjab) quoted in Denzil Ibbetson, DC Gujranwala's No. 119, 27 April 1891, Rev and Agr (LR) November 1891, 35-37A.
84. Total number of immigrants in the Chenab Canal Colony from 1901 to 1911 from the major eight districts of the province.

District	1901	1911
1	2	3
Sialkot	1,03,390	96,984
Amritsar	67,963	81,144
Jullundur	56,983	70,847
Gurdaspur	43,593	52,701
Hoshiarpur	35,099	44,234
Lahore	28,620	28,176
Gujrat	25,352	25,174
Ludhiana	17,807	28,306

Source : *Chenab Colony S.R., 1915*, 34.

85. *Ibid.*, 37-8.
86. *Ibid.*, 39.
87. *Ibid.*, 41.
88. Chander Prabha, *op. cit.*, 339-40.
89. Recently Dr. Elizabeth Whitcombe in connection with her research work on the rural economy of the United Provinces (*Agrarian Conditions in Northern India*, I, *The United Provinces under British Rule, 1860-1900*, Thompson Press, New Delhi, 1971, 75-7) pointed out that canal irrigation brought in its train various 'deleterious' effects. 'With the decline of the numbers of wells in use, cultivators were deprived of a good source of manure. Further there is the problem of over-watering. This over-watering as well as unmanuring land led inevitably to hardening of the soil and even to *reh* . . . .' But this view does not seem to hold good in the case of the Punjab of our period. Actually with the increase of the area under canal irrigation, the number of wells did not necessarily decrease; their number rather increased over the years. Further, the problem of the decline of the use of green manure due to decline in the number of well-bullocks also did not occur for there was no such decline in the number of wells in use. Finally, canal irrigation, as we shall subsequently see, no doubt resulted in the *kalar* in the Chenab Colony as well as in the south-eastern districts of the province. But other benefits, viz., extension of cultivation in the central *bar* lands, development of healthy canal villages, increased yield of certain valuable crops like wheat, cotton, sugar-cane and *toria*, improvement in the techniques of cultivation among the nomad Janglis and the inducement to the zamindars of the densely populated districts to migrate to the Chenab Colony far outweigh the evil effects of water-logging. For a similar view, see also Ian Stone, 'Canal Irrigation and Agrarian Change: The Experience of the Ganges Canal Tract, Muzaffarnagar District (U.P.), 1840-1900', K.N. Chaudhuri and C.J. Dewey, eds., *Economy and Society: Essays in Indian Economic and Social History* (Oxford University Press, New Delhi, 1979), 86-112.

90. *Annual Report for the Chenab, Jhang, Chunian and Sohag Para Colonies, 1901-02*, 39-40; *Ibid., 1902-03*, 11; *Ibid., 1907-08*, 8.
91. Darling, *Punjab Peasant*, 117.
92. The following remarks of the settlement officer about the productivity of the new canal holdings deserve our special attention: 'The tract as a whole is remarkably uniform in the matter of soil and the light loam, of which it is mainly composed, is peculiarly suited to canal irrigation and of great fertility'. *Chenab Colony S.R., 1915*, 54.
93. In the Chenab Colony 'yeoman' grant included 4 to 5 squares or 111 to 139 acres. Similarly each 'capitalist' grantee was generally given 6 to 20 squares or 167 to 556 acres. Personal residence was not made compulsory in the case of 'yeoman' and 'capitalist' grantees. They were allowed to hold their lands on lease for the term of settlement, with power of purchase at any time after 5 years, on condition of bringing under cultivation one-third of their grants within first three years and one-half within first five years. Failure to fulfil this condition would expose these grants to resumption without compensation. For details, see Report on the colonization of the government waste lands situated in the Rechna Doab and commanded by the Chenab Canal, Rev and Agr (LR) September 1897, 60A.
94 The small peasant proprietors were very much elated with their success and it finds an eloquent expression in the following ballad:

    'I will tell a new tale to-day
    How of old the Bar was the prey of thieves,
    The shelter of deer, jackals and rats,
    Now no barren jungle is left,
    Young Sahib has peopled the land'.

    Chenab Canal Colony Gazetteer, 1904, 34.
95. *Punjab Peasant*, 114-5.
96. Annual colony reports frequently referred to the rise in the standard of living in the different colonies and the consequent changes in their social life. The following remarks of the colonization officer will further illustrate this point: 'In matters of social custom, as also in agriculture there is a decided tendency to assimilate new ideas . . . . In matters of social custom the Gurdaspur peasants have gradually overcome their deep-seated fear of buildings of burnt brick and the Arain women of Jullundur have supplemented their scanty petticoats with voluminous trousers. In Jullundur their previous style of clothing was too well known to excite comment, here they have found that trousers on holidays are essential to dignity and the social status to which they aspire. To European mind this change may seem insignificant, but it strikes natives as peculiarly remarkable in view of the fundamental aversion in which Arain women used to hold this peculiar form of habiliment'. *Annual Report for the Chenab, Jhang, Chunian and Sohag Para Colonies, 1902-03*, 11.
97. *Ibid.*, 7; Deva Singh, *Colonization of the Rechna Doab* (Punjab Government Record Office Publications, Monograph No. 7, Lahore, n.d.), 25-6.

98. Actually the Janglis were harshly treated even in the present century when new irrigational projects were undertaken in the different *bar* lands. For it, see Darling, *Wisdom and Waste in the Punjab Village* (Oxford University Press, London, 1934, hereafter *Wisdom and Waste*), 10.

99. Agrarian operations in the tahsils of Gugera, Pakpattan and Montgomery depended greatly on the Ravi, the *sailab* from which usually reached the villages on either bank to a distance of about ten miles. In this arid tract the advantages of *sailab* were obvious. It was the most natural and the least expensive means of irrigation. It improved the soil with the silt it threw up. This form of cultivation was 'very near to the heart of the Montgomery farmer'. But from the early 1870s with some significant changes in the course of the Ravi, cultivators faced enormous difficulties in matters of the *sailab* cultivation. In the 1890s condition of this tract further deteriorated. In 1896-97 the settlement officer had to reduce the fixed land revenue demand in the *bet* circles. In the Ravi *bet* circles a great decrease in cultivation occurred and it was equally very marked in the Montgomery tahsil. In fact, the settlement officer wrote, 'its cultivated area is a good deal less than what it was at the last settlement' (1878). In Gugera also the same story was repeated. Towards the close of the century a number of Ravi villages suffered miserably and the following table will illustrate this point.

Changes in the matured rabi area in four tahsils of the Montgomery district.

Year	Montgomery	Gugera	Dipalpur	Pakpattan
1	2	3	4	5
1898	29,392	57,329	154,352	94,035
1899	14,630	32,597	132,197	67,398
1900	4,264	15,822	98,996	53,132

Source: Remarks by A.J.W. Kitchin, DC Montgomery, *ERR 1899-1900*, 5.

For details, see *Montgomery S.R., 1878*, 157, 162; *Ibid., 1899*, 18, 54; *Census of India, 1901*, XVII, Part I, 68.

100. Thorburn, *P.P.W.*, 283.

101. But this sudden influx of wealth in the colony tract was not an unmixed evil. It left behind a demoralising effect on the immigrant peasant families. For it, see Darling, *Wisdom and Waste*, 16; FC Punjab's review, *Kasur A.R., 1891*, 2.

102. Thorburn, *P.P.W.*, 283.

103. *Jhang S.R., 1882*, 15.

104. In the Punjab districts during the dry months of the year, the surface of the ground often became covered with an efflorescence caused by over-irrigation or by faulty alignments of canals. The salt which

formed this efflorescence was known as *reh*. It was first detected in the neighbourhood of Delhi along the territory irrigated by the Western Jumna Canal. Here the bed of the canal was high above the level of the surrounding country, and water, when percolating, has a tendency to rise up to its own level, and consequently pressed upwards to the surface. 'When thus percolating, the water finds soluble salts in the soil, which it carries up to the surface; and hence the saline efflorescence so destructive to vegetables production'. It rendered lands practically unfit for cultivation. The approach of this problem was marked by certain distinct stages. During the first two years *barani* crops were unusually successful and there was spontaneous growth of a rich crop of *maina*. But in the third year, patches of *reh* began to appear on the affected field, and seeds did not germinate on the patches. Yield started diminishing and these patches of *reh* gradually covered the whole field. Finally, the affected land was turned into a swamp and the surface water developed a rusty colour. *India Selections* (*P.W.D.*), No. XLII, Correspondence Relating to the Deterioration of Lands from the Presence in the Soil of Reh, 1.

105. *Ibid*.
106. *Punjab Selections*, New Series, No. VI, Sanitary Surveys of Villages Watered by the Western Jumna Canal, para 15. See also, *Gohana A.R.*, *1878*, 18.
107. Malaria was a frequent phenomenon in certain parts of the south-eastern and submontane districts where water-logging widely prevailed in the countryside. In these districts stagnant pools with edges over-grown with weeds, provided ideal conditions for the breeding and proliferation of anopheles mosquitoes—the carriers of malaria. germ. Thus from Ambala it was reported: 'The disease is attributed to the water-logging of the country, the standing crops preventing evaporation and quick drying up of the soil, helping to keep up the malaria'. Almost a similar condition prevailed in Karnal. In two other south-eastern districts, namely, Gurgaon and Delhi, water-logging caused by the *jhils* contributed much to the spread of malaria. It is, however, extremely difficult to assess correctly where and when the fever first broke out in the province. It was very much in existence in the south-eastern districts even before the establishment of British rule. But the large-scale destructiveness with which the fever was associated in the districts of Karnal, Rohtak, Delhi, Ambala and Gurgaon was a development mainly of the second half of the 19th century. In Karnal, malaria was causing concern even in the early 1840s while in the 1880s it became almost an annual occurrence. Incidentally malaria also operated with damaging consequences during the winter months, when the kharif was ready for harvesting or the early preparations of the rabi were to start. Consequently, it often led to a contraction of cultivation in certain villages lying along the Western Jumna Canal. Adam Taylor's (Civil Surgeon, Amritsar)

enquiry took note of many 'sick women and diseased children crouching among the ruins of their swamps, watching their sickly crops'. Here contraction of cultivation amounted to nearly 10 per cent while in Mauza Baoli it amounted to nearly 100 per cent. In Delhi, it was pointed out that in many villages along the banks of the Western Jumna Canal malaria and spleen disease contributed much to the misery of the rural folk. Zamindars often found it difficult to procure labour for harvesting their crops. Similarly in Gurgaon the settlement officer found many villages once inhabited by strong Jat communities 'have been decidedly weakened by the loss of a large proportion of their labourers'. According to the same authority, cultivation declined by nearly 10 per cent during the period 1877 and 1882. In the submontane districts like Ambala, Hoshiarpur and Sialkot malaria recurred almost throughout the second half of the century and it led to a 'listlessness and lassitude in the ordinary occupations of life'. For a further discussion on the incidence of malaria and its effects on agriculture, see the author's unpublished Ph.D. thesis, 'Agrarian Society of the Punjab, 1849-1901', (Calcutta, 1976), 63-74.

108. *Chenab Colony S.R., 1915*, 28.
109. Proceedings of the Governor of the Punjab in Council in the Department of Revenue (R), No. 1933-R., 19 September 1927, *RR 1927*, 3.
110. Many contemporary folk songs refer to it and a few of their lines may be quoted here:

> '. . . *mere bebehe naddion par dharti dedehe,*
> *mere bhaiyone nahron par dharti baiyo ne*'.
> [Oh sister give me some canal land,
> Oh brother sow some land on the canal]

Rohtak S.R., 1880, 49.

3

Growth of Commercial Agriculture

After the annexation, the Punjab became an integral part of the British India's foreign and internal trade which witnessed a phase of rapid change during the period under review. With the rapid industrialization of the West a need arose for new sources of raw materials and India was thought to be a potential source. Modern means of communications like the railways and steamships also brought India closer to the West and contributed much to the rapid increase of her external trade. It was the opening of the Suez Canal (1869), synchronizing with the fast growth of steam navigation, that 'simply revolutionized India's trade with the West'. Another important development was the introduction of telegraphic communications between England and India (1855) which further broadened the contact, making possible a more accurate and quicker study of the demand and supply position and of other related phenomena. The liberalization of the tariff policy by the Government of India, particularly after 1867, by abolishing or reducing export duties[1] on a number of commodities, and the gradual fall in ocean freight also contributed to the expansion of India's foreign trade. These developments not only affected the volume, but also the commodity composition of the trade. It was no longer practically confined to 'drugs, dyes and luxuries'; it now included increasing quantities of food-grains, fibres and other great staples of universal consumption.

During this period internal trade and commerce was also stimulated by a gradual development of communications.

Soon after the annexation, macadamized roads were first introduced in the Punjab. The early metalled roads were devised mainly to serve 'military purposes'. Subsequently, however, with their increasing mileage, they were destined to become 'the great channels for the import and export trade of this province'.[2] Attempts were also made to improve the existing river communication system. Previously native boats plied on all the major rivers of the Punjab and offered to traders an easy means of communication from one part of the province to another. The Punjab Government with a view to introducing further improvements in this field put into operation a number of steamers on the Indus (1858-59). But they were not very useful for commercial purposes;[3] consequently, the country boats, capable of carrying from 400 to 600 maunds at a cheaper rate, continued to play an important role in the export-import trade of the province. In this connection, the downward Indus trade by these boats deserves our special attention. During the first twenty years of British rule, when the Indus Valley Railway was yet to appear in this region, the boat traffic served as the readiest as well as the cheapest means of transport to Karachi.

But this brisk country boat traffic did not last long. It steadily declined particularly after the 1880s, when the Government decided to build roads and railways on an extensive scale. The Government, however, had no intention of completely dislocating this river-borne trade; it rather hoped to use it as a feeder to the railways. But even then, it could not compete with the railways. The opening of the Indus Valley Railway lines connecting Karachi with the major wheat and cotton-producing districts offered to traders a safer, quicker and cheaper means of transport. River traffic was thus gradually losing its early predominant position as an important means of export trade of the province.[4] At the beginning of the present century it was found that the Punjab rivers 'were able to hold their own in competition with the railway only in the transport of heavy and bulky goods'. Otherwise, their trade had mostly been taken over by the railways.

Actually the introduction of the railways in the 1860s marked an important landmark in the economic history of the Punjab.

In course of the first forty years of its inception, its mileage increased quite remarkably. The Sind-Punjab and Delhi-Guaranteed Railways Company, registered in 1855, first began its operations between Karachi and Kotri in 1861. But the oldest line within the Punjab proper, connecting Amritsar and Lahore, was, however, ready in 1862. In 1865 Lahore was further linked with Multan and this was soon extended up to Muzaffargarh (1870). On the other hand, Amritsar was also connected with Delhi through important wheat-producing districts like Ludhiana and Jullundur. In 1878 the Indus Valley Railways opened new lines from Kotri to Multan via Lodhran while in the north Lahore was brought closer to Peshawar via Jhelum and Multan. Actually by 1883 railways linked the metropolis not only with most districts but also with numerous agricultural regions and trade centres in other parts of India, thus widening the internal and external markets of the agricultural produce of the Punjab.

An indirect outcome of this growth of railway communication was the development of Karachi as the most important port of the province.[6] But the Karachi-bound trade had its limitations, three of which deserve special mention here. The first one was the absence of a railway bridge on the Indus near Sukkur because it greatly impeded trade along this route. The ferry arrangements were found insufficient to cope with any large expansion of trade. Hence, from a commercial point of view, an early completion of this bridge was undoubtedly of the highest importance. Another limitation was the want of return traffic from Karachi and 'the wheat has to bear the cost of its own haulage and of the return of the empty wagons in which it has been carried'. The third one was that still in the 1880s certain rich wheat-producing tracts of the province remained unconnected by the railways. For example, a line from Raiwind to Ganda Singhwala on the bank of the Sutlej opposite Ferozepore was badly needed. Equally important was a line from Ludhiana to Ferozepore. It was expected to touch a very fertile wheat-producing tract of the province. Another much demanded line was the Karnal-Delhi line.[7]

With a view to overcoming these limitations, it was decided to construct a bridge over the Indus near Sukkur. This was finally completed in 1889. Secondly, attempts were also made to obtain cheaper transit charges for the downward Karachi-bound trade and soon favourable results followed.[8] Finally, the various railway administrations were amalgamated under the name of the North-Western Railways (1886), a state concern, and thereafter a rapid progress was made in the construction of new lines. Now the Raiwind-Ferozepore line via Ganda Singhwala as also the Nowana-Kaithal line were completed. But crowning all these projects came the Wazirabad-Khanewal line in the years between 1896-1900 connecting newly developing trading centres like Lyallpur (1896), Toba Tek Singh (1899) and Khanewal (1900) in the Chenab Canal Colony area of the central *bar* lands. Already the Chenab Canal had converted these arid waste lands into rich fertile tracts; soon the railways carried their agricultural products to the different trading marts and ports of India. The Chenab Canal Colony would perhaps never have been a financial success without the railways to serve its needs.[9]

The opening of the railways thus brought about a great change in the rural economy of the province. With and increasing mileage the railways made possible a faster movement of various agricultural commodities at a cheaper rate from one part of the province to another. They equally assured an easy access to previously inaccessible areas; from Pathankot to Peshawar or from Karnal to Kotri, all important fertile tracts were directly or indirectly brought into closer contact with Karachi, offering traders newer avenues of export of various agricultural commodities to the outside world. Prior to the opening of the railways, a good harvest often caused a glut in the rural economy, while in times of scarcity and famine, no immediate relief could be carried to the famine-stricken multitude because of the absence of any faster means of communications. Under these circumstances, prices depended entirely on local conditions and their violent fluctuations were almost an established pattern of the day. But the opening of the railways largely eliminated this possibility and led to a greater equalization of prices in the different markets of the province.[10] It also stimulated the cultivation or certain valuable crops like wheat, cotton and sugar-cane.[11] Already canal irrigation had made possible a large-scale waste land reclamation. Now the railways gave an added impetus to the increase of cultivation. These improvements in the general communication system[12] stimulated the process of commercialization of agriculture which may conveniently be studied with reference to three important crops, namely, wheat, cotton and sugar-cane which were widely cultivated in the province during the second half of the 19th century.

Wheat occupied a much larger area than any other crop in the Punjab during the period under review. It was not only the staple food of most of the Punjabis but also the chief crop for sale and export in most of the districts. It was also an important source of dry fodder and commonly used in religious rituals. This unique importance of wheat in the second half of the 19th century drew the attention of a number of British wheat experts; one of them even went to the extent of predicting[13] that the Punjab was not only destined to become the future granary of India but also 'probably the chief wheat-exporting province of Hindustan'.

The Punjab was traditionally famous for her wheat. Even during Sikh rule, cultivation of wheat was quite widespread throughout the province[14] and it was sometimes 'carried to foreign markets'. During the second half of the 19th century also the Punjab started exporting wheat to the different European markets, particularly after the opening of the Suez Canal (1869) and the removal of the export duty of three annas on each maund (1873). The steady rise of overseas demand was a very significant aspect of the wheat trade of this period and it greatly encouraged the increase of wheat acreage within the province. Of all the overseas markets, England, because of her direct trade links with India, was the chief centre of this trade. Previously, England almost solely relied on the Russian and the U.S. wheats. But with the improvement in the communication system and the great economy introduced in the transport of wheat from India, British traders slowly tended to shift their attention also towards the Punjab. This was largely due to the fact that wheat from this part of India usually reached London at a time when wheat from the other countries was not generally available. The Punjab wheat was also of a very good quality for baking.

This preference of the British millers for the Indian wheat was also largely due to its dryness which again contributed to its added popularity in the different English markets.

It should, however, be borne in mind that this trade with England depended on a number of circumstances.[15] Whenever these circumstances appeared to be favourable, the trade increased. Actually in the 1880s when the cost of transportation of wheat was greatly economised, the Punjab witnessed a series of favourable harvests. This period also synchronized with occasional crop failures in the United States and Russia, resulting in an increased demand for wheat from the Punjab and its increased cultivation and export trade during the last two decades of the 19th century.

On the eve of British rule in the Punjab, wheat, though widely cultivated, had only a small external market largely because of the absence of modern means of communication. There was then only 'very little trade between villages and town, little enough between neighbouring villages and none of great value between places far apart'. Consequently, the price of wheat depended upon local causes and fluctuated widely. Taking Dera Ismail Khan as a case study, we find that in 1842 wheat was sold at 22 seers to the rupee; a good harvest in 1850 brought the price down to 50 seers, while a bad one in 1868 sent it up to 13 seers. A good year 'brought such a glut that it was unsaleable, while a bad season sent the price soaring beyond the reach of the poorer people'. In 1858 also the merchants of Amritsar were placed under extreme difficulties when the prices collapsed following a supply of wheat 'far beyond the demand'.

Even during this period of price fluctuations, trade in wheat, however, showed signs of very slow development. Various attempts were then made to put an end to the endless customs barriers which restricted trade during the Sikh regime.[16] These measures greatly facilitated the movement of wheat from one part of the province to another. In 1854 alone, it was estimated that wheat worth nearly £66,000 were exported from the province to the various outside markets. In the 1860s, the situation further improved with the introduction of the railways connecting some of the important wheat-producing tracts of the province to the sea ports of Bombay and

Karachi. Accordingly in the mid-1860s an increased demand for the Punjab wheat, caused by the 'opening out of new markets',[17] was first significantly felt. But this trade soon fell-off in 1868-69 with the beginning of scarcity, failure of rains and the rise in the price of wheat in the province. In the 1870s, with the return of favourable seasons and the falling prices of wheat, this languishing export trade revived.

This decade started with a favourable spring harvest but ended with two consecutive short seasons. In between these two extreme points, the trade often greatly fluctuated with a corresponding change in the nature and outturn of harvest and the prevailing price level. In 1873-74, for example, the spring crop was 'a most abundant one' and there was an 'extraordinary export of food-grains to the Bengal famine districts'. Between 15th November 1873 and the end of March 1874, 5,94,788 maunds of wheat were exported from the Punjab to Bengal. In the next year also, Bengal continued to depend very largely on the Punjab wheat to feed her famine-stricken population; 'there was an export of 1,000,345 maunds chiefly on account of the Bengal famine'.[18] But in 1875-76, agricultural prospects in the eastern India improved resulting in a slackening of demand. Consequently, there came a quick falling off in the export trade. The Punjab Government admitted that 'the most remarkable feature in the returns of 1875-76' was the 'decrease in export of grain'[19] and a fall in the price of wheat. In 1876-77, the province had a bumper harvest and the trade in wheat revived in the 'face of a great demand for export to the famine districts of Bombay and to Europe'.[20] But this large-scale export received a check in the last quarter of 1877 owing to the failure of the autumn harvest in the Punjab and the rise in the price of wheat. In the first quarter of 1878 the trade was stimulated again by the increasing demand for wheat from the famine-stricken districts of Bombay and Madras.[21] Against this background of rising export trade, the province, however, suffered from a very lean harvest year in 1878-79 resulting in a sudden decline of outturn of wheat and a corresponding rise in its price in the different provincial markets.[22]

The stock of wheat was also low and the trade therefore inevitably languished. In 1879-80 also, almost a similar state of affairs prevailed. But in 1881-82 the trade greatly revived and 'reached a figure yet to be attained before'.

The year 1881-82 may rightly be described as an important landmark in the development of wheat trade in India. The total export of Indian wheat amounted to 19,863,520 cwt.,[23] out of which the contribution of the Punjab was nearly 2,262,425 cwt. (a ten-fold increase since 1877-78).[24] In this year the wheat crop was an abundant one in India. In the Punjab also there was a favourable harvest resulting in a fall in the price. Already a great economy had been introduced in the exportation of wheat through the port of Karachi. At this point came the report of a deficient wheat harvest from the United States (nearly 24 per cent) on which the English consumers largely depended.[25] Consequently, the Punjab wheat trade assumed a position of importance in 1881-82. This position continued to be maintained throughout the 1880s.[26]

Actually till 1885-86 there was a steady increase in the export trade of wheat carried chiefly through Karachi for shipments to Europe. The year 1885-86 was another important landmark of this trade in the 1880s. The export of wheat occurred on such a scale that during this year the Punjab was practically depleted of its old stocks. The next year was an unfavourable season for the cultivation of wheat. This fact, coupled with the depletion of stocks, led to a rise in the prices in the provincial markets. On the other hand, in Europe, the price of wheat fell because of favouarble wheat outturn in the United States. Under such circumstances, export of wheat to Europe from the Punjab appeared 'unprofitable' and the export of 1886-87 was below the normal figures. In 1887-88, this trade further declined 'due to two causes: (1) extraordinary depletion of stocks of all food-grains resulting from (a) exportation of previous years, (b) bad harvests of 1886-87. (2) The bad wheat harvest of 1887'. There prevailed almost a famine condition in the province; price rise and scarcity in several districts prevented any large-scale export of wheat from the province.[27]

However, this lull in the export trade did not last long. With the return of favourable spring and autumn harvests the price of wheat fell. Actually the wheat crop of 1888-89 was a favourable one and the total outturn was nearly 23.1 per cent higher than that of the preceding year.[28] Prices ruled cheaper in the two important provincial markets, namely, Amritsar and Ferozepore. With this the trade prospect improved, particularly towards the port of Karachi where a comparatively higher rate prevailed. It was particularly reported from Ludhiana that there was a considerable trade during the year in wheat which kept up the prices. Taken as a whole, the export during this year was larger than that of the preceding year.

It is interesting to note that 1888-89 marks the beginning of a long period of brisk export trade which reached its high water-mark in 1891-92. But this trade suffered greatly on three occasions in the 1890s and at least once, it returned to the pre-1888-89 figure. In 1892-93, for example, the wheat trade suffered partly due to following reasons: in the first place, owing to great depletion of stock of wheat, 'caused by the outgoings of last year, prices remained very high in the Punjab' (13.57 seers per rupee as against 18.18 seers per rupee in 1890), and secondly, owing to the abnormally low prices prevailing in England (for the United States had 'a harvest of unparallel dimension' supplying the needs of British consumers), the export of wheat was not profitable; 'the quantity which left the Punjab between July and December 1892 being only about one-eighth of that of the corresponding months of 1891'.

In 1896-97 also the trade suffered quite strikingly. Now this fall in the volume and value of the export trade was not due to cessation of the external demand (as it was in 1892-93), but largely to a widespread scarcity and a general famine condition prevailing over the vast tracts of the Indian peninsula. This led to a general rise in the price of all food-grains, including wheat.[29] In the Ferozepore and Amritsar markets, prices varied from 15 seers a rupee in April 1896 to 8 seers a rupee in March 1897. This high price of wheat in the provincial markets left little margin for profit on exports to Europe. The export trade, during this year of high prices and low stocks, was naturally dull.

Leaving aside these two lean years, the wheat trade of the last decade of the 19th century appeared to have codsiderably increased. In this period, favourable outturn and fall in the price level in the provincial markets made conditions favourable for a large-scale export of wheat. On many occasions, 'practically the whole of the surplus produce of wheat above what is needed for food consumption in the Punjab itself' was 'bought up for foreign export almost irrespective of variations in the cost of transport or in the market price of wheat'.[30] This spectacular rise of the wheat trade of this period ultimately convinced the Punjab Government that 'if stocks are low and prices in India sufficiently high, the wheat export may be checked [i.e. 1886-87 and 1896-97], but if prices are sufficiently high in Europe to make the export of wheat profitable, it cannot be safely predicted that even low stocks would not be exported.'[31] This prediction would appear to be true if its nature is analysed in the background of the wheat trade of 1891-92. In that year, actually a brisk export trade was carried on with England in the background of higher prices in the different provincial markets.

The spring crop of 1890 was an unfavourable one while the succeeding autumn harvest equally turned out to be below the average. In 1891-92, once again the wheat harvest was below the normal yield resulting in a price rise in the period from November to January. This rise was no less precipitated by the various military movements along the extreme north-western frontiers of the province. In this background came an extraordinary demand for wheat from the European markets where wheat either failed or threatened to fail leading to a steady price rise particularly in the United States. This steady European demand for wheat at a higher price (9-7/10 and 12-1/7 seers per rupee at London and Karachi respectively)[32] induced the exporters not only to buy up old stocks largely at Rs. 2-4-0 and Rs. 2-8-0 per maund, but also to make 'forward' purchases of wheat to be supplied from the new crop at similar prices. Thus an enormous amount of wheat was purchased at a higher price to be exported to Europe resulting in a general depletion of stock within the province.

This depletion of wheat stock greatly affected the food supply of the provincial population. Now the cry was that people could not get enough food to eat because exports to England had pushed up the prices to famine rates.[33] The price rise was often 'severely felt by certain classes of the population' and it raised a storm of protest in the Native Press.[34] The *Ataliq-i-Hind*, in its issue dated 22nd December 1891, gave an account of the distress prevailing in parts of the province and requested the Government to 'allow the export of only the surplus produce of the country'. But this appeal went practically unheeded and the wheat export trade showed signs of increase towards the close of the century. This not only led to a sudden depletion of the provincial stock of grain, but also caused considerable hardship to the poorer section of rural population in the late 1890s.

Like wheat, cotton also enjoyed a position of great importance in the agrarian economy of the province. It was cultivated under certain favourable conditions. Early British cotton experts were also quite confident that the Punjab could produce cotton of a good quality with the aid of irrigation since the climate of this tract was warm and stood 'beyond the influence of deluging rains'. 'Along the banks of the Punjab rivers lie tracts of land, at present waste, but which are admirably suited' for the 'finest specimen of cotton' grown in India. 'The cotton thus grown might, at trifling cost, be carried in country boats' to Karachi, and from 'thence be shipped for England'.[35] But this early optimism of the cotton experts was not shared by the Punjab Government. The Financial Commissioner, for example, sharply criticised it; he even came to the conclusion that the Punjab could never 'compete with other parts of India, as a cotton exporting country, notwithstanding its great advantage in the matter of water carriage'.[36]

Despite all this, cultivation of cotton increased remarkably in the Punjab. The first significant stimulus came with the beginning of the American Civil War (1861-64). In the early 1860s the vital trade connections between England and the American Southern States were virtually stopped, resulting in a great cotton famine in the British cotton mills. England was now in search of a new source of raw cotton and the vast Indian peninsula appeared to be an alternative source of supply. This new demand was indirectly responsible for a rapid increase of cotton cultivation in the Punjab. In the pre-Civil War period the cultivation of cotton was approximately confined to 3,10,611 acres[37] but in 1864-65, when the demand for cotton was at its 'unnatural height', the cultivated area increased to 8,91,082 acres.[38] In the next two years also, the Financial Commissioner found that its cultivation was one 'steadily relied on by the agriculturists' and it was likely to maintain a steady position.

Indeed, cotton cultivation was found so very remunerative that in many districts sugar-cane was replaced by it. With this increase in cultivation, trade in cotton also correspondingly expanded during these years. In 1861 nearly 40 per cent of the total outturn was exported.[39] Next year the demand for cotton was even greater, resulting in a rise in the price to Rs. 22 per maund (the former prices being 8, 9 and 10 maunds a rupee) and the total export trade amounted to 2,90,829 maunds (an increase of nearly 25 per cent). It was reported that in this year every available seer appeared to have been bought up and exported down the Indus by the country boats.[40] This brisk export trade continued in 1863-64 and the cotton of the Derajat was then 'highly rated in the Bombay market'.[41] In 1864-65 the demand was found to have attained an 'unnatural height' and its price also increased. In Amritsar, it was thirty to thirty-five rupees a maund resulting in a widespread diversion of capital from other trades to cotton. This 'mania for cotton speculation', as it was called in the administration report, continued till the end of the year.

But soon the cotton boom collapsed and the next year (1865) started with a sharp fall in the cotton price. In Dera Ghazi Khan, the price of a field of cotton fell from Rs. 1,000 to Rs. 300. In Amritsar, the price per maund of 80 lbs. fell from Rs. 35 to Rs. 12 and in Delhi from Rs. 32 to Rs. 7. Now with the cessation of the Civil War and the slow normalisation of trade relations of England with the United States, the English cotton mills could once again safely rely on the supply of cotton from the American Southern States. This naturally affected the volume of the export trade in 1865-66; the Punjab exported only 2,59,976 maunds of cotton (a decline of 11.7 per cent since 1862-63). This fall in the export as well as in the price of cotton inevitably led to a shrinkage of cultivation of cotton in 1866-67. Against this background the Punjab Government developed a pessimistic attitude.[42] With a steady decline in the provincial cotton acreage in the late 1860s, an impression gradually gained ground that the Punjab cotton would perhaps no longer be in demand. This gloomy official prediction was not entirely well-founded.

The area of cotton cultivation no doubt partially declined during the years immediately following the cessation of the

American Civil War. It was, however, still very much above the figures of the pre-Civil War period. Even in 1865-66, shortly after the cessation of English demand, its acreage was nearly three-fourths of what it was in 1864-65, when the trade was said to have attained 'an unnatural height'. The price of cotton per maund was equally not far below that of the Civil War period while it was very much higher than that of the period of the pre-Civil War.[43] This higher price as well as its favourable acreage clearly indicate that even after the end of the Civil War boom, it still appeared to be a remunerative crop. In fact the cultivation of cotton tended to increase during the later years of 1860s, the only exception being 1868-69.[44] The small fall in acreage in 1868-69 was perhaps partly due to the unfavourable trading condition of 1867-68 when a steady decline on the Indus-bound export occurred resulting in a price fall in the provincial markets. But in 1868-69 once again the prices rose to a large extent due to the prevailing famine condition in the province. 'Owing to the scarcity of food' 'the cheap and durable native made cotton cloth has been increasing in demand among the classes who are unable to purchase the dearer and lighter imported cloth, and the result has been to detain a considerable proportion of the stock of raw cotton for local consumption'.[45] The demand for raw cotton within the province made its cultivation quite profitable; further, there was a steady demand from the other Indian markets. Consequently, in 1869-70 its acreage increased remarkably. Besides supplying the domestic needs, the export trade during the year amounted to one lakh maunds, valued at 17½ lakhs of rupees. It was nearly four times larger than that of the previous year. This favourable condition of the export trade in the closing years of the 1860s convinced the Government that on the whole, 'the prospects of the cotton cultivation in the Punjab are encouraging. It is extending in some of the districts best suited for it. Prices are steady, with a tendency to rise, so that the cultivation may be considered to be beyond the risks of loss, except for unfavourable seasons'.

Actually the prevalence of unfavourable seasons often discouraged any large-scale increase of the cultivation of cotton. In 1868-69, as we have already seen, a shortfall in acreage and outturn of cotton was partly due to failure of regular rains at the time of sowing. In the 1870s similar things recurred. In 1873-74, for example, the cotton crop was a failure, even more than in the year 1872-73.[46] But still the prices ruled very low throughout the year and cotton trade also declined. This peculiar condition arose out of two factors: in the first place, wheat, being the predominant rabi crop usually dominated the price level in the different markets of the province. The wheat crop was 'a most abundant one', resulting in a fall in the price of cotton; further, Bombay and Calcutta which were the two major channels of the Punjab cotton export trade, where then passing through a long spell of drought and scarcity. They were badly in need of cereals and not so much of cotton. Consequently, the fall in the demand from Bombay and Calcutta with a corresponding good rabi crop within the province led to a fall in the price as well as in its export trade in 1873-74. Once again in 1875-76 and 1877-78 within a very short interval, two bad years visited the Punjab. In 1875-76, the province was so hard hit that the price of cotton increased strikingly[47] while the export trade also declined by nearly 11 per cent as compared to that of the preceding year.[48] Similarly in 1877-78, which was a period of agricultural distress in a large portion of northern India, the Punjab also suffered, the outturn of cotton having been only half of the average.[49] Of the area sown, a great proportion produced practically nothing or yielded an insignificant return, the total outturn being only 3,52,180 cwts., as compared with 5,29,011 cwts. in 1876-77, and 4,36,904 cwts. in 1875-76. The average yield fell from 86 lbs. per acre to 58 lbs. Against this general decline in acreage and outturn, export of raw cotton also suffered by 21.6 per cent from that of the preceding year.

The year 1880 was once again an unfavourable season for the cultivation of cotton. Drought and unseasonable rain reduced its acreage by 5.5 per cent in 1880-81. There 'was a general rise of prices in the local markets accompanied by a remarkable decrease in exports'.[50] The total export in 1880-81 was only 111,174 maunds compared with 3,03,789 maunds in 1879-80 (a decrease of nearly 63 per cent). The export trade towards Calcutta from the eastern Punjab districts suffered quite strikingly—it was merely one-fifth of its total volume exported in the previous year. This sudden fall in the Calcutta-bound trade was largely due to two reasons: within the province the price of cotton rose from Rs. 20-2-3 to Rs. 21-7-3 per cwt. in 1880-81 while the prices in Calcutta declined by about 10 or 12 annas per cwt. As a result of this price movement, the ordinary course of the Calcutta-bound cotton trade of which Ambala was the centre was reversed. Ambala, 'instead of, as is usual, receiving large amounts of cotton from Ludhiana and Amritsar, for despatch to Calcutta, exported a great deal of its surplus produce to these districts'.

But from 1881-82 onwards, the province witnessed a series of favourable seasons for the cultivation of cotton. This continued till 1889-90 with at least one significant falling-off in 1887-88. During these years, the acreage under cotton increased quite satisfactorily accompanied by a steady development of its export trade. In 1881-82, the total volume of the export trade amounted to 1,29,946 maunds,[51] chiefly going to Calcutta by rail and to Karachi by the country boats. In the next year it increased further till it reached 4,58,716 maunds[52] in 1889-90. This spectacular increase of the export trade of this period was the result of various factors such as the favourable price level, a greater reliance of the cultivators for an increased outturn on the various irrigational facilities, improved means of communications and the steady demand for cotton from the different Indian and overseas markets. As a result the export trade in cotton increased quite steadily during the 1880s.[53] But this brisk period was followed by a lull and the last decade of the century started with two consecutive bad years: 1891 and 1892, particularly the former. It was observed in the annual cotton crop report of 1892 that the harvest of the previous year was the 'smallest which had been known in the Punjab for years'. This failure was ascribed to the 'long deferment of rainy season in 1891 and to the ravages of locusts in most districts west of the Chenab'. As a result of all these factors the total outturn of this year was 35.8 per cent below that of the last year (1890).[54] In the next year (1892) precarious rainfall once again caused a shortfall in the production; the total outturn was nearly 20 per cent below the normal yield of 1,48,391 bales. In this year, it was estimated that cotton acreage 'is the lowest area, 1891 only excepted, which has been returned in the last five years'. This sudden fall in acreage and outturn in these two successive years correspondingly greatly affected the volume of export trade. In 1891-92 in particular there was also a diminution of demand for cotton from the European as well as Indian markets. It also led to a fall in the price of cotton within the province. 'The average price fell from Rs. 15 per maund in 1890-91 to Rs. 13 in the present year, and probably all these three circumstances combined to check exportation, while Bombay, the principal cotton-market in India, displayed a preference for the cotton of other provinces'.[55] Consequently, the export trade fell from 2,01,590 maunds in 1890-91 to only 51,864 maunds in 1891-92. During the same period export towards Bombay also declined by nearly 85 per cent. In the next year, however, things improved with the revival of demand from the Bombay and other overseas markets. The export trade which went down to the insignificant amount of 6¾ lakhs of rupees (1891-92), gradually increased to 36 lakhs in value (1892-93).[56]

In the remaining years of the 1890s, the province once again enjoyed, with minor exceptions, a series of favourable seasons which greatly helped the extension of cotton cultivation during this period. Actually with the exception of 1898-99 and 1899-1900 the cultivation of cotton and its outturn reached an unprecedented height.[57] At the same time increasing demands from the Indian and other overseas markets led to a very considerable expansion of the export of this article, particularly in 1895-96.[58] This trade, however, suffered in 1898-99 and 1899-1900, but soon attained a comfortable dimension in 1900-01. In 1901-02 once again the export trade declined by nearly 40 lakhs. This was due to the fact that the Punjab cotton crop of kharif 1900, though very 'plentiful', was of a poor quality while the crop of Berar and Khandesh was an extraordinarily good one and were able to outbid the Punjab crop.[59] Further the short size of the Punjab cotton was its another great limitation which was faced repeatedly by the cotton exporting agencies throughout the century. The Punjab Government thought of introducing 'American cotton' of a longer size. But the early attempts did not succeed during the period under review. Consequently, the local varieties of cotton with a shorter staple, popularly known as the *desi* cotton, constituted the bulk of the export trade and hence they could not often compete with long staple cotton of Khandesh and Berar. But the situation changed greately later when the 4F American came to be extensively cultivated in the Chenab Canal Colony, slowly relegating the *desi* cotton to a position of secondary importance.[60]

In the Punjab sugar-cane was very widely cultivated in the tract lying between the Jumna in the east and the Chenab in the west. Even within this region, districts such as Jullundur, Hoshiarpur, Gurdaspur, Ludhiana and Sialkot, which had a regular rainfall, fertile alluvial soil and a temperate climate, were particularly well-known for producing the best types of sugar-canes like *katha* and *dhaula*. In this province, as in other parts of India, the cultivation of sugar-cane had some distinctive features. In the first place, it was not produced in large consolidated blocks or plantations at certain intervals, but in small scattered plots by the cultivators who put in a patch of sugar-cane in their holdings of such size as suited them in rotation with other crops. This small area was often less than an acre, protected by a well or other means of artificial irrigation. In most cases, the family supplied the main labour force for ploughing or manuring fields. Outside help was occasionally taken at the time of cutting and crushing sugar-cane for manufacturing *gur* or *shakkar*, immediatedly after the harvest. Secondly, unlike wheat or cotton, the bulk of sugar-cane was grown and *gur* was manufactured chiefly for local or even home consumption and not for exportation to any overseas and other Indian markets outside the province.[61] It was essentially with this home or provincial market that the Punjab sugar-cane growers and manufacturers were chiefly concerned.

During the period under review, the cultivation of sugar-cane considerably increased. There were four major reasons for this. To begin with, increase of population in towns like Delhi, Lahore, Amritsar and Multan (where the purchasing power was usually greater than in the rural areas) led to a greater demand for sugar-cane within the province. The increased demand, particularly in its urban areas, could possibly have resulted in two things: (i) an increased importation of refined sugar from outside the province and (ii) a simultaneous extension of sugar-cane cultivation within the province. In the urban areas the import of refined sugar did increase, but in the rural areas which constituted the main sugar market, its popularity was not so easily established. This was largely due to the fact that 'unrefined sugar was sweeter and more adapted to the necessities of the zamindar; it was also very much cheaper than refined sugar'.[62] On the other hand, the increased demand for unrefined sugar within the province encouraged its cultivation.

Another factor in this growth was the development of various irrigational facilities during the period under review. Sugar-cane is a very thirsty crop and requires quite a good number of waterings for proper harvesting.[63] The increasing popularity of irrigation from wells and canals stimulated its cultivation at least in some parts of the province.

The increase in the cultivation of sugar-cane resulted also from the introduction of a new sugar-cane crushing machine in the province. It was known as the Behia mill after a Sahabad (Bihar) estate whose proprietors Thompson and Mylne had invented it. Its commercial success in other parts of India encouraged its introduction in the Punjab. The new mill crushed nearly 1.3 times as many sugar-canes as the old mill (*belna*) and that, more effectively. The juice extracted was much clearer and its yield was higher by nearly 20 per cent. It was then also found that the saving in money obtained by operating the new mill amounted to Rs. 20 a month. Further, the '*belna* usually requires three pairs of bullocks, and cannot be used with less than two; whereas Messers Mylne & Thompson's machine works easily with one pair, and may be efficiently kept going by a single bullock'.[64] The machine gradually became so much popular in different districts of the province[65] that the old *belna* was found surviving only 'in a few of the most backward villages' at the beginning of the present century. Thus the new mill did greatly 'shorten, facilitate and cheapen'[66] the extraction of juice from sugar-cane. Finally, sugar-cane was also a very remunerative crop for the affluent zamindars. In spite of its heavy initial investment, zamindars usually expected to reap a higher amount of profit from its cultivation which they could hardly expect by sowing other cash crops like cotton.[67]

Under the circumstances, the cultivation of sugar-cane increased. It was found that in course of the first two decades of British rule its acreage nearly doubled.[68] In the early 1880s it continued to be popular in a number of districts across the Chenab and Indus.[69] In most of the central and submontane districts also, the increase in its cultivation was remarkable. In Jullundur, for example, an increase of nearly 16 per cent in acreage took place largely due to widespread popularity of well-irrigation.[70] In Gurdaspur, the rapid extension of the use of the iron roller mills, resulted in 'a wonderful expansion' of the cultivation of the same crop. Similarly in Gujranwala sugar-cane was regarded as the 'most remunerative of all produce'[71] and its acreage strikingly increased during the early 1860s largely due to this reason.

But this rate of increase of sugar-cane acreage was not, however, maintained in the last two decades of the 19th century. In fact, the increase in the sugar-cane acreage was smaller than the increase in the cultivation of other crops like wheat and cotton. A comparative study of the acreages under these three crops would also reveal that while the areas under cotton and wheat increased steadily, sugar-cane merely maintained the level it had attained before the 1880s. The reasons for this are not far to seek. Broadly speaking, this period witnessed a widespread commercial success of wheat in the different Indian and overseas markets. Its cultivation was comparatively easier, demanded lesser amount of labour and attention than either cotton or sugar-cane. It was less prone to failures on account of natural vagaries. Similarly the market of the Punjab cotton had steadily increased during these years, and the result was a large increase in cotton cultivation in this period. On the other hand, sugar-cane had no such comparable market and it had a very limited market in the Native States of Rajputana and central India. Further, the cultivation of sugar-cane also occupied the soil much longer than any other crop. From the time of sowing to ripening, it kept the ground occupied for nearly a year. In the case of cotton and wheat this period was much shorter. This problem was, however, nothing new. Now with the greater commercial success of wheat and cotton, zamindars found it convenient to change over to their cultivation. In the canal irrigated regions of the province, this problem prevented any major increase in its cultivation in newly broken-up waste land.[72]

Besides the sugar-cane cultivation was also more expensive. Indeed 'a single farmer, with no relations to supply cheap labour and without a good supply of manure, could not possibly cultivate sugar-cane with profit'.[73] Thus from Gujranwala, the district officer reported (1890s) that the cultivation of sugar-cane underwent a partial decline largely because of the greater outlay of capital which the crop required and the extra demand it made upon the zamindar's labour. An almost similar report came from the Amritsar district where also a decline in the sugar-cane cultivation took place largely because of the 'vast amount of labour' it required and the high cost of cultivation. The Indian Sugar Committee also admitted the fact that 'heavy expenditure on labour' greatly impeded the extension of sugar-cane cultivation in the central Punjab canal colonies. Actually the heavy initial investment, required for the cultivation of sugar-cane, often necessitated borrowing from the money-lenders. Their exorbitant rate of interest and the numerous fraudulent transactions during the whole period of cultivation considerably reduced its attractiveness and popularity.

Further, the Punjab, in spite of the improvement in the techniques of crushing sugar-cane, could scarcely meet the increasing metropolitan demand. And the province had to depend for this on the adjoining provinces. The cheapness of the imported variety combined with its attractive appearance and its palpable superiority as an article of food, greatly popularised it in most of the metropolitan towns of the province. It 'sells at from Rs. 9 to Rs.15'. 'It requires moreover in the preparation of sweetmeats less than half the labour which has to be spent on country sugar'. 'Customers have been known to leave hundreds of rupees with the manager [of sweetmeat shops] for long periods in order to be sure of their supply'. Finally, with growing laxity in caste regulations in metropolitan towns, the refined sugar came also to be used at all social and public gatherings. All these factors encouraged importation of refined sugar from the outside markets and it amounted to an increase of nearly 187 per cent during the last decade of the century.[74]

One immediate effect of this increased import of refined sugar was the closing down of a number of sugar refineries in three important sugar-cane-producing districts of the province.[75] The size of sugar-cane cultivation in these districts inevitably declined as a result. The Director of the Land Records and Agriculture also admitted that 'the foreign imports have prevented to a slight extent the area under sugar-cane from increasing so largely as it would presumably have done under the old conditions'.

The growth of commercial agriculture produced certain significant effects on the rural economy of the province during the period under review. It greatly stimulated the process of substitution of inferior crops by the superior ones. In this connection wheat deserves our special attention. Its commercial success prompted many zamindars to switch over to its cultivation in many of the districts of the province. In the central Punjab districts and the canal colonies also *jowar, bajra, china, kangi* and *maddul* were largely substituted by wheat.[76] The process continued till the close of the century and the Director of the Land Records and Agriculture in his annual report of 1893-94 clearly admitted that with the spread of irrigation 'lands formerly under inferior crops' were 'brought under wheat'[77] Similarly the cultivation of cotton steadily increased over the years and during the period of the American Civil War, sugar-cane was often replaced by cotton in the central Punjab districts.[78]

This commercialization of agriculture also raises an interesting problem: did the zamindars reap any profit out of it? It is commonly believed that it brought little benefit to them. They were generally indebted to the *sahukars* who compelled them to sell their produce at a low market price. The *sahukars* 'took away almost everything except a few months' supply' for the needs of zamindars and their families. In many cases they financed the cultivation of these commercial crops and carried them away from the zamindars' threshing floor[79] as soon as the harvesting was done. Consequently the zamindars could not respond to the market stimulus and in their cases commercialization of agriculture only increased their indebtedness.[80] But in a number of districts of the province, big zamindars did benefit by the commercialization of agriculture, and to them its benefits did not always remain 'hazy and illusory'. They did not sell their produce at a price arbitrarily fixed by the *sahukars*. They gradually evolved the practice of 'shaking off the trammels of the *bania*', and learnt to 'keep their money themselves and manage their own affairs'. They often held up their grain till their prices rose, sold them directly to the actual exporters and secured a comfortable margin of profit out of their own labour. In districts like Montgomery, Amritsar and Karnal this form of marketing of wheat was becoming increasingly popular towards the close of the century. Similarly the Jats of Ferozepore and Ludhiana reaped a good deal of profit out of it. In the different canal colonies also enterprising zamindars did not fail to respond to the market stimulus. In the Sidhnai Colony, for example, colonists preferred the rabi to the kharif. 'They say that wheat pays them better than any other crops'. A similar response was also evident in the Chenab Canal Colony towards the close of the last century.[81]

NOTES

1. Statement of the Trade of British India with British Possessions and Foreign Countries for the five years, 1887-88 to 1891-92, *Parl. Papers, 1893*, LXVI, 21.
2. For details, see K.M. Sarkar, *The Grand Trunk Road in the Punjab* (Languages Department, Punjab, Patiala, 1971), 12-5.
3. They were mostly occupied by passengers, troops and government stores and had little accommodation for commercial goods. Further, they had to compete with the native boats which plied up and down the rivers to Karachi. Incidentally the freightage for native boats from Lahore to Karachi was about one rupee per maund, while that of the steamer was 'sixty or eighty per cent in excess of the rate of the native craft'. This difference in rates was sufficient in itself to make these steamers 'useless for the purposes of the Punjab commerce'. Actually they were 'incapable of materially helping the export or import trade of the Punjab as they were not sufficiently numerous, spacious or economic'. For details, see Arora, *op. cit.*, 17-8.
4. *Ludhiana D.G., 1888-89*, 193; *Attock D.G., 1907*, 207.
5. *Administration Report on the Railways of India for the Calendar Year 1900* (London, 1901), Appendix 7.

6. Already in the early 1860s the total value of the export trade carried through Karachi was nearly 28 times higher than that of 1857-58. Now the railways, tapping the Indus traffic at Kotri, were extended through the Punjab (1878) which greatly stimulated the export trade. In 1882-83 the Punjab Government found that it had strikingly increased in course of the last two years. It was then firmly believed that this trade had 'a great future before it'. Actually at the beginning of the present century it was estimated that this port alone, excluding Sindh, sent down 37 per cent of the imports and received 54 per cent exports of the province. LG Punjab's No. 6436, 28 November 1882 (P.W.D.), Rev and Agr (A) March 1884, 49-66B; *Internal Trade Report, 1883-84*, 4; *Ibid., 1884-85*, 2.
7. Memorandum by Major A.S. Roberts, DC Karnal, 12 July 1883, *Punjab Wheat: Its Varieties, Distribution and Husbandry* (Lahore, 1884), 11.
8. In November 1882, the cost of wheat delivered at the port of Karachi was Rs. 3-2-0 per maund whereas in 1885 it was exported along the same route at Rs. 2-7-0. During this period the sea freight from Karachi to London was also reduced by 43 per cent. 'This quick reduction in the transit charges is sufficient to show how greatly the importance of the Punjab wheat trade has increased during the last few years'. In 1879 the export of wheat to Karachi was valued at Rs. 74,668. In 1882-83 the money value of the wheat trade consigned by train to that port, exclusive of river traffic, amounted to Rs. 51,42,886, and in 1884-85 to Rs. 54,71,950. For details, see LG Punjab's No. 95, 19 March 1885, Rev and Agr (A) March 1885, 58A.
9. In the early 1890s when the Chenab Canal Colony witnessed a bumper harvest, there were practically no railways and the result was a sudden fall in the prices. Wheat and cotton were actually rotting at different points of this tract. But with the opening of the Wazirabad-Khanewal line they were quickly exported to the outside markets. The following table will illustrate this point.
   Statistics of 3 important articles of trade carried by the railways at the beginning of the present century from the Chenab Canal Colony.

Commodity	Export in maunds
1	2
Wheat	8,134,607
Raw cotton	567,212
Cotton seed	449,754

Source : *Chenab Canal Colony Gazetteer, 1904*, 115.

10. Price of wheat per rupee in seers in three important districts of the Punjab.

Year	Delhi	Multan	Peshawar
1	2	3	4
1861	14.7	15.62	17.62
1871	21.87	16.49	15.33
1881	19.37	16.34	9.68
1891	14.04	13.00	14.92
1901	13.31	14.35	15.12

Source: *Prices and Wages in India, 1902*, 19th Issue (Calcutta, 1902), Table 2.

11. Report on the wheat production and wheat trade of India, Rev and Agr (AH) January 1880, 41-82A; L.M. Dane, SC Gurdaspur's No. 343, 20 July 1888, Rev and Agr (A) October 1888, 28-36B.
12. Development of Public Works in the Punjab, 1872-73 to 1902-03.

Year	Railway mileage	Canal mileage	Metalled road mileage	Cultivated area (millions of acres)
1	2	3	4	5
1872-73	410	2,744	1,036	18.8
1882-83	600	4,583	1,467	23.4
1892-93	1,725	12,368	2,142	26.7
1902-03	3,086	16,893	...	26.8

Source: H.H. Calvert, *The Wealth and Welfare of the Punjab* (Civil and Military Gazette Press, Lahore, 1922), 107.

13. LG Punjab's No. 95, 19 March 1885, Rev and Agr (A) March 1885, 58A.
14. This extensive cultivation of wheat during Sikh rule was, however, due to various factors and a few of them are noted below. The arid and dry climate of the Punjab, coupled with the winter rains, often at the time of sowing, were quite favourable to the cultivation of wheat in the central Punjab districts. In the south-western districts like Muzaffargarh and Multan water from the numerous inundation canals was also available in the early summer months when the wheat seedlings began to sprout. Secondly, the winter frost in the Punjab often damaged the late kharif crops, but it was seldom too severe to have any serious adverse effect on wheat. Thirdly, cultivation of wheat required lesser amount of capital and labour from the agriculturists than did other crops, particularly sugar-cane. For example, for sowing sugar-cane, the land had to be ploughed, as one proverb goes, 100 times whereas wheat required no such elaborate tillage and hoeing. Further for sugar-cane, 10 to 15 waterings were often needed, for it was

regarded to be a very thirsty crop. But a maximum of 5 waterings were sufficient for wheat. From the point of capital investment, wheat could also be cultivated at a lesser cost than sugar-cane. *Report on Condition of Crops: on Wheat in India* (Washington, 1884), Rev and Agr (A) January 1885, 7-8B; W. Hamilton, *A Geographical, Statistical and Historical Description of Hindostan and the Adjacent Countries,* I (John Murray & Co., London, 1820), 557; R.L. Bhalla, *An Economic Survey of Bairampur in the Hoshiarpur District* (The Board of Economic Enquiry, Punjab, Publication No. 1, Lahore, 1922), 122-6.

15. The following remarks of the Punjab Government deserves special attention: 'The export of *wheat*, at all events, seems to depend partly on the nature of the crops of this Province, partly on the variations in cost of transport both by land and sea, and partly on the nature of the crops in America and Russia, and on the variations in cost of transport from those countries to the consumers in England and in Western Europe'. *Internal Trade Report, 1888-89*, 6.
16. Circular No. 1 of 1850, 5 January 1850, *Circular Orders issued by the Board of Administration in the Revenue Department during the years 1849 to 1853*, I ((Calcutta, 1856), 19.
17. *P.A.R.*, 1865-66, quoted in Brij Narain's *Eighty Years of Punjab Food Prices, 1841-1920* (The Board of Economic Enquiry, Punjab, Publication No. 13, Lahore, 1926), 37.
18. Extracts from the Proceedings of the Government of India, 28 October 1879, Rev and Agr (AH) January 1880, No. 66A.
19. For example, wheat which constituted the bulk of the export trade declined strikingly from 16,11,248 maunds in 1874-75 to 7,42,161 maunds in 1875-76. *Note on the Trade Statistics of the Punjab, 1875-76*, 7.
20. *P.A.R., 1876-77*, 82.
21. *Ibid., 1877-78*, 115-6.
22. Besides this rise in the prices, the trade in wheat declined due to crop failure in India, fall in the prices of wheat in the English markets (56 shilling 9 pence per quarter in 1877 to 46 shilling 5 pence) and good supply of wheat from Russia and the United States. Extracts from the Proceedings of the Government of India, 28 October 1879, Rev and Agr (AH) January 1880, 66A.
23. Statement of the Trade of British India with British Possessions and Foreign Countries for the five years, 1879-80 to 1883-84, *Parl. Papers, 1885*, LVIII, 45.
24. LG Punjab's No. 6436, 28 November 1882 (P.W.D), Rev and Agr (A) March 1884, 49-66B.
25. Statement of the Trade of British India with British Possessions and Foreign Countries for the five years, 1878-79 to 1882-83, *Parl. Papers, 1884*, LIX, 63.
26. Acreage and export of wheat from 1882-83 to 1889-90.

Year	Area in lakh acres	Export in thousand maunds
1	2	3
1882-83	66	4,101
1883-84	67	5,187
1884-85	72	9,688
1885-86	78	14,924
1886-87	72	3,335
1887-88	61	865
1888-89	66	4,700
1889-90	74	8,327

Source: *Internal Trade Report, 1888-89*, 6; *Ibid., 1891-92*, 7.

27. *P.A.R., 1887-88*, 97.
28. Note on the wheat crop of the Punjab, 1888-89, *RR 1888-89*, Appendix C (I), vii.
29. Final report on the wheat crop of the Punjab, 1896-97, *Ibid., 1896-97*, Appendix C, x.
30. *Internal Trade Report, 1891-92*, 7.
31. Report on fluctuations in prices of wheat and the trade in that cereal in the Punjab, Rev and Agr (A) December 1895, 7-9A.
32. Final report on the wheat crop of the Punjab, 1891-92, *RR 1891-92*, Appendix C, viii.
33. LG Punjab's No. 61S, 29 May 1894, *Ibid., 1892-93*, 1.
34. LG Punjab's No. 420S, 10 July 1893, *Ibid., 1891-92*, 1.
35. J. Forbes Royle, *Review of the Measures which have been adopted in India for the Improved Culture of Cotton* (Smith, Elder & Co., London, 1857), 76-7.
36. Possibly the Financial Commissioner based his arguments on the following considerations. In the first place, irregular annual rainfall during the kharif season often caused havoc and in years like 1873, 1877, 1884, 1891 and 1892 failure of cotton crop was largely due to this cause. Secondly, the Punjab cotton, with the exception of that of Peshawar, was essentially one of short staple, its maximum length being 5/8 of an inch. It could scarcely compete in the different European markets with the cotton of bigger staples. Thirdly, the Punjab cotton was also exported in an extremely dirty condition admixtured with inferior fibres, thus bringing a great 'disrepute' to it. Finally, the early November frosts also impeded the growth of good healthy pods in the Punjab. For details, see *RR 1861-62* quoted in Baden Powell's *Hand Book of the Economic Products of the Punjab*, I (T.C.E. College Press, Roorkee, 1869, hereafter *Hand Book*), 490-2; *RR 1862-63*, 44.
37. FC's office, Statement No. II, 2 August 1858, Home (Public) Consultation, No. 48, 24 September 1858.

38. *P.A.R., 1864-65*, 118.
39. FC's office, 1 October 1863, *RR 1862-63*, Appendix III.
40. *P.A.R., 1862-63*, 140.
41. *Ibid., 1863-64*, 107.
42. *RR 1868-69*, 71.
43. Remarks by Major Farrington, CR Amritsar division, *ERR 1862-63*, 44; FC's circular No. 20/1100, 9 March 1867, quoted in Baden H. Powell, *Hand Book*, I, 481.
44. Changes in cotton acreage from 1866-67 to 1869-70.

Year	Area in acres
1	2
1866-67	6,24,193
1867-68	6,87,321
1868-69	6,79,294
1869-70	8,11,749

Source: Baden-Powell, *Hand Book*, I, 481; *RR 1869-70*, 45; *Report on the Cotton Cultivation of the Punjab, 1874*, 1.

45. *RR* 1869-70, 46.
46. *Note on the Trade Statistics of the Punjab*, 1873-74, 3.
47. *Report on the Cotton Cultivation of the Punjab*, 1875-76, 1.
48. *Note on the Trade Statistics of the Punjab*, 1874-75, 4.
49. William Hoey, *A Monograph on Trade and Manufactures in Northern India* (American Methodist Press, Lucknow, 1880), 7.
50. *Report on the Cotton Cultivation of the Punjab*, 1880-81, 1
51. *Internal Trade Report*, 1882-83, 33.
52. *Ibid., 1889-90*, Statement Nos. I and IV.
53. Export of raw cotton in maunds from 1881-82 to 1889-90.

Year	Export in maunds
1	2
1881-82	1,29,946
1882-83	1,52,548
1883-84	1,60,338
1884-85	2,53,914
1885-86	3,05,756
1886-87	4,58,512
1887-88	5,14,699
1888-89	4,08,118
1889-90	4,58,716

Source: *Internal Trade Reports* for the respective years.

54. Note on the cotton crop of the Punjab, 1891, *RR* 1891-92, Appendix C (II), xi.

55. *Internal Trade Report*, 1891-92, 6.
56. *Ibid.*, *1892-93*, 3.
57. Area and yield of cotton from 1893-94 to 1901-02.

Year	Area in acres	Yield (bales of 400 lbs)
1	2	3
1893-94	948,300	200,900
1894-95	1,124,500	231,997
1895-96	1,161,200	241,667
1896-97	1,176,700	204,806
1897-98	1,128,400	223,947
1898-99	788,600	166,907
1899-1900	988,400	138,926
1900-01	1,215,400	205,203
1901-02	1,080,200	219,646

Source: *Area and Yield of Rice, Wheat, Cotton, etc., for various periods from 1891-92 to 1901-02*, 26.

58. *Internal Trade Report*, 1895-96, 4
59. *Ibid.*, *1900-01*, 3.
60. *Census of India*, 1931, XVII, Part I, 34.
61. Extracts of the memorandum by Messers Thompson and Mylne on sugar cultivation and manufacture in India, Rev and Agr (A) December 1891, 1A.
62. J.R. Dunlop-Smith, DLRA Punjab's No. 508, 3 March 1898, Rev and Agr (A) June 1899, 7-8A.

63. Crop	Number of waterings
1	2
Wheat	5
Cotton (Desi)	8
Sugar-cane	10 to 15

Source : Randhir Singh and W. Roberts, *An Economic Survey of Kala Gaddi Thamman (Chak 73 G.B.)—a Village in the Lyallpur District* (The Board of Economic Enquiry, Punjab, Village Surveys No. 4, Publication No. 27, Lahore, 1932), Table XIV, 34-5.

64. Remarks by Major Wood, DC Jullundur, *ERR 1884-85*, 34.
65. Remarks by Colonel A. Munroe, CR Derajāt, *Ibid.*, *1878-79*, 27; Remarks by G.G. Young, CR Delhi divisions, *Ibid.*, *1880-81*, 2; Remarks by A.S. Roberts, DC Karnal, *Ibid.*, 1881-82, 5; Remarks by J. Frizelle, DC Ambala, *Ibid.*, 12; Remarks by E.C. Corbyn, DC

Shahpur, *Ibid.*, 34; Remarks by Colonel E.R. Conolly, DC Bannu, *Ibid.*, *1884-85*, 76; *Bannu S.R.*, *1879*, 79; List of agricultural implements found useful in India, Rev and Agr (A) March 1883, 24A; *Karnal D.G.*, *1883-84*, 163.

66. Average daily production and expenditure on the Belna and Behia mills.

Machine employed	Sugar-cane crushed in maunds	Weight of juice per 100 maunds of sugar-cane	Cost of working		
1	2	3	4		
			Rs.	As.	P.
Belna	12	56-5	4	12	0
Behia	16	65-5	1	12	0

Source : Remarks by C. Roe, DC Hoshiarpur, *ERR 1882-83*, 56.

67. Bhalla, *op. cit.*, 123-6.
68. In 1858 sugar-cane acreage was approximately 1,61,230 acres while in 1878-79 it was 3,80,579 acres. FC's office, Statement No. II, 2 August 1858, Home (Public) Consultation, No. 48, 24 September 1858; *RR 1878-79*, Statement XXIX.
69. *RR 1881-82*, Statement XXIX.
70. W.E. Purser, DCS Jullundur, Report on sugar industry in the Jullundur district, Part II, Rev and Agr (A) July 1884, 4-8A.
71. *Gujranwala S.R.*, *1874*, 27.
72. Actually in the canal irrigated districts, sugar-cane acreage did not increase like that of either cotton or wheat. To a large extent this was due to the absence of timely irrigational facilities supplied to its cultivation. For example, in the south-western districts sugar-cane acreage, irrigated by the numerous inundation canals, not only fluctuated enormously, but the supply of water from them could not be depended upon with certainty before May, whereas sugar-cane was usually sown in March. Similarly, the cultivation of sugar-cane, protected by the Western Jumna Canal, did not increase strikingly during the period under review. It was largely due to the fact that it could not provide the optimum possible supply until the beginning of June whereas the sugar-cane 'land requires water from the beginning of March'. For details, see *Report of the Indian Sugar Committee*, 68, 70.
73. *Delhi D.G.*, *1912*, 112.
74. Imports of refined sugar in maunds during the 1890s.

Year	Import of refined sugar in maunds
1	2
1890-91	474,180
1892-93	373,429
1894-95	509,327
1896-97	769,411
1898-99	803,664
1900-01	1,364,708

Source: *Internal Trade Reports* for the respective years.

75. Number of refineries at work in three important sugar producing districts of the province.

District	Number of refineries at work in		Decrease in
	1887-88	1897-98	per cent
1	2	3	4
Hoshiarpur	138	102	26
Jullundur	77	62	19.5
Gurdaspur	50	41	18
Total	265	205	22.5

Source: J.R. Dunlop-Smith, DLRA Punjab's No. 508, 3 March 1898, Rev and Agr (A) June 1899, 6-8A.

76. Note on the wheat crop of the Punjab, 1887-88, *RR 1887-88*, Appendix C (I), xiii; *Amritsar A.R., 1892*, 26.
77. Note on the wheat crop of the Punjab, 1893-94, *RR 1893-94*, Appendix C (III), ix.
78. *P.A.R., 1864-65*, 118.
79. Note by W. Coldstream, DC Simla, Rev and Agr (R), December 1891, 10-11A; Memorandum on the Raya A.R. by D. Ibbetson, CR Rawalpindi division, PGR Rev and Agr (R), June 1893, 15A; Remarks by R.E. Younghusband, DC Dera Ghazi Khan, *ERR 1890-91*, 10; *Sharakpur A.R., 1893*, 4; F.A. Shah and L.R. Dawar, *Finance and Marketing of cultivators' wheat in the Punjab—Being a report of investigation in the Lyallpur, Ferozepore and Attock Districts during 1930-31* (The Board of Economic Enquiry, Punjab, Publication No. 38, Lahore, 1934), 17.
80. Whitcombe, *op.cit.*, 170-9; Bipan Chandra, 'Reinterpretation of the Nineteenth Century Indian Economic History', *IESHR*, V, No. 1, March 1968, 51.
81. Memorandum J.B. Hutchinson, DC Multan, Rev and Agr (R), July 1890, 14A; Remarks by M. Macauliffe, DC Montgomery, *ERR 1876-77*, 34; Remarks by A.H. Benton, DC Karnal, *Ibid., 1880-81*, 4; Note on the wheat crop of the Punjab, 1888-89, *RR 1889-90*, Appendix C(I), xi; *Revenue Report of the Irrigation Department, Punjab, 1891-92*, 84; *Amritsar A.R., 1892*, 3; *Tarn Taran A.R., 1891*, 26.

4

Land Revenue Administration

The early land revenue settlement system of the Punjab under British rule was virtually an extension of the system of the North-Western Provinces as it stood in 1849.[1] It was largely due to the fact that the first batch of the Punjab settlement officers as well as their subordinate native officials were mostly brought from the North-Western Provinces; they were very closely associated with Thomason's[2] *Directions for Settlement Officers and Collectors* (published in three parts between 1844 and 1848 containing a 'masterly exposition' of the land revenue system prevailing in that province) which formed the Revenue Code for newly annexed Punjab. In this way the Punjab 'obtained ready-made a system which had been gradually evolved by the labours of many able officers in the districts between the Jamna and the Ganges'.[3] This settlement system had its 'own distinctive features like a detailed enquiry into the rights and liabilities of all persons having an interest in the land' and 'a moderate assessment of land revenue with persons having proprietary rights over land' for the payment of the state share.

The first task that confronted these officers was to determine who were actually in possession of such permanent rights in the soil so as to settle land revenue with them. But this was not an easy task in view of the infinite varieties of rights over land in different districts of the province. They generally found[4] that the administration of the Sikhs had not only had a levelling impact on the superior landowning families (*ala maliks*) but had greatly strengthened the position of the inferior proprietors like *chakdars* and *sildars* who frequently participated in the cultivation of their holdings. The former were entitled to some proprietary dues from the latter (for example, in Muzaffargarh and Multan); but sometimes they were denied even this in the districts of Rawalpindi, Jhelum and Gujrat. Similarly, the position of the different forms of quasi-proprietary tenures varied from district to district. In the south-west, they generally paid some dues to their superior overlords though in the extreme north-west they were under no such obligations. These striking differences in land tenures naturally made the task of the early settlement officers an extremely difficult one.

But from the very beginning it became an agreed policy among these officers to settle land in favour of persons who held land and had paid the revenue for twelve years prior to the introduction of the first land revenue settlement (of a particular district which was introduced shortly after the annexation of the province). Consequently, they generally settled land revenue with the inferior proprietors and allowed them the sole management of the estate while the claim of the superior owner to a share of the crop was 'commuted into a moderate sum levied as a surcharge upon the revenue' and was 'calculated at a small percentage on its amount'.[5] The former were looked upon 'as the valuable element in the community' while the latter 'as an interesting survival of a state of society which had passed away and should not be revived'.

Accordingly in the south-eastern districts where the village land was predominantly held and cultivated by the 'proprietary bodies of kinsfolk' with ancestral rights the settlement officers found little difficulty in settling land with them. They were confirmed on their ancestral holdings and they were declared jointly responsible for the payment of land revenue. To represent these village proprietary bodies in their dealings with the Government, a few of their leading members were selected as hereditary headmen (*lambardars*), their most important function being to collect revenue from the village proprietors and pay it to the revenue officials. Unlike the south-eastern Punjab, the arid south-west, however, reported no such homogenous village proprietary body closely related by ties of kinship. Here the unit of property was the well and the climate by itself was 'enough to account for the prevalence of holdings in severalty'. Further here the tillage entirely depended on artificial means of irrigation; cohesion among the holders of lands was very weak and the proprietary right was often 'split up in a curious way between the inferior and superior proprietors'. While introducing land revenue settlement, the settlement officers not only 'forcibly engrafted' the joint village system in this tract but also treated the inferior proprietors very favourably. They granted proprietary right to the inferior proprietors while the claim of the superiors to a share of the produce was recognized and 'commuted into a surcharge on the assessment calculated at the percentage of Re. 1 annas 12 on its amount'. This might not have been 'an equivalent to the grain payments hitherto received, but it had at least the effect of establishing the tenure on a firm basis'.[6]

Again the north-west of the province was characterised by the 'juxtaposition of dominant families and clans and a miscellaneous collection of inferior tribes', many of whom had fared badly at the hands of the Sikhs. When the early settlement officers introduced land revenue settlement in this tract, they often tried to get back their dominant position in the rural society. The settlements of this tract were however not completed till after the Mutiny, 'when official opinion was more sympathetic to the claims of those martial clans, who had rendered excellent services against the mutineers and whose rights were recognised roughly in inverse proportion to their distance from the Indus'.[7] Thus to the east of this region the rights of the 'old warlike tribes, when actually admitted, were restricted to a small surcharge on the land revenue; but in the further west, they did receive in addition the full proprietary right over the entire village waste while the inferior proprietors' rights were limited to the ownership of the holdings they actually held and cultivated' (*malikan kabza*). It was only in Hazara that the old superior families were able to obtain full ownership rights in their own villages.[8]

While settling lands with the actual tillers of the soil as far as possible, the early settlement officers had also to determine the amount of land revenue of the Government. Under Ranjit Singh, the Government demand was heavy and it was usually fixed at half the produce.[9] The British administration also considered it to be high, and felt that this demand must be sufficiently lowered in order to leave a 'fair and liberal margin to the occupiers of the soil'. Accordingly, the land revenue demands of the closing years of Sikh rule as shown in the official accounts,were taken as the main guide to the amount of the new cash assessment, but deductions of various amounts (for example, the striking out the cesses and allowing a deduction of 5 per cent for *inam*) were allowed. In many cases, a committee of village elders accepted the demand and agreed to pay it for a short term of years.

Broadly speaking, these settlements, popularly known as the summary settlements,[10] almost everywhere reduced the demands of the Sikhs, but it would seem that the new system of cash payment and the rigidity of collection largely set off the advantages resulting from such reductions to the cultivators. The summary settlements of the Jullundur *Doab* (1846) by John Lawrence and his Assistants 'were much more reasonable', especially in the two plain districts where the settlement officers were considerably 'influenced by their knowledge of the success of Misr Rup Lal's assessments. Nearly the whole of the Punjab, west of the Beas, with the exception of the districts included in the Governorship of Diwan Sawan Mall and his successor Diwan Mulraj, was summarily settled in the cold weather of 1847-48 by the Assistants of the Resident at Lahore'. The districts, which had not been assessed before the outbreak of the second Sikh War, were put under summary settlements shortly after the annexation. The work was done 'hastily by young officers with only such local knowledge as they could get in the course of their hurried tours'.[13]

These settlements were, however, welcomed by the peasantry and as long as the harvests were good, and the markets were steady, these cash assessments worked satisfactorily. But this happy condition lasted only for two years, for then the prices began to fall. The drop continued until grain sold at fifty per cent below its settlement valuation. These assessments 'though on paper at least a good deal lighter than the demands which they superseded', largely broke down with this extraordinary fall in the prices[12] which began in the late 1840s.[13] 'Grain in consequence became a glut in the market. In 1851 and 1852 wheat fetched only half as much as the average price of the five years before annexation'.[14] The situation, therefore, became quite critical and the zamindars had to face an extremely grave condition; the cry of over-assessment was raised from different parts of the province. In Ambala, for example, the assessment was pitched so high that the Commissioner of the Ambala division noted in his review of the settlement report of the early 1850s that he frequently came across a 'complaining tenantry, broken villages and deserted fields' in a considerable part of the district.[15] In Sialkot also heavy assessment in parts of this district gave rise to unfortunate consequences.[16] In Gujranwala the situation was equally alarming because the zamindars expressed 'remarkable distaste to fixed assessments'; sometimes 'they would say that they would renounce their proprietorship rather than engage for any fixed assessment'.[17]

Such cases of recusancy were sternly dealt with by the settlement officers. They frequently transferred the shares of such recusants to more solvent shareholders who agreed to pay the Government revenue or sold them to the highest bidders. In the Gujranwala tahsil 15 estates wholly and 2 partly were transferred to outsiders; in the Wazirabad tahsil one whole estate and one-third of another were similarly transferred while in Hafizabad the transfer covered one whole estate, one-half of two, one-third of two, one-fourth of two and one-sixth of three estates. In addition to these, transfers of holdings covering about 14,000 acres took place; the old owners in most cases owing to poverty or the pressure of assessment had to alienate their shares to more solvent shareholders.[18] In Amritsar, particularly in its Narowal pargana, the situation was equally grave. In a memorandum to the Government, the Extra Assistant Commissioner admitted that the summary settlements had increased the 'embarrassments' of the zamindars because these assessments 'continued to bear heavily on the people, and some villages were thereby impoverished'.[19] In Thaneswar (Karnal) the high assessment brought immense misery to the rural folk. But the 'revenue continued to be realised with the greatest severity, coercive measures were constantly adopted, and farms and transfers of revenue paying lands and even of whole villages, were frequent'.[20]

In view of this general distress of the people, the Punjab Government was forced to reduce these high revenue demands. Accordingly from 1850-51 onwards attempts were made to reduce this exorbitant rate of assessment and in 1856 it was found that the permanent reduction in the assessment since the annexation amounted to nearly 25 per cent. At the same time steps were taken to reinstate the old owners to their ancestral holdings.[21] Finally, these harsh summary settlements were replaced by regular settlements. With these regular settlements the settlement system in the Punjab took its first definite shape and it may conveniently be divided into five distinct phases during the period under review.[22]

The first period lasted till the year 1863. It began with the settlement of the districts in the cis-Sutlej and trans-Sutlej territories after the first Sikh War and ended with the appointment of Prinsep as the Settlement Commisioner. During this period assessments were based on 'general considerations', such as a careful enquiry into the resources and the past history of the estates which had governed the assessment procedure in the North-Western Provinces.[23] At first the standard assessment was fixed at two-thirds and at the end of the period at one-half of the net assets, i.e., the average surplus after deducting the cost of cultivation. These assessments were not, however, 'founded on any attempt to determine with exactness by the help of rents what the amount of a standard revenue demand really was'.[24] Further, these officers hardly paid any regard to 'natural varieties of soil' which later on played a very important part in calculating the standard assessment in the province. But in distributing this assessment over the village, there was, however, a decided tendency among the settlement officers to assess leniently those zamindars whose antecedent conditions had given them less opportunity of developing agricultural skill. Again in the region irrigated by the Western Jumna Canal, a new water rate was levied on the land actually irrigated in each harvest. This was in addition to the fixed assessment on land normally irrigated from wells, and was itself higher than that on unirrigated land. Ont he whole the amount assessed in the first regular settlements was considerably lower than the demands of the summary settlements, which had generally been accepted as too severe. Actually the 'low range of prices from annexation down to the famine of 1860-61' coupled with the widespread distress of the zamindars prompted the Government to reduce its high rate of land revenue assessment at the earliest possible opportunity.[25] The amount of reduction varied from district to district and it came to be enforced when a particular district came under the operation of a regular settlement.

This 'moderation of demand' characterised the Punjab settlement system even during its second period which started in 1863 when Prinsep assumed the office of the Settlement Commissioner and ended with the enactment of the First Land Revenue Act in 1871. During the early 1860s irrigation from the Bari Doab Canal brought new tracts under cultivation; naturally the question of assessing the irrigated lands received serious attention from the Settlement Commissioner. In connection with his settlement operations in the Sialkot district, he was very 'much struck with the expense and risk involved in well-irrigation'. He held that the existing settlement policy of the British Government frequently led to over-assessment of the irrigated lands. The state had no doubt 'a right to assess water as a cause of increased fertility when it became available for use', he continued, but this 'demand must be very light, otherwise capital would be taxed, and improvements discouraged'.[25] Thus while assessing the area irrigated by the new canal, the principle adopted by Prinsep was to first make a 'dry' assessment at the rate which would have been imposed had there been no well or canal, and then to add a 'water advantage rate', i.e., an extra assessment on the advantages due to irrigation. In the case of canal lands this was paid by 'acreage rates on the area actually irrigated each year. Prinsep's proposal to apply this principle to well-irrigation also, was not adopted, as it made no allowance for the great differences in efficiency between various wells. It also violated the principle that the state was entitled to half the net assets'.

The third period of the Punjab settlement system embraced the eight years from 1871 to 1879. It was marked by certain distinctive features of which the 'steady extension of the authority of the Indian Government in settlement matters' deserves special attention. Prior to it, all Punjab settlements had been undertaken without its 'legal sanction'. To remedy this defect, the Land Revenue Act was passed in 1871. It laid down that from then on a 'settlement could only be undertaken with the sanction of the Government of India'; further the officer placed in charge of it was furnished with clear instructions 'stating the principle on which the revenue was to be assessed, approved by the same authority'. Accordingly in the assessment instructions issued to the settlement officers of Delhi, Gurgaon and Karnal, the Government of India clearly pointed out (1873) that 'one-half of the share of the produce of an estate ordinarily receivable by the landlord either in money or in kind' should be the basis of assessment.[27] In these instructions the importance of the produce estimate was emphasized while due weightage was given to the existing general considerations principle. Actually till the enactment of the second Land Revenue Act in 1887, all assessments were made in the Punjab in accordance with the instructions issued in 1873. This period also witnessed the 'wide extension of the plan of fluctuating assessments' in different districts of the province. It was already 'adopted in the districts watered by the Western Jumna Canal; and in substance also in the tracts in Montgomery dependent on inundation canals from the Sutlej'. Soon this principle was also introduced in the *sailab* tracts of Bannu, Dera Ismail Khan, Multan and Muzaffargarh.

The fourth period of the system lasted from 1879 to 1889. These years also witnessed certain significant changes in the 'settlement procedure culminating in the system embodied in the Land Revenue Act of 1887 and the rules under it, and in the instructions under section 49 of the Act and the assessment circular issued in 1888'. The basic principle underlying the changes introduced was the assimilation of settlement work and ordinary district revenue work. Its success depended 'on the possibility of so improving the latter as to avoid the necessity of extensive surveys and revisions of records at future settlements' by basing the 'assessments largely on a continuous record of agricultural statistics compiled by a well-trained staff of *patwaris*'. About the year 1874 this new policy first took shape in the North-Western Provinces and in 1885 it was introduced in this province.[28] These reforms envisaged among other things 'an accurate registration of the crops of both harvests at the time when they ripened and a detailed enquiry into the prices and the carrying out of numerous experiments by the settlement staff to determine the yield of the crops'.

Further steps were taken to make *jamabandi* and other revenue settlement records correct to date for this would enable the setttlement officers 'to dispense with fresh surveys and revision of records as far as possible'. These correct settlement statistics were asked to be maintained in the village registers which soon took the place of the old village note books. This policy of 'assimilating settlement and ordinary revenue work was carried to its logical conclusions' by the Land Revenue Act of 1887. It placed the records drawn up at settlement and the annual revenue records prepared by the *patwaris* 'precisely on the same legal footing'. It was followed by the assessment instructions under section 49 of the Land Revenue Act of 1887 and a circular which clearly laid down that the Government demand for land revenue should not as a rule generally exceed 'the estimated value of half the net produce of an estate'.

During the fifth and final period of the Punjab settlement (from 1889 onwards), the new procedures were put to test. Some of their fundamental limitations were revealed. The success of the new procedures depended largely on the effective maintenance of different annual revenue papers at the village level by the *patwaris.* But the latter miserably failed in maintaining these records correctly. Besides measures prescribed for the keeping up of village maps, and record of rights were not properly carried out at different levels. Orders were not promptly passed on matters relating to alienation of holdings. Consequently, the general revision of land records, which it had been hoped could be avoided under the new system, still continued to delay the work of assessment.[29]

These changes in the settlement policy also brought in their train a steady increase in the land revenue demand over the years. In this connection table 1, given on page 86, merits special attention. It appears that in course of the last forty years of the 19th century land revenue demand increased from Rs. 1,90,18,132 to Rs. 2,22,34,850. This period also witnessed a steady price rise. It seems that prices of food-grains and the land revenue demand rose more or less at a same rate during these years. In other words, this increased land revenue demand of the Government did not apparently suggest any significant increase in the burden of revenue for the zamindars. But this did not necessarily mean that this land revenue demand of the Government had no adverse effect on the agrarian economy of the province, or that the zamindars faced little difficulty in paying this official demand in due time. A critical analysis of the different village surveys would reveal that zamindars were placed in great difficulty in paying the land revenue of the Government. Actually their small, scattered and fragmented holdings, failure of crops, as well as their increasing volume of debt and the extreme rigidity in the collection of land revenue frequently compelled them to borrow from the *sahukars*. In order to have a better understanding of the problem, one village (Bairampur) enquiry in the Hoshiarpur district may be cited. This enquiry established one point beyond doubt that nearly 40 per cent of the zamindars could not meet their revenue obligations out of their own income.[30] Some of them had to borrow while some others got it from other sources, often not directly connected with their cultivation. Further, the dates of payment of revenue and the harvesting often coincided. 'In

TABLE 1: **Increase of land revenue and the rise in the price of food-grains from 1860-61 to 1901 (Rabi)**

Year	Price of food-grains in seers per rupee	Index No. (1860-61 =100)	Land Revenue (including Nazrana and service commutation) demand	Index No. (1860-61 =100)
1	2	3	4	5
1860-61*	17.46	100	1,90,18,132	100
1871-72	21.08	82.8	1,87,64,491	98.9
1881-82	17.33	100.7	1,91,91,755	101
1891-92	14.91	117.2	2,08,76,476	109.9
1901 (Rabi)	15.20	114.9	2,22,34,850	116.8

Source : *RR* for the respective years.
*The early years of the 1850s have not been taken into consideration because these years were marked by low prices of grain.

order to meet the demand of the Government they are frequently compelled to sell their produce at unfavourable prices'.

Thus even in a district like Hoshiarpur (traditionally regarded as an important region of the Punjab agriculture) zamindars had to face difficulties in paying the land revenue of the Government. The situation was even worse in many of the extreme south-western districts where its extreme rigidity was causing great anxiety among the zamindars. Here they often refused to accept the fixed assessment because its inelasticity did not assist them 'in meeting unforseeable losses, the collapse of a well, etc., and in such necessities they were to borrow at heavy interest'. From Bannu also Thorburn, the settlement officer, reported that over-assessment and extreme rigidity in the collection of land revenue universally led to indebtedness of the zamindars.[31] In his monograph on the indebtedness of the Muhammedan zamindars of the western districts, he reiterated that the inelastic revenue administration was an important cause of debt. He further suggested that the landowning Musalman tribes of the western districts 'were generally indebted and sinking into the position of serfs or villeins to Hindu money-lenders, and that their degradation was directly due to our [British] system of administration, particularly to the innovations of fixed assessments'. The remedial measures, he suggested, were the 'substitution of elasticity for fixity in collecting the land revenue'.[32] Many experienced officials also realised the futility of maintaining this type of land revenue assessment in the 'dry' areas of the province; they repeatedly urged upon the Government the need for a fluctuating assessment in the riverain tracts of the province. Accordingly, a fluctuating form of assessment (as it has already been pointed out) was introduced in different districts of the Punjab. In spite of its steady extension, there remained wider tracts of the province yet to be brought under a similar land revenue arrangement. Further, it came at a time when the zamindars had already got themselves seriously involved at the hands of money-lenders in many of the districts across Chenab.

This widespread indebtedness led to steady displacement of the zamindars from their ancestral holdings.[33] An enquiry of the early 1890s clearly revealed that in one particular year

(1887-88) out of 8,634 cases of alienations, at least 926 were due to the strain which the payment of the Government revenue involved. These transfers of lands, however, raised a storm of debate among contemporary officials. Many of them expressed their deep anxiety and held the view that this process of expropriation of the zamindars would give rise to 'a grave political danger' in the rural society of the province.[34] But at the commencement of British rule, though indebtedness and alienation of lands were very much in existence in different parts of the province, local officers were then under the impression that alienation of lands in the 1850s was of a very limited nature and hence they did not attract any serious attention.[35]

But in the late 1860s and the early 1870s when this alienation sharply increased due to widespread scarcity and famine in a number of districts of the province, senior officials like Brandreth and others tried to explain it in greater details. As the Commissioner of the Multan division, Brandreth pointed out (1869) that this process of alienation involved a 'political question of extreme importance' and accordingly he asked (1871) the Government not to allow free alienations by zamindars.[36] Like Brandreth, Melvill, as officiating Judge of the Chief Court, felt (1872) the need of some legislative actions to protect these zamindars against their creditors.[37] But the Lieutenant-Governor was not in a position to accept and implement those restrictions suggested by Melvill. He held the view that in number and extent transfers of lands were insignificant and there was also no reason to assume that all these transactions were made under the pressure of debt. He firmly believed that the condition of the peasantry was in general prosperous and, therefore, 'no legislative interference was needed to save them'. According to him any legislative interference would only 'stave off and ultimately intensify the evil which it aimed to stop'.[38] His views were fully endorsed by Egerton, the Financial Commissioner of the province.[39]

These views of the Lieutenant-Governor and the Financial Commissioner were not shared by all.[40] Thorburn, for example, was then convinced that legislation was badly needed to avert future agrarian trouble in the province.[41] In 1884 he sent a detailed report on the indebtedness of the Muslim zamindars of the frontier districts of the Punjab.[42] In 1886 he published his monograph on the rural indebtedness and transfers of lands: *Musalmans and Money-lenders in the Punjab*. On the basis of 'official literature and personal experience', he graphically described that almost everywhere in the western Punjab expropriation of the zamindars by the money-lenders was going on over the years.

This monograph of Thorburn soon drew the attention of the Secretary of State for India. He immediately asked for a report from the Punjab Government[43] and the Lieutenant-Governor endorsed it. Accordingly the latter requested the district officers to report whether alienations were increasing and whether such increase indicated any political danger.[44] The detailed replies of some forty-four revenue officers (1888-89) established it beyond doubt that alienations of lands to money-lenders and indebtedness of the zamindars were steadily increasing. They were particularly of a serious nature in the frontier districts where the landowners and money-lenders were sharply divided by religion as well as by interests. The former group was vastly superior in point of number and made excellent soldiers while the loyalty of the latter to the Government 'was of a doubtful nature'. Naturally the steady expropriation of the zamindars by the *sahukars* would create a discontented agricultural community, ready for violence against the money-lenders. The problem, therefore, required an immediate attention from the Government since the security of the British Raj in the Punjab was at stake.[45]

In order to combating this evil, these officers including the Lieutenant-Governor himself, were more or less then agreed that a legislative measure was badly needed. The Lieutenant-Governor suggested the extension of some of the stronger provisions of the Deccan Relief Act to the whole of the Punjab[46] while many others were prepared to go even further in this direction. But the Government of India 'refused to legislate along the lines suggested by the retiring Lieutenant-Governor, Sir J.B. Lyall'. His successor Dennis Fitzpatrick soon assumed the office with this conviction that a direct restriction of the power of transfer could put a stop to alienation of lands by the zamindars to the *sahukars*. Simultaneously he also requested Thorburn, now the Commissioner of the Rawalpindi division, to select four or five assessment circles in his own division in which he considered the evils of transfers of lands were the greatest and make a minute investigation into the problems.[47]

Thorburn's findings were quite revealing. It was found that in his division money-lenders held 15 per cent of the agricultural land in full proprietorship and another 13 per cent under mortgage. He, therefore, suggested that permanent alienation of land to non-agriculturists without official sanction should be declared illegal.[48] His views were also shared by the two Financial Commissioners of the province.[49] Accordingly a committee of revenue experts of the province[50] was appointed by the new Lieutenant-Governor Sir Macworth Young who succeeded Sir Dennis Fitzpatrick in March 1897. This body also suggested that a measure of general application would only be effective in restricting the process of expropriation of the zamindars from their holdings.[51] The resolutions of the Punjab Committee deeply influenced Rivaz. He was now in the Governor-General's Council and he accordingly presented the draft of the Punjab Alienation of Land Bill in September 1899. Once again he expressed his opinion in favour of a general restriction on alienation.[52] The Viceroy also described this measure as the 'first serious step' to 'free' agricultural communities from 'an incubus' which was 'slowly but steadily wearing them down'. The bill received the consent of the Secretary of State for India. Thus was passed the Punjab Alienation of Land Act (Act XIII of 1900) on 8 June 1901.[53]

Broadly speaking, under the new Act permanent alienation of land between members of agricultural tribes was permitted while sales by agriculturists to persons not belonging to agricultural tribes were virtually prohibited. Restrictions as to the form and period of mortgages by members of non-agricultural tribes or by members of agricultural tribes to members of same tribes were removed. The maximum period of usufructuary mortgage, as also of lease, was fixed at 20 years and another form of mortgage was added under which the mortgagor could remain in possession of land as an occupancy tenant for any period on a rent to be fixed in case only of dispute by a revenue officer. The mortgagor could be evicted for arrears of rent only. Hypothecation of produce for a period of one year and mortgage in any other form might be permitted by the Government at its discretion. As regards enumeration and grouping of agricultural tribes it was generally decided to include the market-gardening tribes (for example, the Malis) and tribes like the Jats, Gujars and others, 'whose pursuits were distinctly agricultural or pastoral'. Village artisans and menials were proposed to be excluded from the list of agricultural tribes. 'Tribes of low status, like the Labanas, and tribes which contained both agricultural and non-agricultural elements like the Sheikhs were sometimes included and sometimes excluded. The Muslim religious tribes, like the Sayads, and other high status Muslim tribes, like the Pathans and Mughals, were usually, though not invariably, included.'[54] The Act came into operation amidst much criticism by the native press.[55] The Punjab Government kept a close watch over the working of this Act for the next eight years and at the end of that period it was claimed that the Act proved to be a great success 'in not only stopping the process of expropriation of the hereditary landowners of the Province from their ancestral land, but in enabling the agricultural classes as a whole to recover much of the land they had lost'.[56]

The process of expropriation of the hereditary landowners may be said to have largely stopped with the disability placed upon the non-agriculturist *sahukars* to own permanently the alienated land of the former. After 1901 sales of land to them practically ceased and applications for sanction to sell land to non-agriculturists were also not very numerous during the first eight years (1901-08) when the Act was under a close scrutiny.[57] At first the professional money-lenders were equally shy of the new forms of mortgages.[58] Subsequently, however, they 'expressed their willingness to accept mortgages permitted under the Act, particularly the self-redeeming usufructuary mortgages'. The *sahukars* also made a futile bid to evade the provisions of the Act and cases of *benami* tractions were frequently detected by many officers.[59] Actually under the Act 'the legal position of the alienee was also too insecure for evasion to be generally credited with success'. Further the process of expropriation of the hereditary landowner was also to a great extent arrested; this again may be related to a general decrease of the alienated area in each year following the year of this enactment. The area under redemption, except during the first few years following the enforcement of this Act, also indicated a definite sign of increase.[60]

But when viewed from the standpoint of the weaker agricultural tribes the Act ultimately turned out to be a very dangerous weapon in the hands of the powerful to be frequently used against the weak. Actually it was often seen that those thrifty enterprising tribes (for example, the Jats) who required little protection most strikingly benefited from this enactment while the weaker ones were placed under extreme duress to preserve their very existence; the latter, instead of being swallowed up by the professional money-lenders, were now faced with a similar process of expropriation at the hands of the former.[61] The Act also sought to restrict the process of acquisition of lands by the village artisans and menials.[62] Consequently, many agriculturists, not notified as agricultural tribes, suffered a similar fate. In this connection agriculturists belonging to the Labana and Ramgharia communities who were equally debarred from acquiring lands under this Act merit special attention. Many of them often applied to the Government for their inclusion in the list of agricultural tribes. A few of them wanted to acquire land in the canal colonies since these grants were virtually confined to the members of the agricultural tribes. Many others were anxious to have the protection of the Act. In several districts membership of an agricultural tribe conferred a sort of social status. This also prompted many to apply to the Government. The Government, after an extensive enquiry, agreed to notify the Labanas while the claims of the Ramgharias and others were not recognized. This official refusal to sanction the status of agricultural tribes must have greatly restricted their acquisitive instinct. With them this enactment was naturally very unpopular.[63]

Further the Act, as anticipated by many, was responsible for an immediate contraction of credit[64] (largely because of the elimination of the *sahukars* from the land market) and strengthened the position of the agriculturist money-lenders.[65] It led to a temporary depreciation in the value of land,[66] but it was not of a permanent nature. In fact the price of land after a brief fall began to rise after 1902-03 and by 1906-07 it certainly reached a higher level than ever before.[67] But this Act did not necessarily mark the virtual withdrawal of the *sahukars* from the rural economy. They continued to extend credit to the zamindars; but advances were then made with care and discrimination, and with reference to the circumstances and position of the client. They agreed to extend loan to a poor zamindar only 'on the intervention of some strong and reputaable zamindar'.[68] The money-lenders continued their trade because they successfully learnt to manipulate the law. They secured long leases and nineteen-year mortgages with insured rights of renewal. The Act was also evaded by marrying into an agricultural family.[69] A new type of *benami* mortgage was devised through which these *sahukars* used to 'get rich agriculturist to buy land and then transfer the property sub rosa to non-agriculturists'.

In some cases, however, the Act also resulted in a partial diversion of capital from money-lending to trade and commerce. With the restrictions placed on the money-lenders from holding the lands of the notified agricultural tribes, many of them often found little interest in their traditional avocations and started shifting to trade. In several districts money-lenders showed a greater interest in wholesale and retail trade in foodstuffs and other commodities.[70] This diversion of capital to trade and industry (like cotton factory) marked the beginning of a new chapter in the rural economy of the province. This process was no doubt very slow and gradual, but it was expected 'to promote, in some degree, the industrial as opposed to agricultural development of the more advanced portions of the province'.[71]

While all this have been said in favour of the Act, a critical perusal of its working would reveal that it did not alleviate the poverty and indebtedness of the zamindars of the Punjab. In his evidence before the Provincial Banking Enquiry Commission (1927), Darling, Registrar, Co-operative Department, pointed out that the Punjab, particularly its Muslim districts, were deeply in debt. The Commission also found that the total debt in the Punjab increased from Rs. 90 crores in 1921 to Rs. 135 crores in 1929.[72] It was then also revealed that money-lending to agriculturists had become the Punjab's largest industry in the province and old debts like 'large boulders on a hill road' blocked the path of advance.[73] Thus the problem of rural indebtedness continued to remain in the rural society of the province and it assumed a serious proportion particularly during the period of depression in the 1930s.

NOTES

1. *S.M.*, 8.
2. Sir James Thomason (1804-1853) was the Lieutenant-Governor of the North-Western Provinces (1843-1853). He laboured for nearly twelve years to complete his monumental work on the land system of Northern India. For details, see Sir Richard Temple, *James Thomason* (Oxford University Press, 1893).
3. *S.M.*, 8.
4. *Supra*, 2-4.
5. *S.M.*, 68.
6. *Ibid.*, 82.
7. Hugh G. Trevaskis, *The Land of the Five Rivers* (Oxford University Press, 1928), 248.
8. *S.M.*, 86-7; Baden-Powell, *Land Systems*, II, 630. Similarly in the Baluch area across the Indus the tribal chiefs (*tumandars*) retained 'important magisterial and administrative functions' in consideration of which they were allowed to collect in grain the land revenue of particular villages, which were assigned to them as payment for their services. 'This was a highly valued privilege', as they were thus enabled to 'collect an amount which approximated to the pre-British land revenue, and was therefore considerably higher than that which would have been obtained from the British cash assessment'. Sir James Douie, *Punjab Land Administration Manual* (Superintendent, Government Printing, Lahore, 1931), 136-7.
9. The Sikhs, however, took even more from lands with exceptional fertility. References were not uncommon where as much as 54 per cent of the actual produce was taken as the share of the Government. As a rule the state demand 'may be said to have varied from two-fifths to one-third of the gross produce'. This proportion generally prevailed in all the districts which the Sikhs had conquered and which were fully cultivated. This system was equally in force in all their cis-Indus districts, except the province administered by Diwan Sawan Mall. Beyond the Indus, owing to the distance from the seat of the Sikh power, and the warlike character of the local population, the revenue demand of the Sikhs 'pressed more lightly on the people'. In all these tracts, except perhaps the rich land around Rawalpindi, the Government share never exceeded one-third, and usually averaged one-fourth or one-fifth, and was in some cases as low as one-eighth of the crop. For certain crops such as sugar-cane, cotton, indigo, tobacco and vegetables which could not be 'conveniently' divided, money-rates were

always paid. Where the demand consisted of a share of the crop, whether by *batai* (actual division) or by *kankut* (appraisement of the outturn by inspection of the crop), the Government officials sometimes disposed of the grain themselves, but more commonly obliged the zamindars to pay for it in cash, at prices rather than higher those quoted in the ordinary markets. This system of collection of land revenue in kind, was not, however, universal. Some local Governors often assessed their revenue in money, and towards the close of Ranjit Singh's reign, a portion of the kingdom was thus assessed. In this connection the very 'equitable' money assessment of Misr Rup Lal in the two plain districts of the Jullundur *Doab* deserves our special attention. For details, see *P.A.R., 1849-50 and 1850-51,* 81; *S.M.*, 19-20; Jullundur *D.G., 1883-84,* 58-9; Kohli, *op. cit.*, 437-44; Banga, *op. cit.*, 88-107.

10. A summary settlement has been defined in the first Land Revenue Act (XXXIII of 1871) as a 'provisional settlement made pending a first regular settlement'. Legally the chief difference between the two lies in the fact that 'no presumption of truth, such as is attached to entries in records-of-rights prepared at regular settlements (section 16 of Act XXXIII of 1871), belongs to similar entries made at a summary settlement'. *S.M.*, 23.
11. *Ibid.*, 22.
12. This fall in the price was largely due to the fact that during the first three years following the annexation, the harvests with a few isolated exceptions were remarkably favourable. Cultivation was extended even on *barani* lands without much exertion on the part of the zamindars. These circumstances, joined to the general peace and security of the country, 'contributed to cause so great an increase of produce as to reduce prices to an unprecedented extent'. It also fell due to the closing down of the mints and scarcity of silver. During Sikh rule regular cash remittance of the soldiers employed in the *khalsa* to their home constituted a very important source of income to zamindars and greatly helped them to meet the land revenue demand of the Government. 'Many a highly taxed village paid half its revenue from its military earnings. Thus money circulated freely'. This remittance of the Sikh soldiers also increased the purchasing power of the consumers in the rural tracts of the Punjab. But shortly after the annexation, the *khalsa* was disbanded and with it also the cash remittance of the soldiers to their home was practically stopped leading to a great scarcity of silver. Further, during these years 'the Indian portion of the army employed in the Punjab was largely Hindustanee. A considerable share of the Punjab revenues was paid to them as their wages, of which they spent a part in the Punjab, and remitted the remainder to their homes. Many lakhs of rupees were thus annually drained from the Punjab'. For details, see *P.A.R., 1849-50* and *1850-51*, 11, 81; Brij Narain, *op. cit.*, 39-40.
13. Prices of wheat in maunds, seers and chattacks per rupee in Lahore from 1848 to 1851.

Year	Prices of wheat in maunds, seers and chattacks per rupee
1	2
1848	0 27 2¼
1849	0 19 3
1850	0 21 12
1851	1 4 4¾

Source : *P.A.R. 1849-50* and *1850-51*, Appendix A.

14. According to another estimate of the early 1850s 'the price of the staple produce, wheat, has fallen by 35 per cent; that the zamindar has now to part with 88 seers of wheat for one rupee, whereas at the time of the summary settlement he gave only 65 seers'. Letter from R.H. Davies, Secy. to the Government of the Punjab to the Secy. to the Offg. FC Punjab, quoted in G.W. Leitner, *History of Indigenous Education in the Punjab* (Languages Department, Punjab, Patiala, 1971), 196.
15. *Ambala S.R., 1893*, 20.
16. *Sialkot S.R., 1865*, 55-6, 77.
17. Remarks by R. Temple, CR Lahore division, *Gujranwala S.R., 1874*, 33.
18. *Gujranwala D.G., 1893-94*, 146-7.
19. Memorandum by W. Blyth, EAC Narowal, *Amritsar S R., 1873*, 164-5.
20. *Karnal-Ambala S.R., 1891*, 16.
21. In Gujranwala, for examble, all such transfers for arrears of revenue, were annulled. Here these measures were generally 'successful except in cases where whole estates had been transferred to wealthy capitalists like the Dewans of Eminabad and the Sardars of Butala, who claimed to hold on the ground that they had spent money on the property'. *Gujranwala D.G., 1893-94*, 147.
22. *S.M.*, 24.
23. Actually what was really done by the settlement officers in determining the standard of assessment, the following remarks of Sir James Douie, the Settlement Commissioner, is worth mentioning in this connection: 'Great stress was laid on the working of the summary settlements. Villages were sometimes grouped with reference to their past revenue history as highly, moderately, and lightly assessed. The rates paid by estates of the second class gave a clue to the rates which would probably be suitable as general average rates. The opinions of native officials and of respectable landowners were weighed, those of the latter being considered specially useful as regards the distribution of the gross assessment over estates. Statistics of cultivation, irrigation, population, ploughs, wells, and other matters throwing light on the economic condition of each estate and circle were tabulated'. *Ibid.*, 26. See also Baden-Powell, *Land Systems*, II, 570-1.

24. The settlement officers generally held the view that cash rents in the true sense of the word hardly then existed in the Punjab and hence in framing the standard assessment their calculations were not 'seriously' taken into consideration. Similarly when 'estimates were framed, a fraction of the gross produce, generally one-fourth, was assumed as the share of Government throughout a whole district with small reference to the varying *batai* rates which actually prevailed'. *S.M.*, 25.
25. The following remarks of Sir John Lawrence thus aptly summed up the character of the assessments of this period: 'Moderation of demand is not only due morally and actually to the people, but is also conducive to the best interests of the Government'. *Ibid.*, 27. See also R. Bosworth Smith, *Life of Lord Lawrence*, I (Elder & Co., London, 1883), 394.
26. *S.M.*, 29.
27. *Ibid.*, Appendix I B.
28. Actually the need for reform of the village revenue records was long felt in the Punjab because they were extremely 'unreliable and worthless' for assessment purposes. Everything was then practically done by a host of 'ill-paid and ill-taught' village *patwaris* who often performed their functions relating to annual statements of cultivation and wells (*milan khasra*), crops (*jinswar*) and transfers (*naksha intikal*) without any periodic field-to-field inspection. Even the *jamabandi* (record of right) records were 'little better than waste papers'. Naturally when the time for a new settlement arrived, 'much money and labour had to be spent in entirely re-casting them'. These evils in the village revenue records naturally required an immediate rectification. *Ibid.*, 36.
29. *Ibid.*, 42-3.
30. Bhalla, *op.cit.*, 94.
31. *Bannu S.R., 1879*, 59.
32. Thorburn, *P.P.W.*, 252.
33. For details, see Chapter V.
34. These officers believed that the zamindars were 'unjustly being deprived of their ancestral holdings'. These expropriated zamindars frequently took to violent means in the frontier districts and *sahukars* (who mostly purchased their alienated holdings) were their main target of attack. They were frequently manhandled; their account books or *bahis* were destroyed; their houses were even indiscriminately burnt down. This widespread rioting and unrest among the zamindars produced apprehensions of mutiny in the British Indian army. The army was chiefly recruited from those warlike agrarian communities who were slowly losing their ancestral holdings. They also pointed out that alienations of lands mostly affected Muhammedan zamindars of the frontier districts while their creditors were almost universally Hindu *sahukars*. Here communal antagonism further complicated the problem. This view was generally held by officers like S.S. Thorburn, DC Bannu, C.M. Rivaz, CR Lahore division, T.J. Kennedy, DC Montgomery, J.C. Brown, DC

Gurdaspur and J. Wilson, DC Shahpur. For their views, see G.R. Elsmie, FC Punjab's memorandum, 15 August 1889, Rev and Agr (R) December 1891, 10-11A. See also John R. McLane, 'Peasants, Money-lenders and Nationalists at the end of the Nineteenth Century', *IESHR*, I, No. 3, September 1963, 71.

35. According to Dr P.H.M. van den Dungen, the remarks of the local officials 'on the state of indebtendness, the onerous terms on which money was borrowed, and the transfers which had occurred' were marked by an 'optimistic tone'. Their attitude, the same authority further added, was consistent with contemporary evidence which yielded 'no indications of special anxiety' on land transfers. (For it, see P.H.M. van den Dungen, *The Punjab Tradition : Influence aud Authority in Nineteenth Century India*, George Allen & Unwin, London, 1972, 49). This view seems to be based on a misreading of the contemporary evidence. A critical perusal of the official records would reveal that no such 'optimistic tone' characterised official opinion in the 1850s; there are also other grounds to believe that the Punjab Government was well aware of the problem of indebtedness and expressed a deep concern about it. For example, the Punjab Board of Administration made it a principle to maintain and preserve the hereditary village communities 'in all their integrity'. It also expressed its strong aversion to sub-letting village lands to bankers. The Punjab Civil Code (prepared under the direct supervision of Robert Montgomery, a junior member of the Board) also reflected this concern. The Code of 1854 reiterated the rule of pre-emption in regard to permanent transfers of lands. It was then also pointed out that all transfers of lands should be reported immediately to the Divisional Commissioners. Simultaneously, a great care was taken 'that landed property shall not unnecessarily be brought to the hammer'. Further, shortly after the Mutiny, Sir John Lawrence proposed to place certain restrictions on the compulsory sale of land for debt because such transfers of lands would foster 'hatred between classes' in the rural society. For details, see *P.A.R., 1849-50* and *1850-51*, 78; Extract from Government of India's No. 418, 31 March 1849, para 7, C.L. Tupper, ed., *Punjab Customary Law*, I (Superintendent of Government Printing, Calcutta, 1881), 49; Extract from the Secy. to CC Punjab's No. 325-787, 22 October 1858, paras 3 to 14, D.G. Barkley, ed., *The Non-Regulation Laws of the Punjab* (Punjab Printing Company, Lahore, 1871), 165.

Remarks by A. Brandreth, CR Multan division, *ERR 1868-69*, 53; *Ibid.*, *1869-70*, 73-4; as CR Jullundur division, *Ibid.*, *1870-71*, 44.

37. P.S. Melvill's attitude on land transfers underwent a definite change over the years. In the 1850s as the settlement officer of the Ambala district, he attached no particular significance to the existing indebtedness and the land transfers resulting from the high rate of assessment. He found that the deadly climate from which the tract suffered

rendered it inevitable that the villages would be indebted to *sahukars*. He accordingly pointed out that the faster these villages were bought up by the money-lenders the better. The Punjab Government would then have some security for its revenue, while the villagers would be no worse off. He felt so strongly about it that he did not even recommend any revision of assessment, though he believed that this tract had been assessed high. According to him any reduction in revenue would do no good to the villagers. Speculative purchasers, on the other hand, must take the risk of loss—a risk which might lead to exert themselves to improve the condition of the tract. For it, see *Ambala S.R., 1893*, 33. But in the early 1870s his views underwent a definite change. He was then convinced that this steady rise in the number and area of alienations of lands required an immediate legislative interference. He suggested a number of measures of which two deserve special attention —(i) that 'no transfer of land shall be permitted in payment of debt to a creditor', and (ii) that 'no mortgage shall be valid for more than the lifetime of the mortgagor without the sanction of official authority'. For details, see *Punjab Selections*, New Series, No. XIII, LG Punjab's No. 4609, 23 December 1874, Papers Regarding Alienation of Estates of Insolvent Proprietors to the Money-lending Class, 3.

38. *Ibid.*, 7.
39. On the basis of the annual revenue statistics, the Financial Commissioner pointed out that transfers of lands represented 'a natural and healthy process' in the rural society of the province. Land value was now increasing and almost every year the disinclination on the part of the zamindars to part with their valuable holdings was also fast disappearing. Consequently, if the powerful machinery of the state was employed to prevent the voluntary transfers of lands, the result would only be 'depreciation in the value of the land itself and deterioration of its productive power'. He asserted that legislative interference was nothing but an attempt 'to introduce a disturbing element in the self-adjusting process'. He regarded this move both as unnecessary and undesirable. For details, see *RR 1873-74*, 67-8.
40. Arthur Brandreth, the Commissioner of the Jullundur division, urged for an immediate stringent measure against the actual debtor; otherwise, he believed, this process of transfers of lands would bring about some disastrous consequences on the rural economy of the province. Similarly, McMahon, the Commissioner of the Amritsar division, also found that professional money-lenders were getting more lands into their hands and this created a grave political situation in the province. In Gurgaon also, steady expropriation of the Meo proprietors by the *sahukars* drew the attention of the settlement officer, James Wilson (1882). He sought approval for a scheme whereby the Government advances would be applied to the redemption of mortgages made by the Meo proprietors. Among other things he suggested that the power of alienating lands should be entirely withdrawn from the zamindars. For their views, see Remarks by A. Brandreth, CR

Jullundur division, *ERR 1876-77*, 19; Remarks by C.A. McMahon, CR Amritsar division, *Ibid., 1881-82*, 19; Note by J. Wilson, DC Gurgaon, on the redemption of mortgages in the Gurgaon district, Rev and Agr (R) June 1883, 30A.

41. Remarks by S.S. Thorburn, DC Dera Ismail Khan, *ERR 1882-83*, 148, 150.
42. According to Thorburn nearly 8 per cent of the cultivated area in Dera Ismail Khan were alienated to the Hindu money-lenders. But this did not wholly explain the gravity of the situation. Here the expropriated proprietors mostly came from the warlike Muslim tribes of western Punjab. He thought that the loyalty of these Muslim landowners would be greatly strained if this process was allowed to continue. He warned that the danger of allowing the Hindu *sahukars* to assume 'a position of domination over the more warlike Muhammadans would create a state of things which would tempt the latter to welcome the subversion of our government'. He suggested among other things, the introduction of a number of changes in the legal system which would make the 'civil courts less of a tool in the hands of money-lender and more of a protective shield for the proprietors'. For details, see *FC Selections*, New Series, No. 11, No. 37, No. LXV, Note by S.S. Thorburn, DC Dera Ismail Khan, 29 June 1884, Papers on Indebtedness of Agriculturists in the Punjab and Foreclosure of Mortgages, 930-55.
43. Secretary of State's No. 27, 24 March 1887, Rev and Agr (R) May 1887, 33A.
44. LG Punjab's No. 231, 7 November 1888, quoted in Rev and Agr (LR) October 1895, 72-73A.
45. In this connection opinions of Rivaz, CR Lahore division, Kennedy, DC Montgomery, Brown, DC Gurdaspur, Wilson, DC Shahpur and Hutchinson, DC Multan merit special attention. For their replies, see Rev and Agr (R) December 1891, 10-11A.
46. This Act sought to introduce certain checks on the powers of the money-lenders. The Punjab Government's views are in the following important files: Rev and Agr (R) April 1894, 1A; Home (J) December 1891, 234-300A; Home (J) June 1894, 329-364A.
47. Note by Dennis Fitzpatrick, LG Punjab, 26 December 1895, *Agricultural Indebtedness*, II, Rev and Agr (LR) November 1898, 3-22A.
48. Thorburn also suggested numerous other urgent remedial measures. For details, see *Ibid.*, General Report, para 86, Rev and Agr (LR) November 1898, 3-22A.
49. The two Financial Commissioners felt that the measure should apply at once to the whole province because if it was only applied to selected areas it would render the zamindars of these areas an isolated group with whom the money-lenders would refuse to deal on account of their inability to offer land as security, whereas in the neighbouring tracts where the restrictive measures had not been clamped, zamindars would be in a better position to make terms with the

money-lenders. Note by C.L. Tupper, FC Punjab, 7 September 1896; Note by C.M. Rivaz, FC Punjab, 16 August 1896; *Ibid.*, Rev and Agr (LR) November 1898, 3-22A.

50. It met on 1-2 July 1898 with Sir Macworth Young on the chair; its members were C.L. Tupper, J.A.L. Montgomery, S.S. Thorburn, R. Clark, L.W. Dane, J.M. Douie, G.C. Walker and Captain J.R. Dunlop-Smith; M.M. Penton was its Secretary. Dungen, *The Punjab Tradition*, 247.

51. The Committee also suggested that the Punjab Government should be given wide discretionary powers to exempt areas from this legislation. Permanent alienation of agricultural land to non-agriculturists without the sanction of the collector should be prohibited. Temporary alienation was to be permissible in the form of usufructuary mortgage for 20 years, or mortgage without possession, the mortgagee having power to usufruct in default of payment as stipulated, or lease for life of the lesser but not exceeding 20 years. Hypothecation of land-produce for more than a year should be prohibited. Finally, the Committee permitted free alienation when the alienee was an agriculturist in the same village or a descendant in the male line of a common ancestor. For details, see Resolutions of the Punjab Officials' Committee, 1-14, Rev and Agr (LR) November, 3-22A.

52. Speech by C.M. Rivaz, FC Punjab in the Legislative Council, 27 September 1899, *Abstracts of the Proceedings of the Council of the Governor-General of India Assembled for the Purpose of Making Laws and Regulations, 1900*, XXXVIII (Calcutta, 1901), 318-27.

53. Despatch from the Secretary of State, 20 December 1900, Rev and Agr (LR) January 1901, 47-48B. See also Notification in the *Gazette of India, Extraordinary*, 8 June 1901, Rev and Agr (LR) June 1901, 35B.

54. The Punjab Government's correspondence on grouping of agricultural tribes is in Rev and Agr (LR) May 1901, 11-12A.

55. The Punjab newspapers like the *Akhbar-i-Am* (Lahore), *Aftab-i-Punjab* (Lahore), *Siraj-ul-Akhbar* (Jhelum), *Chaudwin Sadi* (Rawalpindi) and *Tribune* (Lahore) strongly condemned and sharply criticised the various provisions of this Act. For details, see *Selections from Punjab Native Papers*, 1901-02 (sections headed 'Punjab Land Alienation Act').

56. *LAR 1907-08*, para 28.

57. These applications were sanctioned only in extreme cases where the land was required for building sites or to provide necessary means for redeeming other property from mortgage. Otherwise sanction was not granted. *Ibid., 1903-04*, para 16; *Ibid., 1906-07*, para 19.

58. They were then extremely 'eager to come to terms with the mortgagees in order to release their capital for more profitable employment'. *Ibid., 1901-02*, para 8.

59. *Ibid.*, para 28; *Ibid., 1904-05*, para 19; *Ibid., 1905-06*, para 26; *RR 1909-10*, 14; *Ibid., 1910-11*, 14; *Ibid., 1911-12*, 14; *Ibid., 1912-13*, 17.

60. This pattern of land transfers after the enforcement of the Land Alienation Act would be more clear if two unfavourable years (1898-99 and 1907-08—the former belonging to the pre-enactment and the latter to the post-enactment period) were taken into account.
Cultivated area sold, mortgaged and redeemed in 1898-99 and 1907-08

in acres.

Cultivated area in acres	1898-99	1907-08
1	2	3
Sale	167,229	131,865
Mortgage	382,813	249,573
Redeemed	255,804	325,173

Source: *LAR 1906-07*, paras 30-1; *Ibid., 1907-08*, para 28.

61. In connection with his enquiry in the Bairampur (Hoshiarpur) village, Prof. Bhalla also noticed the utter helplessness of the poorer proprietors. He wrote: 'It has failed to save and protect the poorer and helpless zamindars; land is still passing out of the hands of the poor into those of the rich—the bigger fishes have eaten and are eating the small ones.... It has saved those for whom there was a chance of being saved and who wanted simply time and opportunity to get out of the clutches of the money-lender'. Bhalla, *op. cit*,, 110-1. See also *P.P.B.E.C.* II, 858, 873. The Punjab Government, however, refused to share this view that the small landowners were being 'swallowed up' by the big landlords. See Cyril P.K. Fazal, *A Note on Sales of Land between the Notified Agricultural Tribes in the Punjab during the Quinquennium 1922-23 to 1926-27* (The Board of Economic Enquiry, Punjab, Publication No. 32, Lahore, 1931), 1-2.
62. For details, see Chapter VII.
63. *LAR 1905-06*, para 22.
64. *Ibid., 1900-01*, para 19,
65. Agriculturist money-lenders were nothing new in the Punjab. But in the present century, with the elimination of the *sahukars* from the land market, they virtually established their complete domination in a number of central and south-eastern districts of the province. It was estimated in 1929 'that 75 per cent or more of the land mortgaged in the last 25 years has been mortgaged to agricultural tribes' while three-fourths of the mortgage debt of the province came from their purse. For details, see *P.P.B.E.C*, I, 138-41.
66. E.D. Lucas, *The Economic Life of a Punjab Village* (Civil and Military Gazette Press, Lahore, n.d.), 97.
67. Sale price of the cultivated land per acre in rupees from 1896-97 to 1907-08.

Year	Sale price of cultivated land per acre in rupees	1896-97=100
1	2	3
1896-97	74	100
1897-98	77	104
1898-99	79	106
1899-1900	78	105
1900-01	80	108
1901-02	66	89
1902-03	66	89
1903-04	80	108
1904-05	82	110
1905-06	82	110
1906-07	98	132
1907-08	97	131

Source: *LAR 1906-07*, para 30; *Ibid., 1907-08*, para 11. For land prices of the Punjab during the present century, see Gulsan Rai, *Agricultural Statistics of the Punjab, 1901-02* to *1935-06* (The Board of Economic Enquiry, Punjab, Publication No. 49, Lahore, 1937), Table 52.

68. *LAR 1901-02*, para 29.
69. Norman G. Barrier, *The Punjab Alienation of Land Bill of 1900* (Duke University Press, N.C., Durham, 1966), 82.
70. *LAR 1905-06*, para 23; *P.P.B.E.C.*, II, 858.
71. *LAR 1902-03*, para 16.
72. *P.P.B.E.C.*, I, 165.
73. While analysing the effects of this Act, Prof. Barrier pointed out that it had an indirect role in 'widening the rift between the rural and urban areas' of the province. The Act disallowed the urban rich to acquire the cultivable lands of the agricultural tribes in the rural tracts. This created a widespread disaffection among them and made them indifferent to rural interests. However, the urban gentlemen did not always react in this way. Even after the enforcement of this Act, they continued to purchase lands, often in the form of *benami* transactions. Further, rural-urban differentiation, as suggested by the same authority, should have encouraged the *sahukars* to migrate towards the nearby towns. But no such large-scale migration of the *sahukars* took place during this century; they rather continued to remain in the rural areas maintaining an important link in the rural-urban trade in agricultural produce. This period also witnessed the development of communal politics in the rural Punjab with an active support from the educated middle class of the towns. Finally, the agitation of 1907 over the Colonization Bill created a real rural-urban solidarity which Prof. Barrier himself did not fail to record. He thus wrote:

'The agitation [of 1907] was unlike any other agitation previously witnessed in the Punjab. . . . They [local leaders] sent out printed invitations before each meeting, released news to the local press, and got several rich yeomen to donate a 'war chest' to support colonists who refused to pay fines. The *Zamindar* was in charge of publicity. . . . Representatives from the Lahore Indian Association, a branch of the Indian National Congress, attended the Lyallpur meeting. . . . After a number of patriotic songs, Lajpat Rai and Ajit Singh . . . made the major speeches. . . .'

Actually without an active support from the urban native press, the success of the rural mass during this period would not have been possible. For details, see N.G. Barrier, 'The Punjab Disturbances of 1907: the Response of the British Government in India to Agrarian Unrest', *The Punjab Past and Present*, VIII-II, October 1974, 456-9. See also, Kenneth W. Jones, *Arya Dharam* (Manohar Book Service, New Delhi, 1976), 272.

5

Rural Credit and Land Alienation

The growing indebtedness of the zamindars to the *sahukars*, which had often been described as one of the most glaring domestic problems faced by the Punjab Government during the period under review,[1] had complex origins.[2] Of the various factors contributing to this widespread indebtedness, we should first take note of natural fluctuations in the province. In the Punjab, as in other parts of India, agriculture depended largely on the rains and failure of rains was a common phenomenon in the south-eastern districts of the province. Famines thus recurred, and their disastrous effects on the rural economy had been noted in most of the famine literatures of this period.[3] Such famines and scarcities undoubtedly drove the zamindars in the arms of the *sahukars*. Thorburn in his enquiry in the 12 villages of the Rawalpindi division also recognized the fact that the beginning of indebtedness was usually due to seasonal variations in rainfall causing fluctuations in the yields of grain and fodder.[4] The money-lenders took advantage of the plight of the zamindars and reaped enormous profits 'by storing up the grain, by mixing inferior grains with wheat, and by raising the prices quickly and continuously'. In extreme cases the debtors were often 'compelled to alienate lands on any terms to *sahukars*'.

The small and fragmented holdings of zamindars were no less responsible for the growth of indebtedness.[5] As a result of the steady fragmentation of their holdings, zamindars often had to work at a small margin of profit; indeed, many of them had no margin at all, so that mishaps such as cattle mortality and continual drought forced them into the clutches of village money-lenders; and once they fell into their hands, there was no getting out of it. Thorburn's enquiry in Sialkot and Shahpur clearly pointed out that quite a sizable number of proprietors, because of their uneconomic holdings, were forced to borrow from the money-lenders even in years of good harvests.[6] Similarly in Bannu, in a majority of cases a zamindar parted with his land owing to poverty caused by the 'holding being economically too small to support the number of mouths dependent on it'.[7]

The fixed, rigid and inelastic land revenue demand of the Government, as it has already been pointed out, had of course a role to play in the growing rural indebtedness. During Sikh rule, the Lahore administration usually did not ask for a fixed land revenue in areas where cultivation was insecure and depended almost wholly on *sailab* or precarious rainfall.[8] Shortly after the annexation, a fixed land revenue assessment was introduced even in the western Punjab districts which the zamindars could hardly pay because of insecurity of cultivation. Many experienced officers admitted the grave error of the Government in thus suddenly introducing a rigid annual cash assessment immediately after the annexation.[9] They repeatedly pointed out that zamindars were very reluctant to accept fixed assessments.[10] In Amritsar it was found that many borrowed from the *sahukars* to meet the Government demand[11] and indebtedness extensively prevailed in the 'more highly farmed parts of the district'[12] while in a number of riverside villages of Montgomery it gradually developed due to fixed assessment of the *sailab* lands.[13] In the Rawalpindi division also Thorburn estimated that nearly 12 per cent of the total debt of the rural population was due to the payment of the fixed land revenue demand of the Government.

In some cases bad canal administration and high canal water rate also led to indebtedness. In Lahore, Clark, the settlement officer, found that in many rich canal-irrigated villages extensive alienation of lands had taken place.[14] An enquiry in the late 1860s clearly revealed that in the *reh* affected areas of the Rohtak district, many zamindars frequently borrowed from the *sahukars*. Here the main source of evil was the wrong alignment of the Western Jumna Canal. It was also responsible for the outbreak of malaria and led to a large-scale contraction of cultivation in a number of villages of the Rohtak district.

Paradoxically, cultivation of certain crops also greatly aggravated the evil of rural indebtedness at least in some parts of the province. For example, in a number of south-eastern and submontane districts small peasant proprietors universally depended on money-lenders for seeds, etc. These creditors who were often petty village traders, served as an important channel of wheat trade at the village level. They advanced necessary credit to those proprietors with a view to acquiring their crops as soon as the harvest was over. The indebted producers were compelled to sell their crops 'at fixed rate considerably cheaper than the market price'. This evidently increased their burden of debt.[15]

Actually money-lenders were more active in those parts of the province, where the lands were very fertile and the agricultural produce could be readily sold.[16] By virtue of their position as creditors, they often imposed harsh terms on the debtor-zamindars. An enquiry in the Dasuya *bet* villages revealed that as soon as harvest was ready, the *sahukars* proceeded to the threshing floor and the grain was laden on the carts of the zamindars and borne off to the granaries of the town. All was taken away except a few months' supply for the needs of the zamindars and their families. 'This very grain', reported the Deputy Commissioner, 'they are forced to take back at a valuation perhaps 50 per cent higher than that at which they had parted with it'. Thus they went on living from hand-to-mouth hardly anticipating the time 'when their proprietary rights would cease to exist even in name'.[17]

However, rural indebtedness was not always explicable merely in terms of the 'poverty of the zamindars' or to their 'irrational, irresponsible management of the family's economic affairs'. Sometimes it could be due to productive ventures as well. In the central Punjab districts like Ludhiana, Ferozepore and Jullundur, enterprising Jat zamindars frequently borrowed from the *sahukars* and mortgaged their holdings 'to get money for outfits, etc., to join the army or for a trading venture'.[18] In many cases credit was also taken by the small peasant proprietors for the construction of wells or for the use of the Behia mills from the money-lenders.[19]

Soon the problem of rural indebtednees assumed a universal dimension during the period under ıeview. According to an enquiry of the late 1870s, indebtedness was most widespread among the peasant proprietors of Gujranwala. As early as 1860 the settlement officer found *sahukars* advancing credit to zamindars at exorbitant rates of interest, receiving the produce of their labour in return.[20] This domination by the village grain dealers cum money-lenders continued unabated in the 1870s. In 1879 it was estimated that 80 per cent of the owners, 20 per cent of the occupancy tenants and 10 per cent of the tenants-at-will were indebted.[21] This general indebtedness of the proprietary body alarmed the settlement officer so greatly that he even recommended the introduction of 'a system of State loans, accompanied by a more liberal elastic revenue policy'.[22] In Ludhiana, zamindars were equally miserable. In the Ludhiana *bet*, a considerable number of Muhammedan proprietors were 'entirely at the mercy of the money-lender'.[23] They were generally 'dependent for their daily food on the money-lenders, whose terms precluded the chance of any part of the produce remaining in their hands'. The influence of the *bet* was seen at its worst in Ferozepore along whose border the Sutlej 'glides like a snake'; here almost every proprietor had, 'his account with the village money-lender'. Generally, zamindar had to hand over the bulk of his produce to the creditor and was often unable to retain enough to keep his family until the harvest time.[24]

Things were not far different in the *manjha* tract. In Amritsar, for example, the money-lenders were firmly established even before the beginning of British rule. In Narowal they were creating an immense trouble since the late 1850s. In 1879 the district officer frankly admitted before the Famine Commission that very 'few agriculturists' were free from debt. 'Nearly all' were 'in debt'.[25] The situation was even worse in the south-western districts like Muzaffargarh, Multan and Montgomery. Thorburn observed that the peasantry were more involved as the Salt Range was approached, 'and south of it almost universally so'.[26]

This view of universal indebtedness of the proprietors along the cis-Salt Range region finds corroboration from the writings of the settlement officers like Steedman, O'Brien and

Purser who had carefully studied this problem. In Montgomery district, Purser found that except in the canal villages seed grains were almost universally 'borrowed from the Karars' and there were very few villages which were not deeply indebted.[27] Subsequently, the situation deteriorated so rapidly that in the late 1920s it was estimated that nearly 99 per cent of the proprietors were in debt.[28] In Muzaffargarh, according to one estimate, only 39 per cent of the Muhammedan zamindars were free from debt.[29] Here they were so deeply involved that they were practically unable to get food and clothing or to celebrate a marriage, as the Extra Assistant Commissioner wrote, without borrowing.[30] In Shahpur also, 'the peasantry are generally in debt'.[31] Thorburn's enquiry in the six villages of this district revealed that in the mid 1890s nearly 46.5 per cent of the cultivated area had been transferred[32] and a little over 72.5 per cent of the old proprietors were indebted. Similarly in Multan, of the Muhammedan proprietors (who constituted the bulk of the proprietary body) 50 per cent were in debt as early as 1878-79[33] while towards the close of the century it was revealed that nearly one-fourth of the total area of the district was alienated by them.[34]

In Dera Ghazi Khan, Bannu and Dera Ismail Khan, the situation was not much different. In Bannu, Thorburn found that the zamindars were mostly indebted in the poor sandy tracts of Marwat as well as in the lands of the Bannuchis. 'With both the struggle for existence is terrible'. The indebtedness of a greater portion of Marwat was due, as Thorburn pointed out,[35] chiefly to over-assessment and rigidity of British revenue system while in the land of the Bannuchis, indebtedness was ascribed to the smallness of their holdings. In Dera Ghazi Khan the condition of the zamindars was equally bad. As early as 1878-79 it was found that nearly two-thirds of the Muslim land-owners were deeply in debt and their volume of indebtedness varied from Rs. 100 to 5,000.[36] In Dera Ismail Khan an enquiry by Thorburn as Deputy Commissioner (1884) revealed that, 'excluding the 5 or 8 lakhs of petty debts, most of which could be easily paid off after any average harvest, the debts at present owned by Muhammadans to Hindus in this district amount to between 12 and 14 lakhs of rupees'.[37]

In the submontane districts like Sialkot, Ambala, Hoshiarpur and Gurdaspur indebtedness was similarly universal. In Ambala many Rajput landholders were fast 'dropping out of sight' towards the close of the century, as a local report put it. While explaining this, the settlement officer pointed out that their indebtedness assumed 'a dangerous proportion', particularly in the four southern tahsils of this district. He believed this tract to be 'the worst affected' region in the eastern portion of the province.[38] In Gurdaspur the dominant position of the money-lenders could be traced even during Sikh rule. In the late 1870s the situation was so grave that nearly three-fourths of them were in debt,[39] many of them belonging to the Rajput and the Pathan communities. The result, wrote the district officer, 'is the seething feeling of discontent' among the peasantry. A critical perusal of the contemporary official literature would reveal that Hoshiarpur was one of the most indebted districts of the province. As early as 1879 the district officer in his note to the Famine Commission admitted that nearly 70 per cent of the zamindars throughout the district were in debt. It increased further towards the close of the century, when scarcity and high prices of grain crippled zamindars of small means.[40] In Sialkot district, alienation of land started in the mid 1860s and by 1894, 27 per cent of the total area had been transferred by way of sale and mortgage.[41] Thorburn's enquiry in the three villages of this district clearly brings out this problem. According to him in two (Karowal and Sihoki) of these villages indebtedness had become considerable as early as 1865 and by 1894-95, nearly 42 per cent of the total area was alienated by the zamindars. In the third village (Kot Ghumman) the situation was even worse; here during the same period (1865 to 1894-95), nearly 51 per cent of the total area was transferred, most of it to money-lenders.[42]

It is, therefore, evident that zamindars were universally indebted to the money-lenders during the period under review. The *Report of the Punjab Provincial Banking Enquiry Committee* divided these money-lenders into three broad groups: (1) urban money-lenders, (2) rural money-lenders (*sahukars*) and (3) agriculturist money-lenders. But this group division appears to be a very vague one because it practically suggested nothing about the various sub-groups. Further, it is also very difficult to say whether a money-lender was urban or rural since he often operated in both the places. Thorburn again divided these money-lenders into four major groups,[43] namely, Bania, Khatri, Arora and Bhatia who in the census of 1881 constituted nearly 7 per cent of the total population. Thorburn, however, did not mention about agriculturist money-lenders and their role in the agrarian economy. Sir Denzil Ibbetson, the Census Superintendent, suggested a five-fold division. His detailed classification appears to be an improvement on that of Thorburn. He, however, equally maintained a complete silence about the agriculturist money-lenders, such as the Jats and the Malis. In vicw of these difficulties, it would be more convenient to divide them into three broad groups: *sahukars*, agriculturist money-lenders and the new credit group which came into existence as a result of commercialization agriculture.

The *sahukars* may broadly be divided into five territorial groups—first of all, Banias, Dhunsars, Bohras and Pahari Mahajans; secondly, Suds and Bhabars; thirdly, Khatris, Khakas and Bhatias; fourthly, Aroras; and lastly, Khojas and Parachas. The territorial distribution of these groups was more or less 'well marked'. The first or Bania group was mainly 'confined to the eastern and south-eastern divisions of Delhi, Hissar and Ambala, and to the Native States, though a few of them spread along the north of the Eastern Plains and into the Hill States'. They were practically unknown west of Lahore. The second or Sud group was found only in districts that lay under the hills on the northern border of the province from Ambala to Rawalpindi divisions. The third or Khatri group was 'most numerous' in the Jullundur, Amritsar, Lohore and Rawalpindi divisions. The fourth or Arora group was chiefly found in the Multan and Derajat divisions and Bahawalpur and then again crossed the Sutlej in Sirsa 'to meet the Bania group of the east'. Finally, the fifth or Khoja group was confined to the central and western districts and the Salt Range tracts.[44] Of these five groups, the second and fifth constituted only a minor portion of the general money-lending community and the credit advanced by them was equally of a limited nature. The remaining three groups were numerous and supplied the bulk of the rural credit to the proprietors.

While writing about these money-lenders an interesting question crops up: were they essentially an alien community in the rural society? Thorburn believed that they did not represent indigenous elements.[45] But it would be difficult to describe all these different money-lending groups as altogether an alien community, constituting a sharply differentiated body from the vast rural folk, though residing side by side with it. At least one important section of them represented indigenous elements. The 'capitalist indigenous to the Punjab was the intellectual Khatri',[46] while the Banias of the south-eastern Punjab and the Aroras of the west came to settle there from outside long before the introduction of British rule.

The Banias of the south-eastern Punjab were well-known to the northern Indian population for their commercial enterprise since the days of Tavernier.[47] But the Banias of rural Punjab were poor creatures, notwithstanding the title of *mahajan*, which was affixed by usage to the caste to which they belonged.[48] They spent their lives 'mostly in their shops, and the results were apparent in their poor physique and utter want of manliness'. The Khatris of the central Punjab were largely represented in districts where Sikhism was predominant though only 9 per cent of them professed that faith. They were traditionally famous for their enterprising zeal as traders and held important administrative posts under Ranjit Singh.[49] Since they were local men, they were not much hated by the rural folk, usually got on better terms with their debtors and were often found readily sharing in the life of those around them.

While the Khatris were concentrated chiefly in the central districts, the stronghold of the Aroras, as money-lenders and traders was in the western part of the Punjab. They were to be found 'everywhere down the Indus and the lower reaches of the Jhelum, Chenab and the Sutlej amidst the rude primitive conditions of the western Punjab'. Like the Khatris and unlike the Banias, 'the Aroras were no mere traders, but would turn their hands to anything'. They were often enterprising cultivators and a large proportion of them on the lower Chenab were purely agricultural while in Bahawalpur many of them were contractors, bankers or money-lenders.[50] In the western districts their harsh treatment towards their Muslim clients made them very unpopular.[51] They were commonly known as *kirar*, a word almost synonymous with coward. They were universally known as 'an exacting master'.

Besides these *sahukars*, agriculturist money-lenders also played an important role in the rural credit relations during the period under review. They were by no means a new feature in village life. In some of the central districts like Ludhiana and Ferozepore they were very much in existence even before the close of the 19th century. These agriculturist money-lenders largely arose out of the richer zamindars who usually had sufficient funds to employ in money-lending.[52] They provided credit to fellow zamindars mainly or sometimes even solely with the object of getting possession of their lands. Of the different agricultural tribes the Arains of Jullundur, the Sainis and Mahtons of Hoshiarpur, and the Sikh Jats of Ferozepore and Ludhiana, the Khakwami Pathans of Mailsi and Lodhran were noted for their thrift. 'So everywhere money-lending and thrift went hand in hand'. In the last quarter of the century, we come across numerous such cases. In Amritsar, as the district officer wrote, it was by no means unusual to hear of a zamindar combining a little money-lending with agriculture.[53] Similarly in the *dhaia* region of the Ludhiana district money-lending was mostly in the hands of the Sikh Jats. 'In very few villages is there a professional money-lender'.[54] In Ferozepore also, the great majority of the mortgages went to them. Thorburn's enquiry testified to their presence in Sialkot while in Dera Ismail Khan they were no less active towards the close of the century.[55]

Of the different sources of credit in the rural society, we have so far studied two: *shaukars* and agriculturist money-lenders. In many villages these two rival agencies of credit lived side by side providing loans to zamindars and Thorburn's enquiry shows that the relationship between them was anything but satisfactory. The *sahukars* might be timid but they knew very well how to reap the maximum profit out of their transactions with the indebted proprietors. But agriculturist money-lenders were admittedly more harsh in their dealings with the indebted clients. On some occasions *sahukars* often wrote off a part of their interest, but the Jats gave up nothing, 'not even a pebble'.[56] In most of the central districts they were universally hated and feared by their debtors. Anderson, the Divisional

Judge of Delhi, also found them 'harder on their debtors than others.'[57]

Besides *sahukars* and agriculturist money-lenders, proprietors got credit also from the new credit group emerging as a result of the cultivation of certain cash crops. Their mode of operation was somewhat different from that of village money-lenders and they could not always be clearly distinguished from the *sahukars*. The *sahukars* advanced loans with the ulterior motive of being repaid on a higher rate of interest. But the new credit group, closely connected with trade in agricultural produce, advanced credit through agents at different levels, largely with a view to getting hold of crops in the post-harvest period. Of the different commercial crops, wheat,[58] sugar-cane,[59] and cotton[60] particularly offered them an attractive field of operation. But the emergence of the new credit group, however, did not necessarily mean a complete breakdown of the old credit relations with the village money-lenders; it did not suggest that the *sahukars* were almost relegated to the background either. The older group continued to persist and on many occasions, their position was consolidated by closer contacts with the newer ones. It was frequently seen that the new credit group connected with trade in agricultural produce, found it convenient to carry on its credit operations through them and the reasons for it are not far to seek.

In the rural economy village money-lenders were closely associated with the proprietors of land through their credit relations over the years while the new credit group, especially when they were outsiders, often had no such direct link with them. The *sahukars* usually lived in the same villages with their indebted clients and enjoyed a position of importance for their financial solvency. In many cases, particularly in the remotest corners of the western districts, they were well acquainted with the techniques of market operations and hence served at the lowest level in the villages as the only regular agency for marketing wheat and cotton to the outside world. Perhaps realising this important role of the village money-lenders, the agents of the wheat or cotton exporting firms with their headquarters at important cities, found it convenient to operate their necessary credit relations through them. This borrowed capital was called *ras*,[61] advanced at 8 or 12 per cent per mensem. This dependence of the new credit group on the village money-lenders consequently appears to have strengthened their position in the rural economy and indirectly placed them at a more favourable position than before in carrying on their credit operations.

In the Punjab, zamindars usually borrowed from money-lenders for four necessary purposes, viz., food, seed, cattle purchase and payment of land revenue. Everywhere in the province, these money-lenders provided necessary grain loans during some particular months of the year and money loans of various kinds against the security of crop or land or other valuable things like ornaments. Grain loans were generally of two forms: grain for seed and grain for food. For seeds zamindars almost universally depended on money-lenders and two village enquiries of the Hoshiarpur district (Kabirpur and Bairampur), carried on at two different times clearly establish this fact.[62]

In some parts of the province zamindars, however, had to depend on money-lenders for necessary grain advances throughout the year. Even shortly after the harvest, they often asked for grain loans from their creditors. It was largely due to the fact that the small produce from the petty holdings of zamindars tended to be gradually depleted by their various compulsory payments. In Thorburn's enquiry it has been clearly established that in widely separated tracts like Sialkot and Gujranwala inhabited by widely differing tribes of peasant proprietors, on well as well as on rain lands, indebted zamindars borrowed, even after good or average harvests, food-grains in winter and spring and seed at sowing time because their creditors appropriated 'a large part of their crops from the threshing floor in full or part payment of debts previously incurred, or of interest due on such debts'.[63] Payment of land revenue had a big role in this depletion of zamindar's stock after the harvest. The time of harvesting and the time of land revenue payment often coincided; consequently, they were 'compelled to sell their produce at unfavourable prices' to meet the land revenue demand of the Government.[64]

This depletion of stock often compelled zamindars to borrow cash from money-lenders for the payment of land revenue. This was a very common practice in the south-eastern districts of the province. In Montgomery also the settlement officer found that the necessary money loans were widely taken by zamindars to pay revenue, and a similar state of affairs prevailed in Gujranwala and Sialkot, and Thorburn found there that the creditors took a part of zamindar's crop from the threshing floor and subsequently accommodated him by paying his revenue.[65]

Another reason for borrowing was the purchase of cattle by zamindars. Widespread cattle mortality, particularly during the famine years, often forced them to borrow. Prinsep, the settlement officer of Sialkot referred to a group of dealers known as the Bedees who used to sell cattle to the rural folk on credit.[66] In Lahore, the case was somewhat different. Here 'often no cash is actually advanced, but the village *bunya* or the cattle trader is authorised to supply the tenant on the owner's responsibility for payment'.[67] In his evidence before the Royal Commission on Agriculture, the Honorary Magistrate of the Siranwali village (Sialkot) also admitted that it was a common practice on the part of the cattle dealers 'to give cattle on credit' to the zamindars; and when the crop was ready, they 'pay them from the sale of the produce of their lands'.[68]

The rate of interest charged by the money-lenders also deserves special attention in this connection. It, however, varied widely. Apart from the general availability of loanable capital, it usually depended on factors like the status of the debtor, his degree of necessity, or the nature of security offered by him. But in all cases the preponderating factor was the 'quality of the security offered, with special reference to the trouble and risk involved in the loan'. In view of all these related factors, generally the rates of interests were slightly higher in the extreme north-western districts like Peshawar and Rawalpindi, for there the money-lenders had to carry on their trade in the midst of a hostile agrarian population. On the other hand, the comparative security of the submontane zone against famine and scarcity accounted for the relatively lower rates of interest there.[69] Further in the north-western districts, it was the difficulty of obtaining possession of land, if the loan was not repaid in time, that also led to a higher rate of interest.[70] Similarly the interests on advances in grains varied widely. In Jullundur, grain was advanced to agriculturists commonly on terms of repaying in grain with the addition of one-fourth at harvest. But their failure to pay off the loan at the agreed time was offten responsible for a sharp rise in the rate of interest. Accordingly the Deputy Commissioner of Jullundur reported: 'If the advance is not repaid for a year, one-half is added'.[71] In the north-western districts, the rates of interest against grain loan, as usual, were always higher. In Rawalpindi, for example, it ranged from 1¼ to twice the quantity of grain advanced.[72] In times of scarcity and famine again this high rate of interest rose further.[73] It inevitably depleted the surplus of small zamindars shortly after the harvest. This often compelled them to purchase at a higher price the very grain which they had to part with in payment to the money-lenders.

Besides high rates of interest, money-lenders had recourse to various malpractices. For example, 'debts are misrepresented in the ledger by entering inferior grains as if they were wheat'. Further, accounts were often kept in such 'a loose and unintelligible' way that the interest could not be separated from principal; these were also maintained in the *Landa*[74] scripts which the *sahukars* in their own neighbourhood could alone understand. Another interesting aspect of this credit transaction was its tendency to accumulate without limit. Darling referred to a case in which a loan of Rs. 2,550 became a debt of Rs. 9,400 in course of a decade.[75]

This widespread indebtedness of the zamindars brought in its train a large-scale alienation of lands. But transfer of lands was by no means a new development in the rural society of the Punjab during the period under review. The available official reports sufficiently support the view that even during Sikh rule, full 'individual proprietary right with power to sell or mortgage was well established in many parts of the Punjab'.[76] From Ganesh Das' *Char Bagh-i-Panjab* we have a detailed list of villages in the Gujrat district, all purchased by the Khatris long before the establishment of British rule.[77] Similarly, 'a market for land, and the practice of buying and selling land' existed in the Jullundur district in the first half of the 19th century. Sir Richard Temple in connection with his settlement operation in this district found Khatris in possession of some lands 'acquired by sale, mortgage and such like transfers.[78] In some parts of Multan and Montgomery also many Aroras coming from central Punjab districts acquired lands under Diwan Swan Mall.[79]

In the second half of the 19th century transfers of lands almost tended to be a general phenomenon. Official statistics on alienation, mostly collected through village *patwaris* and other revenue officials at the lowest level, clearly indicated that such transfers steadily increased over the years. According to one estimate sales averaged about 88,000 acres a year from 1866 to 1874. From 1875 to 1879, sales averaged about 93,000 acres annually; from 1880 to 1884, 160,000 acres; from 1885 to 1889, 310,000 acres; and from 1890 to 1894, 338,000 acres a year.[80] Early British settlement statistics on land transfers of the 1850s revealed that in the Alipur tahsil of Muzaffargarh district a small area had been alienated, nearly three-quarters of which went to Hindu traders. Similarly in 1854 in two tahsils of the Amritsar[81] and Gurdaspur[82] districts, 3 per cent and 6 per cent of the available land respectively had been mortgaged; in several other tahsils of these districts less than 1 per cent was under mortgage. But from the mid 1860s when alienation of land gradually affected almost all the districts of the province, we have a detailed statistical account throwing lights on the various aspects of this problem. According to the available sale statistics, the average annual sale of land increased by nearly 40 per cent between 1865 and 1884[83] while in 1899-1900 it was estimated that transfer of land by sale increased by nearly 431 per cent since 1865.[84] Correspondingly the number of sales rose sharply by nearly 210 per cent during the last quarter of the century.[85] The same period also witnessed a steady increase in the mortgaged area of the province. According to the statistics furnished by the annual revenue reports belween 1875-76 and 1899-1900 the mortgaged area increased slightly over 200 per cent.[86]

Such large-scale alienations of lands by way of sale or mortgage were generally an outcome of two sets of circumstances. Zamindars had to sell or were prepared to sell under certain conditions more lands than before, and the purchasers of such holdings considered it more worthwhile than before to purchase such lands. The compulsion under which zamindars sold their holdings mostly arose out of their permanent indebtedness. The volume of indebtedness was enhanced by a number of factors. One such factor was the bringing of inferior soil under cultivation in some of the densely populated districts of the province, necessitated by population increase in the context of a more or less unchanged technology. Such new cultivation was more vulnerable to natural hazards. A number of developments also led the purchasers of zamindars' holdings to regard such purchases as a secure and worthwhile investment of their capital. Already the completion of different regular settlements of land revenue had put the zamindars' legal rights in their holdings on a sound footing. This security of status coupled with the right to alienate through law courts enabled creditors to acquire lands of the indebted clients against the security of their credit. Further, various other factors contributed to the increasing demand for land. In this connection the rise of population and its effects on land deserve special attention. With the increase of population, as it has already been pointed out, there developed a large-scale movement of population in search of lands for bringing them under the plough. In many of the densely populated central and submontane districts, in the context of a limited scope for new cultivation and of lack of alternative opportunities for the use of zamindars' labour and capital, there developed an increasing demand for land. In some other parts of the province, this demand tended to increase with the opening out of canal irrigation over waste lands. It increased not only the production per acre, but also brought about an increased degree of security against famines and crop failures. All these factors led to a steady rise in the price of land.[87] This increased price of land made it an object of safe investment and purchasers of such lands seldom ran any risk of losing their money, and could easily resell them, if they so intended, often with a clear margin of profit. Such cases of sales had often been reported by many district officers of this period.[88] Finally, land purchase was certainly beneficial to purchasers, particularly when they were mere *sahukars*.[89]

In connection with this large-scale transfer of lands, one interesting question crops up: who were the purchasers of these lands? The local officers usually classified them into three broad categories: (1) old agriculturists, i.e., persons recognized as proprietors of lands at the first regular settlement of a particular district, (2) non-agriculturists, i.e., persons who were not agriculturists by profession but engaged in trade, money-lending or other avocations often belonging to the *sahukar* community, and (3) new-agriculturists, i.e., persons who were not regarded as proprietors at the first regular settlement, but subsequently acquired lands by purchase and became agriculturists by profession; they often came from the different artisan communities such as tarkhans and lohars. The Punjab Government introduced these classifications for the first time in 1876 in the annual revenue report and they had obvious limitations. For example, in Amritsar, Grant, the settlement officer, found that the 'term "old agriculturists" is held to include any man who already owns and cultivates land in any village whatever', and 'it is inevitable that many persons are returned under this head whose real occupation is money-lending and money-lending only'.[90] In many cases, with a view to avoiding income tax assessment, money-lenders often described themselves as agriculturists.[91] Similarly in many of the official statistics[92] new-agriculturists were treated as money-lenders.

This official classification is not entirely acceptable. But from a critical perusal of other official sources some broad indications about the purchasers of land can be had. In the districts of Ludhiana, Amritsar, Jullundur, Ferozepore and Hoshiarpur, as we have already seen, many zamindars were found actively engaged in extending credit to their kinsmen. In these districts also quite a substantial portion of land was alienated to them.[93] Similarly in a number of districts like Sialkot, Ambala, Gurgaon, Gurdaspur, Jhelum, Gujrat, Multan, Dera Ismail Khan, Bannu and Dera Ghazi Khan, *sahukars* achieved equal, if not greater, success in acquiring lands from their indebted clients.[94]

What was the result of such transfers of land to money-lenders or zamindars? An obvious effect would be a large-scale displacement of traditional zamindars (who or whose ancestors held lands even before British rule) from their ancestral holdings. Even where the old zamindars continued to cultivate their transferred lands, the conditions under which they had to work were substantially altered as a consequence of these transfers. Thorburn's enquiry throws important light on the altered position of the zamindars as a result of land transfers. In Sialkot and Gujranwala, Thorburn found that zamindars were often refused permission to cultivate their alienated holdings. They were frequently replaced by the 'outsiders' who cultivated for the *sahukars*. But in Shahpur the case was different. There the 'mortgagee rarely ventures to evict him, however troublesome he may be as a tenant'.[95] This difference in the treatment of zamindar-mortgagors in these districts was largely due to the fact that in Sialkot there was often a competition among cultivators for lands. This competition made things easier[96] for the new purchasers to replace the old proprietors by outsiders, if and when they showed their unwillingness to cultivate lands on terms and conditions imposed by the former. But in Shahpur no such competition for lands existed; further, the ties among the members of the village proprietary body were still strong enough to resist the total eviction of zamindars from their alienated holdings.[97] Similar cases of resistance offered by the village proprietors against the new purchasers of land occurred in Hissar in south-eastern Punjab.[98]

Usually, however, the *sahukars* as mortgagees, allowed the zamindar-mortgagors to cultivate their alienated holdings. Being busy in their trade and money-lending, the *sahukars* found it convenient to leave the cultivation of the transferred lands in the hands of the zamindar-mortgagors, because the latter often agreed to the most onerous terms for this cultivation. In Muzaffargarh, for example, O'Brien, the settlement officer, reported that 'the mortgagor agreed to pay the land revenue, to supply the labour for canal clearance, and to pay the mortgagee one-fourth of the whole crop, or what is harder still, a good round sum in cash or grain, whether crops were produced or not. Thus a purchaser of land gets land only, while mortgagee gets land and a hard-working slave into the bargain'.[99] This process of leaving cultivation to the zamindar-mortgagors often gave rise to a peculiar form of tenure, popularly known as *lekhā-mukhi*. *Lekhā-mukhi* was a form of running mortgage in which the zamindar-mortgagor was allowed to cultivate his transferred land by his creditor (usually *sahukar*) under certain specific conditions. Under this system the 'former surrendered his crop to the latter, who paid all expenses of cultivation for him, deducted interest due to himself, and finally, was supposed to credit the balance, if any, towards the liquidation of the debt, a consummation seldom, if ever, attained. In this form of cultivation the zamindar-mortgagor was fleeced in every possible way'. The debt tended to grow till at last the creditor eventually appropriated the proprietary right of that land. Thorburn found that the *lekhā-mukhi* mortgage was fast spreading throughout the Punjab towards the last quarter of the century.[100]

In many parts of the province, the *sahukars* as mortgagees did not hesitate to claim a higher rate of rent from their zamindar-mortgagors. In his evidence before the Thorburn Commission, the *patwari* of the Kot Ghumman village (Sialkot) admitted that *sahukars* took four maunds of wheat per acre as rent in rabi when a zamindar would only take three.[101] This higher rate of rent often created bitterness between the zamindar-mortgagor and the *sahukar*-mortgagee, but the former knew that his refusal to pay the high rate of rent would only bring about his eventual eviction from lands. So 'to avoid expatriation, the old owner will pay a higher rent than a new tenant, who will only pay a customary rent prevailing in the neighbourhood'. This process of transfer of lands to *sahukars* and their attempts to exact a higher rate of rent from the zamindar-mortgagors deeply affected the rural economy of the province. *Sahukars*' extreme greed, their absenteeism, along with their readiness to arrange the cultivation of their acquired holdings on a crop-sharing basis, inevitably created an increasingly parasitic group in the agrarian society. They also increased the old customary rents, took a share of the straw, attached the plough cattle and sold the houses of their debtors. In many cases they even reduced the indebted zamindars to a status of *sam*.[102]

But land alienations were not always, as we shall presently see, necessarily injurious to the rural economy. Their effects on agricultural production and economic developments largely depended on the characters of the persons who bought and sold the land. Where the land was transferred from a zamindar who did not use, or was unable to use it effectively to one who did, the effects on production were likely to be healthy. To have a better understanding of this problem four major districts from four different zones of the province may be taken up, viz., Gurgaon (south-eastern Punjab), Ferozepore (central Punjab), Multan (south-western Punjab) and Ambala (submontane Punjab).

To begin with, Gurgaon was regarded to be 'one of the most embarrassed districts of the province' towards the close of the century.[103] Here lands were mostly passing out of the hands of the Meo proprietors, commonly known for their slovenly cultivation. In many parts of this district, particularly in its Rewari tahsil, a large area of land was transferred to Banias and Dhunsars. It was a common practice among them to sublet these lands to the zamindar-mortgagors at a rack-rent or ejecting them and putting in strangers as their tenants. But there remained still more areas transferred by poorer zamindars to the wealthier members of the same brotherhood who possessed 'at the time most means of cultivation at their disposal'.[104]

At the revision of settlement (1880s), it was estimated that out of 12 per cent of the mortgaged area of the tahsil Gurgaon 4 per cent went to members of the same proprietary body while the remaining 8 per cent was 'occupied by the outsiders'. A considerable amount of the latter area was held on mortgage by 'comparatively prosperous cultivators belonging to other villages'. Besides a sizable tract was also held by many enterprising village menials on mortgage. Alienation of lands to the village *kamins*, according to the settlement officer, represented a healthy process because they constituted a thrifty group of peasants who could cultivate them effectively and hence their effects on production organization were likely to be healthy. This process of alienation of lands to enterprising cultivators continued even afterwards and at the beginning of the present century it was reported that more than half the transfers were to the members of the agricultural tribes who were again in most cases co-sharers of the village proprietary lands.[105]

In Ferozepore also transfer of land by the Dogar and Gujar zamindars had been drawing attention of the different settlement officers over the decades. They were not always regarded as good agriculturists; the Dogars in particular had been described by one settlement officer as the 'most lawless and discontented tribe in the district' and were 'of the lowest class of husbandmen'.[106] In the Ferozepore *bet*, much of their transferred lands no doubt went to money-lenders and bankers; but the great majority of the mortgages in the upland tracts were in favour of 'more prudent and industrious' agriculturists of the district.[107] They were mostly Jat zamindars, commonly regarded as the 'most thriving agricultural community in the whole Punjab'.[108] Here in Ferozepore, they practically dominated the trade in agricultural produce, controlled the money-lending transactions in the Moga tahsil and occupied a good deal of land alienated by the Muhammedan proprietary tribes. Many of their kinsmen were in the army and sent money to be invested in land. In Moga at least, they were independent of money-lenders[109] and their village sites were made up of most commodious and substantial houses.[110] Consequently, when they took up the alienated lands of the Gujars and Dogars for their own cultivation, they found a unique opportunity of demonstrating their worth as agricultural entrepreneurs.

In Multan also the Aroras coming from the central Punjab districts set up an example of enterprising landlordism even before the establishment of British rule. During the period under review, they continued to be the main purchasers of lands alienated by the Muhammedan proprietors of this district. According to Maclagan, the settlement officer, *sahukars* held by sale and mortgage nearly 26.8 per cent of the total area of this district at the beginning of the present century.[111] Much of this alienated area was kept by the *sahukars* under their direct cultivation. They constituted a very enterprising group of land-owners and invested a considerable amount of their profits in land. 'Improvements are effected by them which other zamindars' 'as a rule would never undertake'. The value of land was thus 'raised and crops rendered more secure'.[112] Besides the *sahukars*, lands also passed into the hands of Muslim zamindars who were 'thrifty, shrewd, and affluent, forming a fine stamp of landed gentry'.[113] They possessed all the shrewdest instincts of the *sahukars* and the necessary attributes of good agriculturists.[114]

A similar development was reported from Ambala. From the standpoint of agricultural indebtedness the four southern tahsils of this district had often been regarded as 'the worst affected tract in the eastern portion of the province'. In Jagadhri, money-lenders who acquired nearly half of the transferred area, were regarded as 'greedy and unimproving landlords'. Similarly in the Naraingarh tahsil, the settlement officer did not notice any improvement in cultivation due to passing out of holdings to them. Against this background, the Pipli tahsil presented a somewhat different picture. Here the inefficient Rajput zamindars were gradually 'disappearing' as a result of land transfers; they were slowly replaced by an enterprising group of Mali cultivators. They were of a much more independent character and more fitted to make a good use of the land. Prior to the coming of the Malis, the Northern and Southern Chachra circles were a very wild waste with a stiff soil and an abundant growth of *dhak* jungle, and intersected by several hill streams. The Southern Chachra circle was an extremely unhealthy tract while in the Northern Chachra, the soil, though good, could not be properly cultivated because of the absence of an enterprising peasantry. Here the proprietary right of village lands belonged mostly to 'broken-down zamindars, or to non-resident proprietors, money-lenders and others'. From them the enterprising Malis purchased a considerable tract of land and they contributed much in turning this 'neglected' zone into 'a new centre of healthy' agrarian community. It was reported that since 1869 about 8,500 acres of lands were purchased by them at a price of nearly Rs. 1,18,000. Their first purchases were in the Northern Chachra tract. Soon this movement was extended to Southern Chachra and Indri Nardak regions where they also acquired some estates from the non-resident Bania landlords. Shortly afterwards, 'a division on ploughs of the land purchased' was speedily effected, thereby reducing the area marked waste within the limits of the district.[115]

It is, therefore, evident that at least in these districts transfers of land from the inefficient proprietors (i.e., generally Rajputs and Gujars) to the enterprising Jats, Arains and Malis often resulted in the emergence of stronger units of cultivation. This process continued even after the passing of the Land Alienation Act (Act XII of 1990) when the agricultural tribes occupied the bulk of the alienated holdings.[116] And of all the agricultural tribes, the Jats achieved the most striking success. During the first eight years (1901 to 1908) they added a considerable tract to their ancestral holdings in the districts of Ferozepore, Lahore and Hissar often at the cost of the Rajputs, Dogars and Gujars. A similar process was also going on over the years in the Panipat and Banger tracts of Karnal as well as in the Jagraon circle of Ludhiana even before the enforcement of this Act. The passing of this Act evidently strengthened the position of the Jats.

As early as 1902-03 this acquisitive instinct of the Jats came to be clearly admitted. In Ferozepore they made 'considerable encroachment on other tribes, especially on Rajputs', while in Hoshiarpur, Lahore and Delhi they took more lands on mortgage than they mortgaged. Their successful bid in replacing the *sahukars* in the land market in different districts of the province was also now an established fact. In the next year also (1903-04) they continued to gain at the cost of the Rajputs and in Ferozepore their dominant position in the land market persisted. Then again from 1904-05 to 1906-07, they continued to acquire more lands throughout the province by sale and mortgage.[117]

This steady success of the Jats in acquiring lands of other proprietary communities had wholesome effects on the rural economy because they were universally regarded as one of the most thriving and industrious peasant proprietors of the central Punjab districts. They were also noted for their thrift and prudence and amassed sufficient capital through various channels, viz., trade and money-lending, which they often invested in land.[118] Naturally this steady acquisition of lands by the Jats represented a healthy aspect of the rural economy of the province. The significance of these transfers would be better illustrated if we contrast the system of cultivation of the Jats with that of the Rajputs.

> Too proud to till the land themselves, they rarely touch a plough or yoke a bullock, but cultivate through the agency of servants, or lease out their land to tenants. In either case they receive only landlord's profits, while the sturdier Jat, cultivating with his own hand, reaps the profits both of landlord and of cultivator.[119]

This attitude of the Rajputs towards cultivation was no doubt an important factor in their gradual expropriation, particularly by the thrifty Jats. They were expropriated by the *sahukars* long before the close of the last century. The land Alienation Act by debarring the *sahukars* from acquiring their lands might have temporarily arrested the expropriation of the Rajputs, but it practically failed to save them completely[120] from the hands of the Jats and other thrifty agricultural tribes. In view of this steady expropriation of the Rajputs (the Gujars also followed their example) it is evident that the Act did not completely stop the process of displacement of the hereditary landowners of the province from their ancestral holdings. It no doubt caused an immediate and marked diminution in the total area under sale and mortgage but placed the thrifty tribes, especially the Jats, at an advantageous position in the land market, while the Rajputs (or even the Gujars) practically found little protection under this Act.

Besides the Jats, the Kambohs and the Arains also considerably added to their existing holdings as a result of the passing of this Act. Their frugal habits as well as their readiness to undertake all kinds of odd jobs in connection with the cultivation of their lands must have greatly led to their enumeration as agricultural tribes under this Act. In the districts of Lahore, Jullundur and Amritsar[121] the Kambohs were regarded as a first rate cultivating community while the Arains were equally known for their vegetable cultivation.[122] With the elimination of professional money-lenders, these two tribes achieved striking success in the acquisition of cultivable lands of other weaker proprietary bodies like the Sayads and the Rajputs. The mortgage statistics of the first few years[121] following the enforcement of this Act clearly indicated that the Arains were particularly successful in a number of central and submontane districts. In the early decades of the present century it was also found in Amritsar that many Arains (who managed to acquire merely the status of occupancy tenants in Rajput villages) were frequently seen growing vegetables and other produce requiring 'constant labour and supervision, which no other tribe would undertake.

From a purely economic standpoint this process of acquisition of land by the thrifty Jats as well as by the enterprising Arains from the indifferent Rajputs and Gujars was far from injurious to agriculture. On the contrary, land was mostly transferred from one group of zamindars who could not make full use to another group who could use it effectively and its effects on agricultural production were most likely to have been healthy. In many central and south-eastern districts, this process often marked a transfer of ownership to zamindars who usually commanded greater capital and energy to be invested in cultivating these lands which the Rajputs and Gujars often refused to undertake.

Transfers of land also paved the way for the consolidation of the fragmented and scattered holdings of the zamindars. This process particularly helped the peasant proprietors to add to their units of cultivation and consequently made for a much better utilisation of their resources, at least in the sense that without this arrangement a larger part of such resources would have remained unemployed, and it also made possible at least in some cases, the emergence of more viable units of cultivation as a result of cluster of splinter holdings. In order to enjoy these benefits an owner often mortgaged the outlying part of the land simply as a matter of convenience and in return held the land of others 'near his own house' on mortgage.[124] This process of consolidation of holdings continued even in the first decade of the present century when the Land Alienation Act came into effect. Under this Act the land market was now virtually thrown open to the more thrifty agriculturists; this they promptly utilised in central and south-eastern districts at the cost of the weaker neighbours like the Rajputs, Gujars, Dogars and Meos.

In some cases the owners transferred a part of their cultivable holding with a view to undertaking various healthy ventures. A Moga Jat frequently mortgaged a part of his land to a fellow zamindar whenever he wanted money for a trading venture; and on his return either redeemed the mortgage or altered it in some way to suit his convenience.[125] It was also a common practice among the zamindars to mortgage their lands to a relative and spend the credit meeting their necessary expenses for joining the army.[126] Simlarly, Thorburn's enquiry also revealed that many zamindars of Sialkot alienated their small fragmented holdings before going to the Chenab Canal Colony. They subsequently invested their mortgage money in the cultivation of their newly acquired holdings in the canal tracts.

NOTES

1. The problem of rural indebtedness was not altogether a novel development during the second half of the 19th century. Early British records clearly reveal that it was widely prevalent in the different districts of the province even before the British take over. *Supra*, 7-8.
2. Among authorities, on the subject, we may mention the opinions of Thorburn and Darling. Thorburn pointed out that contrary to established notions on the subject, it was not the initial harsh land revenue administration of the British in the province which was to be blamed as 'an original cause of debt'. Fixed land revenue demand in cash and conferment of individual proprietary right on the zamindars coupled with the right to alienate it at their will accounted for only a small part of the total rural indebtedness. Indebtedness, in his opinion, spread fast among the village zamindars only in the 1870s when the British administration system, particularly its legal side, lost its early simplicity and began to behave like an insensible machine blindly applying statute laws and often sweeping away general principles of equity in the process. Thorburn said that it was right from 1866 that Punjab fell a prey to all the paraphernalia of British justice—technical laws, courts, barristers and pleaders. It was this harsh 'machine rule of the British civil courts that, according to Thorburn, should be blamed for this widespread indebtedness of the zamindars in the last quarter of the 19th century.

   Thorburn, however, analysed the problem of indebtedness mainly from a legal and juristic standpoint without paying sufficient attention to various other economic and social factors responsible for its rapid growth. He placed too much importance on the role of the civil courts in the rural society. The swift execution of the decrees against the indebted zamindars by these courts might have encouraged the money-lenders to provide more credit to them than before. But this does not wholly explain the problem. Rural creditors provided loans to zamindars not solely because of the easy execution of sale or mortgage deeds through civil courts. They were also encouraged by the prospect of a higher profit from the sale of agricultural produce over which they acquired control in satisfaction of their credit advances. The intervention of the civil courts did not account for the origin of indebtedness; it constituted a culminating point in the long process of rural indebtedness leading to transfers of the debtors' lands. Far his views, see *P.P.W.*, 242-55.

Darling, however, held that debt and prosperity usually go hand in hand almost all over the world. According to him, the great expansion of credit due to high prices and the inflated value of land enabled zamindars to borrow money and their extravagant habits placed them at the mercy of the *sahukars*. It was their prosperity that was the sole cause of their indebtedness. Darling did point out factors like the smallness of holdings and their frequent fragmentations. However, his main emphasis was on the extravagance of zamindars. But Darling's concept of thriftlessness and rural extravagance arose out of his misconception of the social value cherished by every member of the rural society. These ceremonies were an essential part of a man's life through which he subscribed to the universal pattern of social behaviour and thus identified himself as an integral part of human society. It should also be noted that the volume of wealth spent on such occasions was not larger than a man in his position was justified in spending on those occasions. Even Thorburn's enquiry of the late 1890s found that ruinous expenditure on marriage was rare. For Darling's views, see *Punjab Peasant*, 171-227.

3. In 1860-61 a famine devastated many south-eastern districts of the province. In the Delhi district, zamindars suffered a loss of nearly 75 lakhs of rupees by the death of their plough and well bullocks. In 1868-69 zamindars once again saw crops turning 'sickly yellow, while the cattle died and there was nothing but death or ruin before them' and the burden fell heaviest on the districts of Hissar, Karnal, Sirsa, Rohtak and Amritsar. In 1877-78 scarcity and famine again ravaged the province and the principal scene of distress was the Hissar division and the dry tracts of Delhi division. Finally, came the cycle of famine years in the 1890s. In Lahore, only one-fourth of the living stock was fit for work, and in the district of Hissar no less than 54 per cent of the plough cattle were killed off between the 1st May 1896 and the 31st March 1897. According to another estimate for the same district '92 per cent of the plough and well cattle of those found to exist in April 1895, disappeared in the two-and-a-half years following'. For details, see *Report of the Famine of 1860-61*, 24-5; *Report of the Famine in the Punjab during 1869-70*, 9, 47; *Report of the Famine in the Punjab in 1896-97*, 73; Remarks by Lieutenant C.P. Down, AC Lahore, *Ibid.*, Appendix I, ii.
4. *Agricultural Indebtedness*, General Report, para 36, Rev and Agr (LR) November 1898, 3-22A.

5. Fragmentation of holdings became a very serious problem in a number of central and submontane districts like Sialkot, Gurdaspur, Hoshiarpur and Amritsar. Prof. Bhalla's findings furnished the following interesting piece of information on the way the holdings were split up during the period under review.

Fragmentation of holdings in Bairampur from 1851-52 to 1902-03.

Year	Number of fragments	Average area of a
1	2	3
1851-52	605	.54
1884-85	1,236	.27
1890-91	1,517	.225
1894-95	1,752	.18
1898-99	1,632	.20
1902-03	1,736	.181

Source: Bhalla, *op. cit.*, 33.

6. *Agricultural Indebtedness*, Appendix IV, 256-7, 260, 310-1, 399-400, Rev and Agr (LR) November 1898, 3-22A.
7. *Bannu S.R.*, 1879, 60.
8. *F.C. Selections*, New Series, No. 11, No. 37, No. XLV, E.B. Steedman, SO Jhang's No. 90, 9 July 1879, 851.
9. Thorburn, *M.M.*, 48.
10. *Supra*, 81.
11. J.A. Grant, SC Amritsar's No. 553, 15 February 1889. Rev and Agr (R) December 1891, 10-11A.
12. *Amritsar S.R., 1893*, 3.
13. FC Punjab's review, *Montgomery S.R., 1878*, xiii.
14. Remarks by W.O. Clark, DC Lahore, quoted in G.R. Elsmie's memorandum, 15 August 1889, Rev and Agr (R) December 1891, 10-11A.
15. Translation of opinion of Mian Ghulam Farid, EAC Shahpur, Rev and Agr (R) December 1891, 10-11A.
16. L.W. Dane, SC Gurdaspur's No. 4, 4 January 1889, Rev and Agr (R) December 1891, 10-11A.
17. Note by W. Coldstream, DC Simla on the alienation of agriculturists' land in the Punjab and the proposal to introduce measures to check it, Rev and Agr (R) December 1891, 10-11A.
18. Remarks by E.B. Francis, DC Ferozepore, *ERR 1893-94*, 9. See also Note by F.A. Robertson, DLRA Punjab, *Agricultural Indebtedness*, Rev and Agr (LR) November 1898, 3-22A.
19. *Jullundur S.R., 1892*, 107; *Sialkot S.R., 1918*, 11; Remarks by J. Frizelle, DC Ambala, *ERR 1881-82*, 12, Remarks by E.C. Corbyn, DC Shahpur, *Ibid., 1882-83*, 115.
20. *Gujranwala S.R., 1871*, 23.
21. Reply by T.W.H. Tolbert, DC Gujranwala, *Punjab Famine Report, 1878-79*, II, 466

22. *Gujranwala S.R., 1894*, 24.
23. *Ludhiana S.R., 1884*, Appendix XIII, cxi.
24. E.B. Francis, SO Ferozepore's No. 31, 2 February 1888, Rev and Agr (F) December 1888, 1-24A.
25. *Amritsar D.G., 1892-93*, 81.
26. Thorburn, *M.M.*, 92.
27. *Montgomery S.R., 1878*, 128-9.
28. Oral evidence of the zamindars and co-operators of the Montgomery district, *P.P.B.E.C.*, II, 897.
29. Reply from E.O'Brien, SO Muzaffargarh, *Punjab Famine Report, 1878-79*, II, 498.
30. Translation of a memorandum by Kazi Ghulam Murtaza, EAC Muzaffargarh, Rev and Agr (F) December 1888, 1-24A.
31. *Shahpur D.G., 1883-84*, 57.
32. *Agricultural Indebtedness*, Appendix IV, 354, 364, 386, 395, 411, 430, Rev and Agr (LR) November 1898, 3-22A.
33. Thorburn, *M.M.*, 160.
34. *Multan S.R., 1901*, 17.
35. *Bannu S.R., 1879*, 58-9.
36. Reply from Chimman Lal, EAC Dera Ghazi Khan, *Punjab Famine Report, 1878-79*, II, 532-4.
37. Indebtedness in Dera Ismail Khan district.

Percentage of Muhammadans	State of indebtedness, if any
1	2
13	Already ruined
10	Irretrievably involved
28	Seriously, but retrievably, involved
26	Would be free with two good crops and a little thrift
23	Owing nothing, or if anything under Rs. 50, and easily able to pay

Source : *FC Selections*, New Series, No. 11, No. 37, No. XLV, Note by S.S. Thorburn, DC Dera Ismail Khan, 29 July 1884, 936.

38. *Ambala S.R., 1893*, 3.
39. Report of Muhammad Hayat Khan, JAC Gurdaspur, *Punjab Famine Report, 1878-79*, II, 457.
40. Remarks by J.S. Donald, DC Hoshiarpur, *ERR 1897-98*, 21.
41. *Sialkot S.R., 1895*, 9.
42. *Agricultural Indebtedness*, Appendix IV, 265, 278, 293, Rev and Agr (LR) November 1898, 3-22A.
43. Thorburn, *M.M.*, 35.
44. Ibbetson, *op. cit.*, 237.
45. Thorburn wrote: 'Throughout Eastern Europe the Jews are hated and persecuted rather because they are successful aliens . . . than because they are successful. So with the Bunniahs of the Western Punjab'. Thorburn, *M.M.*, 1.

46. Trevaskis, *op. cit.*, 316.
47. Darling, *Punjab Peasant*, 177.
48. H.A. Rose, *A Glossary of the Tribes and Castes of the Punjab and North-Western Frontier Province*, II (Languages Department, Punjab, Patiala, 1971, hereafter *Tribes*), 59.
49. Ganesh Das repeatedly referred to this in his *Char-Bagh-i-Panjab*. They 'became *diwans, nazims, kardars, vakils*', 'without losing their traditional position as *qanungos, mutasaddis* and *munshis*'. Grewal and Banga, *op. cit.*, 26.
50. Rose, *Tribes*, II, 16.
51. Contemporary sayings also indicate the universal hatred of the zamindars towards them:

    '*Kirar howi yar,*
    Dushman dhar na dhar'

    [He who has a *kirar* for a friend, needs not an enemy.]
52. *P.P.B.E.C.*, I, 144-5.
53. *Amritsar D.G., 1883-84*, 32.
54. *Ludhiana D.G., 1888-89*, 105.
55. *Agricultural Indebtedness*, Appendix II, 207, Rev and Agr (LR) November 1898, 3-22A; R.I. Bruce, DC Dera Ismail Khan's No. 429, 13 April 1889, Rev and Agr (R) December 1891, 10-11A.
56. While recognizing the fact that an agriculturist money-lender was more harsh in his dealings with the indebted clients than a *sahukar*, the former in the opinion of Darling, was a lesser evil; for on the whole 'it is better', he argues, 'that land should pass into the hands of those who can both cultivate and defend it than into the hands of those who rarely do either. A Jat, too, is flesh and blood of the village to which he belongs whereas the *sahukar* is apt to become a parasite in its system' (*Punjab Peasant*, 199). But even accepting the first part of Darling's argument, i.e., 'land should pass into the hands of those who can both cultivate and defend' (which obviously meant the Jat or Arain agriculturist money-lenders) the second part, i.e., '*sahukar* is apt to become a parasite' is of doubtful validity. Dr. P.H.M. van den Dungen in an article ('Changes in Status and Occupation in Nineteenth Century Punjab', D.A. Low, ed., *Soundings in Modern South Asian History*, Weidenfeld and Nicholson, London, 1968, 82-3) has clearly indicated that *sahukars*, particularly the Aroras of western Punjab, were not always a parasitic group, as Darling supposes. They showed their enterprising zeal and often played an improving role in the field of agriculture. They approached the land as 'capitalists determined to get the most out of their investment in land'. In the districts of Multan and Montgomery, Darling himself reported, 'if cultivation is anywhere above the average, if the fruit-trees are being tried, it is ten to one that there is a *Kirar* in the background directing and supervising the work'. Actually long before the establishment of British rule in this part of the province, many of them migrated there from the central districts,

took up lands, sank wells and turned this virgin prairie into a fertile plain. They continued this tradition even during the period under review.

57. Note by J.A. Anderson, DJ Delhi division, *Agricultural Indebtedness*, General Report, 288, Rev and Agr (LR) November 1898, 3-22A.

58. As regards wheat, this new credit group operated through their agents posted at different provincial markets. The official reports described them as 'outsiders', perhaps suggesting that they were not local men. They were often agents and sub-agents of foreign wheat exporting firms of Karachi and Delhi and they were frequently on the move from one *mandi* to another, purchasing wheat against advances. In many cases, however, these creditors carried on their trade through *sahukars* to whom they had advanced credit and the latter often settled the prices at the threshing floor of the zamindars as soon as the harvest was over. For details, see W.O. Clark, DC Lahore's No. 2205. 22 August 1883, *Punjab Wheat : Its Varieties, Distribution and Husbandry*, 47; Bhalla, *op. cit.*, 85.

59. The cultivation of sugar-cane was a very costly one. A small peasant proprietor with no relatives to supply cheap labour and a good source of manure could not possibly cultivate sugar-cane with profit. Consequently, he had to borrow frequently from the *khandsaris* (traders of *mal rab* and *shakkar*) 'as much as he pleases on the security of his crop'. In the Ludhiana *bet*, for instance, the settlement officer pointed out, cultivation of sugar-cane or manufacture of *rab* was largely financed by money-lenders and their men supervised its hoiling. Such advances provided the creditors with an opportunity of controlling the manufacture of *rab* from sugar-cane. They were frequently seen posting a man of their choice, popularly known as *rabia* to carry on boiling and to prevent zamindars from resorting to fraudulent practices. In Hoshiarpur also, zamindars took loans from traders. Similarly in Jullundur, zamindars growing sugar-cane maintained running accounts with money-lenders who were also mostly sugar curers. Here again, *rab* was boiled by these men and not by zamindars at their own will. Even at the time of selling their produce to money-lenders, these indebted zamindars often had to 'put up with a price somewhat lower than that ruling in the open market'. But if the zamindar 'sells his goods elsewhere, the creditor charges him for the loss the creditor is supposed to have sustained by being excluded from the bargain. Such a charge is called *sershahi*, and usually amounts to one anna in the rupee or a standard of *ser* per rupee'. Thus if 'a debtor sells cane juice for Rs. 100 to an outsider, his creditor will debit him with Rs. 6-4-0 or charge 100 standard *sers* against him'. For details, see *Ludhiana S.R., 1884*, Appendix XIII, cx; *Hoshiarpur S.R., 1885*, 86; Report on sugar industry in Jullundur district, Part IX, para 38, Rev and Agr (A) July 1884, 4-8A.

60. In the early 1860s when the cultivation of cotton received sudden stimulus due to the American Civil War, 'much borrowed capital'

was invested in it. Official reports did not specifically mention the sources of this credit, but only suggested that 'obscure traders joined in this venture'. It is difficult to know who really constituted this group; they were perhaps not local people, for it is certain that in the early stages of the cotton boom the 'native dealers appeared quite unconscious of it'. This attitude of the local dealers did not last long. The flourishing cotton export trade of this period soon encouraged them to come forward. Many of them were found 'going about from village to village purchasing every seer they can procure, at prices not heretofore thought of'. With the end of this cotton boom in the mid 1860s, the cultivation of cotton declined in many districts of the province. The Deputy Commissioner of Jhelum attributed it to the fact that the money-lenders no longer found it profitable to grow cotton 'on their account by means of advances'. But once again wiih the revival of trade in the late 1860s they resumed their credit transactions. In the early decades of the present century when cotton came to be regarded as the second important commercial crop of the province, zamindars were so much at the mercy of their creditors that they had then seldom a free hand with their produce. In Karnal, for example, many of them were found selling their cotton to creditors who had already made advances to them while in Multan also they were equally expected to sell their cotton through them at a fixed rate, because these men had already made advances to the zamindars. But in the *mandis* of the Chenab Colony, in the present century, there was very little or practically no contract business of cotton. For details, see *RR 1862-63*, 44; FC's Circular No. 20/1100, 9 March 1867, quoted in Baden H. Powell's *Hand Book*, I, 481; Evidence by F.G. Miliadis, Agent, Messrs Ralli Brothers, Lyallpur, *Report of the Indian Cotton Committee*, IV, Part I, Question No. 4259, 59.

61. *Hoshiarpur D.G., 1904*, 152.
62. Lucas, *op. cit.*, 93; Bhalla, *op. cit.*, 80.
63. *Agricultural Indebtedness*, General Report, para 67, Rev and Agr (LR) November 1898, 3-22A.
64. Bhalla, *op. cit.*, 95
65. *Agricultural Indebtedness*, General Report, para 15, Rev and Agr (LR) November 1898, 3-22A.
66. *Sialkot S.R., 1865*, 36.
67. *Lahore D.G., 1893-94*, 127.
68. Evidence by Shiv Dev Singh, Honorary Magistrate, Siranwali, *Royal Commission on Agriculture in India*, VIII, 391.
69. *RR 1875-76*, 63.
70. *Punjab Selection*, New Series, No. XII, C.R. Hawkins, Offg. Secy. to FC Punjab's No. 1138, 18 October 1875, Report on Current Rates of Interest on Loan Transactions in the Punjab, 2. Perhaps another reason was the absence of rival money-lenders. Thorburn's enquiry also referred to the presence of money-lending fraternity in some parts of the western districts where they, far from encouraging competition,

usually followed a policy of co-operation and mutual understanding in dealing with the indebted clients. This also largely accounted for the exaction of a high rate of interest. *Agricultural Indebtedness*, Appendix II, 203, Rev and Agr (LR) November 1898, 3-22A.

71. *Punjab Selections*, New Series, No. XII, Memorandum by D.G. Barkley, DC Jullundur, 4 August 1875, Report on Current Rates of Interest on Loan Transactions in the Punjab, 15.
72. Remarks by J.E. Cracroft, CR Rawalpindi division, *ERR 1875-76*, 33.
73. In Muzaffargarh, for example, the usual rate of interest against grain loan was nearly 25 per cent. But in 1878-79, when there was a partial failure of crop in this district, the Deputy Commissioner pointed out that 'the premium has risen to 50 (*didh*) and 100 (*dor*) per cent'. Remarks by E.O'Brien, DC Muzaffargarh, *Ibid., 1878-79*, 25.
74. The *Landa* scripts have practically no vowels and may be read differently by different men. The following sayings is proverbial about the different readings of *Landa* scripts: *Lalaji Ajmer Gaye, bari bahi bhej do* (Lalaji has gone to Ajmer, send the ledger). It was read as *Lalaji ajmar gaye, Bari bahu bhej do* (*Lalaji* has died today. Send elder wife). Evidence by Chaudhuri Duli Chand, Member, Legislative Council, Rohtak,*P.P.B.E.C.*, II, 979.
75. It has been pointed out by Prof. Morris D. Morris ('Economic Change and Agriculture in Nineteenth Century India, *IESHR*, III, No. 2, June 1966, 204) that in pre-British India rate of interest charged by money-lenders was high due to low price of land, absence of market and lack of legal protection enjoyed by the creditors for the recovery of their loans. During British rule, it is argued, this high rate of interest tended to decline over the years, largely due to greater economic and legal security for the realization of debts. The increased price of land made it a safe security and purchasers of such lands seldom ran any risk of losing their money and could resell them, if they so intended, often with a clear margin of profit. But this view does not seem to hold good with regard to the entire Punjab of our period. Under Sikh rule, as it has already been pointed out, *sahukars* could not demand an exorbitant rate of interest due to the wide prevalence of the *dam dupat* principle , according to which the interest of a loan accumulated only to the extent of the capital and never beyond it. But if the *sahukars* sought to enforce any high rate of interest on the indebted proprietors, the *kardars* immediately intervened and generally settled the debt by scaling down the rate of interest in favour of the zamindars. Consequently, under Sikh rule the rate of interest was not unusually high. Further, the contemporary official records also do not suggest that due to greater legal and economic security rates of interest appreciably declined during British rule. During an official enquiry (1874-75), the Deputy Commissioners of Lahore, Multan and Rawalpindi pointed out that 'the high rate of interest charged on loans made on the security of land' was due to the

'difficulty of obtaining possession of land' in the rural Punjab. Darling also suggested that things became worse under British rule due to the prevailing practice of demanding compound interest from the debtors. For details, see *Punjab Selections*, New Series, No. XII, C.R. Hawkins, Offg. Secy. to FC Punjab's No. 1138, 18 October 1875, Report on Current Rates of Interest on Loan Transactions in the Punjab, 2; Darling, *Punjab Peasant*, 187-8.

76. H.C. Fanshawe, Offg. Jr. Secy. to FC Punjab's No. 231, 7 November 1888, Rev and Agr (R) May 1891, 1-8A. See also *Punjab Government Records*, I, *Records of the Delhi Residency and Agency, 1807-57* (Lahore, 1911), 74.
77. Grewal and Banga, *op. cit*., 27-8.
78. *Jullundur S.R., 1852, Parl. Papers, 1854*, LXIX, 265.
79. R.K. Seth, Faiz Ilahi, H.W. Emerson and E.P. Moon, *An Economic Survey of Durrana Langana—a Village in the Multan District* (The Board of Economic Enquiry, Punjab, Village Surveys No. 11, Publication No. 54, Lahore, 1938), viii, 89.
80. Calvert, *op. cit.*, 263
81. *Amritsar S.R., 1873*, 13.
82. *Gurdaspur S.R., 1859*, 13
83. H.C. Fanshawe, Offg. Jr. Secy's to EC Punjab's No. 231, 7 November 1888, Rev. and Agr (R) May 1891, 1-8A.
84. *Ibid., RR 1899-1900*, Statement No. XA.
85. Increase in the number of sales between 1875-76 and 1899-1900.

Year	Number of sales
1	2
1875-76	6,600
1899-1900	20,584

Source: *RR* for the respective years.

86. The following 12 districts recorded a large-scale mortgage of their cultivated area (in per cent) at the beginning of the present century.

Name of the district	Cultivated area under mortgage in per cent
1	2
Gurdaspur	25.5
Sialkot	25.1
Kohat	20 4
Bannu	19.9
Dera Ghazi Khan	18.7
Amritsar	17.0
Dera Ismail Khan	16.7
Gujrat	16.1
Gurgaon and Shahpur	15.9
Muzaffargarh	15.3
Ambala	15.2

Source: *RR 1900-01*, 13.

87. Rise in the land prices in the Punjab during the period 1870-71 to 1900-01.

Year	Average sale price of cultivated land in rupees per acre
1	2
1870-71	15
1875-76	20
1880-81	18.5
1885-86	36
1890-91	61
1895-96	59
1900-01	77

Source : *RR* for the respective years.
See also Karunamoy Mukherjee, 'Land Prices in the Punjab', M. K. Chaudhuri, ed., *Trends of Socio-Economic Change in India, 1871-1961* (Indian Institute of Advanced Study, Simla, 1969), 520-44.

88. As early as 1865-66 such cases of resale of lands drew the attention of the revenue authorities. For details, see *RR 1866-67*, 142.
89. The reasons for this eagerness of the *sahukars* to purchase land were two-fold: they sought landed property for the sake of acquiring the respectable status of a landowner; further, 'it is so good an investment'. L.J.H. Grey, CR Delhi division's No. 510, 29 July 1889, Rev and Agr (R) December 1891, 10-11A.
90. J.A. Grant, SC Amritsar's No. 553, 15 February 1889, Rev and Agr (R) December 1891, 10-11A.
91. T.J. Kennedy, Offg. DC Montgomery's No. 31 December 1888, Rev and Agr (R) December 1891, 10-11A.
92. A. Anderson, DC Hissar's No. 64G, 11 March 1889, Rev and Agr (R) December 1891, 10-11A.
93. For details, see LG Punjab's No. 81, 28 March 1890, quoted in *Hoshiarpur S.R., 1885*, 4-5; *Jullundur S.R., 1892*, 70-73; *Ludhiana D.G., 1888-89*, 191-6; *Amritsar A.R., 1892*, Statement V; *Tarn Taran A.R., 1891*, 20-1; *Jullundur A.R., 1883*, 9-10; *Phillour A.R., 1883*, 6; *Nawashahr A.R., 1883*, 11; *Zira A.R., 1888*, 32-3; *Ilaka Mamdot A.R., 1875*, 18; *Muktsar A.R., 1893*, 8 9; *Dasuya A.R., 1883*, 9; *Garshankar A. R., 1884*, 11-3.
94. For details, see *Karnal-Ambala S.R., 1891*, 18-9; *Sialkot S.R., 1895*, 9; *Gurgaon A.R., 1883*, para 10; *Gurdaspur A.R., 1890*, 19-20; *Pathankot A.R., 1890*, 28-30; *Shakargar A.R 1891.*, 19-20; *Lodhran A.R., 1900*, 33-4; *Mailsi A.R., 1900*, 28; *Khusab A.R., 1892*, 32; *Preliminary Kharian A.R., 1892*, 54; *Zafarwal A.R., 1892*, 27-31; *Dera Ghazi Khan A.R., 1896*, 42-3; *Rajanpur A.R., 1896*, 38; T.J. Kennedy, DC Multan's No. 223, 9 July 1895, PGR Rev and Agr (R) July, 1896, 15A; FC Punjab's review, *Jampur A.R.*, 1896, PGR Rev and Agr (R) January 1897, 19-24A; *Agricultural Indebtedness*, Appendix IV, 265, 278, 293, Rev and Agr (LR) November 1898,

3-22A; J.B. Hutchinson, CR Lahore division's No. 697, 4 October 1894, Rev and Agr (LR) June 1896, 28A; Note by Captain J.G. Crosthwaite, SO Dera Ismail Khan's No.—, n.d., Rev and Agr (LR) May 1901, 11-12A; Report of M.L. Dames, DC Dera Ghazi Khan's No.—, n.d., Rev and Agr (R) December 1891, 10-11A; Remarks by A.J. Harrison, DC Montgomery, *ERR* 1891-92, 30, para 51, Rev. and Agr (LR) November 1898, 3-22A.

95. *Agricultural Indebtedness*, General Report, para 51 Rev and Agr (LR) November 1898, 3-22A.
96. Evidence by Kartart Baksh, Patwari of Kot Ghumman (Sialkot), *Ibid.*, Appendix II, 206, Rev and Agr (LR) November 1898, 3-22A.
97. *Ibid.*, General Report, para 51, Rev and Agr (LR) November 1898, 3-22A.
98. Remarks by Colonel C.A. McMahon, CR Hissar division, *ERR 1876-77*, 6.
99. Remarks by O' Brien, DC Muzaffargarh, *RR 1881-82*, 15.
100. Thorburn, *M.M.*, 83.
101. *Agricultural Indebtedness*, Appendix II, 206, Rev and Agr (LR) November 1898, 3-22A.
102. Thorburn thus described *sam*: 'Literally *sam* means one-fourth of produce earned by a plough. When a zamindar has transferred all his land and has no assets left except himself and a pair of bullocks, he borrows money on the security of his *sam*, undertaking to pay his *sahukar* each harvest one-fourth of his plough produce in payment of interest, no matter where earned: a debtor without bullocks may give his labour, such as ploughing, building of a wall, ete., as interest on his debt; sometimes a debtor makes over his son or brother to his creditor as a servant in lieu of interest. A *sahukar* sometimes lends out services of his debtor to friends or relatives. *Ibid.*, Appendix II, 222, Rev and Agr (LR) November 1898, 3-22A. See also *Jhang S.R., 1882*, 72.
103. Memorandum by J.R. Maconachie, DC Gurdaspur, *Agricultural Indebtedness*, Rev and Agr (LR) November 1898, 3-22A.
104. *Gurgaon A.R., 1883*, 11.
105. *Gurgaon S.R., 1909*, 14.
106. T.G. Walker, AC Karnal's No. 53, 14 April 1884, Rev and Agr (R) August 1884, 10-12A.
107. E.B. Francis, SO Ferozepore's No. 419, 31 December 1881, Rev and Agr (R) December 1891, 10-11A.
108. Remarks by Colonel C.F. Massy, CR Jullundur division, *ERR 1895-96*, 45.
109. In the present century the Sikh Jats virtually ousted the professional money-lenders from this district. For details, see Darling, *Wisdom and Waste*, 103.
110. T.G. Walker, AC Karnal's No. 53, 14 April 1884, Rev and Agr (R) August 1884, 10-12A.
111. *Multan S.R., 1901*, 17.

112. Major J.B. Hutchinson, DC Multan's No. 645, 31 December 1888, Rev and Agr (R) December 1891, 10-11A.
113. Remarks by C.G. Parsons, DC Multan, *ERR 1888-89*, 14.
114. Remarks by J.R. Maconachie, DC Multan, *Ibid., 1891-92*, 30.
115. *Ambala S.R., 1893*, 6.
116. Sale, mortgage and redeemed areas from 1902-03 to 1907-08 by agricultural tribes (See table on page 141).
117. Net gains of the Jats on sale and mortgage of the cultivated area in acres from 1904-05 to 1906-07.

Year	Net gain of the Jats on sale	Net gain or loss of all agricultural tribes on sale	Net gain of the Jats on mortgage	Net gain or loss of all agricultural tribes on mortgage
1	2	3	4	5
1904–05	+3,614	+1,040	+171	+5,030
1905–06	+4,866	+490	+1,761	+23,523
1906–07	+2,564	+4,000	+4,365	+84,119

Source: *LAR 1904-05*, paras 46-7; *Ibid., 1905-6*, paras 43-4; *Ibid., 1906-07*, paras 25-6, 30-1; *Ibid., 1907-08*, para 28.

118. *Ludhiana D.G., 1888-89*, 82.
119. *Jullundur D.G., 1883-84*, 26.
120. Net loss of the Rajputs on sale and mortgage of the cultivated area in acres from 1903-04 to 1906-07.

Year	Net loss of the Rajputs by sale	Net loss or gains of all agricultural tribes on sale	Net loss of the Rajputs by mortgage	Net loss or gain of all agricultural tribes on mortgage
1	2	3	4	5
1903–04	–1,039	–11,674	–23,058	–30,811
1904–05	–2,342	+ 1,040	–13,381	+5,030
1905–06	–301	+490	–13,240	+23,523
1906–07	–2,286	+4,000	– ...	+84,119

Source: *LAR* for the respective years.

121. *Lahore D.G., 1893-94*, 107; *Jullundur D.G., 1883-84*, 26; *Amritsar D.G., 1914*, 39.
122. Ibbetson, *op. cit.*, 189-95.
123. *LAR 1904-5*, paras 46-7; *Ibid., 1905-06*, paras 43-4; *Ibid., 1906-07*, para 25.
124. Remarks by Captain H.P.P. Leigh, DC Kohat, *ERR* 1888-89, 19.
125. Remarks by E.B. Francis, DC Ferozepore, *Ibid.*, 1893-94, 9.
126. Note by F.A. Robertson, DLRA Punjab, *Agricultural Indebtedness*, Rev and Agr (LR) November 1898, 3-22A.

Year	Sold by agricultural tribes	Sold to agricultural tribes	Net gain or loss of agricultural tribes on sale	Redeemed by agricultural tribes	Mortgaged by agricultural tribes	Net gain or loss by agricultural tribes on mortgage
1	2	3	4	5	6	7
1902–03	132,310	138,290	+ 5,980	124,679	169,858	−45,179
1903–04	153,396	141,722	−11,674	162,829	193,640	−30,811
1904–05	151,041	152,081	+ 1,040	199,179	194,149	+ 5,030
1905–06	163,209	163,699	+ 490	225,118	201,595	+23,523
1906–07	152,445	156,445	+ 4,000	301,073	216,954	+84,119
1907–08	156,492	168,562	+12,070	293,256	232,065	+61,191

Source: *LAR 1906-7*, paras 30-1; *Ibid.*, *1907-8*, para 28.

6

Tenants and Their Relations With the Zamindars

Early settlement reports clearly reveal that at the outset of British rule 'a specially favoured non-proprietary class of cultivators' existed in the Punjab. Many of them brought land under cultivation by either breaking the waste or clearing the jungle; many again sunk wells, erected embankments for irrigation and improved the soil by manuring it and thereby acquired a right to hold and cultivate it so long as they paid the revenue and other village charges to the state. These tenants often held land for over two or three generations and their rights were generally admitted by the village proprietary body.[1] Besides there were other less favoured tenants[2] who generally held land from year to year and their ranks were commonly swelled either by owners of small holdings[3] or by 'village servants, itinerant cultivators, persons who from a variety of causes, might 'have temporarily abandoned their village, and individuals who' did not 'make agriculture their chief occupation, such as weavers, Banyas, etc.' They were, however, at liberty to give up the land when they pleased and were also removable by the landlord.[4]

Accordingly in Sialkot, Prinsep in his settlement report referred to *hissachuk*, *varyoon* and *vasee*, entitled to certain important privileges denied to *asami* and *pahikasht*. The tenure of the former group of tenants was heritable and they were not disturbed so long as they regularly shared the revenue burdens of the village proprietary body. They might cut trees planted by others, but to plant or sell them they would need to consult the owners. They could not also transfer their rights by sale or mortgage. The settlement officer also found that the *hissachuks* again never 'paid the proprietary dues of any kind to any body' though the same was paid by all other categories of tenants.[5] In Shahpur, these privileged tenants were known as *abadkaran* or *banjarshigafan* who often held lands along the banks of the river and enjoyed some concessions regarding rent rates which were denied to the tenants-at-will.[6] In Amritsar, *bhaewals* (relatives or intimates associated as co-partners to cultivate lands) were also entitled to most of these privileges. Their rights were not hereditary but they 'could not be ejected except after an adjustment of accounts'.[7] The thinly populated and sparingly cultivated parts of this district also saw the development of the rights of the *butmars* or 'adventurers from other parts, who sought for waste land to cultivate, and entered into a stipulation with the village proprietors to take up lands which had hitherto been uncultivated'. It was estimated that at the revision of settlement (1854) these privileged tenants held nearly 10 per cent of the total area under their cultivation.[8] In Jhelum also tenants were generally of two categories:[9] *muzarian mustakil* and *muzarian ghairmustakil*. The former group was again subdivided into three smaller subgroups: *asami kadimi*, who had come in before the great famine of 1783; *mustakil purano*, who had been in possession of their holdings around 1810; *mustakil naya* who came in this district after 1810. The *muzarian ghairmustakil* were nothing but mere tenants-at-will with no special rights over land. Similarly in the Dera Ghazi Khan the settlement officer recognized the existence of tenants-at-will who were known as *charyat*. Besides there were tenants like *mundemars* or *butmars* (who cleared jungle), *jhuribands* (who paid *nazrana* to landlord in cash or kind), *latmars* (who erected embankment) and *kuhmars* (who sunk well) swelling the rank of the privileged tenancy. In the opinion of the settlement officer *mundemars* in particular enjoyed certain special privileges like sinking wells, building houses and subletting their holdings temporarily. These privileges were granted to them 'owing to the scarcity of tenants in the district'.[10]

The tenants' appreciation of these special advantages found expression through a docile compliance to share the revenue obligations of the proprietary body on a basis of parity.[11] In a number of districts they also paid some proprietary dues under the name of *ismi*, *biswi* and *malikana*. Thus in Ambala the proprietors received 'a trifling recognition of their proprietary right in the shape of a seer or two in the maund' while in Muzaffargarh it varied from $2\frac{1}{4}$ to $2\frac{1}{2}$ seers in the maund.[12] In some other districts these tenants paid numerous extra dues under the general name of *habubat*.[13]

The question of tenant liabilities automatically gives rise to the question of the stability of their tenure under Sikh rule. The early settlement records point to a widespread belief that since land was abundant and cultivators were scarce in the context of heavy Sikh land revenue demand, these tenants were 'tolerated by the proprietors without any active resistance'[14] so long as they paid the revenue and other necessary charges. The proprietors, however, always had an 'unlimited and unrestrained'[15] right of evicting any tenant whenever they required land for their own use. 'It mattered not how long the cultivator might have been on the land.'[16] But this power was seldom exercised unless the tenant 'made himself obnoxious'. However in such cases the proprietor had to see to an alternate arrangement for the efficient cultivation of the land, since otherwise the removal of the tenant would be opposed by the *kardar*.[17]

This was the background of the introduction of the regular settlements in the Punjab. Among many other things, these settlements also carried on a detailed enquiry into the record of rights of these tenants. In different districts of the province they invariably found many tenants who had not only aided the proprietary body in founding villages and clearing the soil during Sikh rule, but also shared the heavy revenue demand with them at same rates. They were also convinced that the customs of this country 'accorded a privilege' to these tenants since they had tolerated 'the heat and burden of the day' over the years. It 'is not easy', thus wrote Wynyard while conducting the settlement in the southern parganas of the Ambala district in the early 1850s, 'to dismiss the claim of a man, who has for years been bearing up against heavy assessments, and paying his share with the proprietary brotherhood'.[18] Incidentally it may be borne in mind that these settlements were mostly undertaken by young officers from the North-Western

Provinces[19] where twelve years' uninterrputed possession of a holding at the same rate of rent was regarded to be a sufficient proof of occupancy right. In fixing the record of rights of these tenants, twelve years' rule[20] was taken up as a safe guide by these officers.

Accordingly these officers found little difficulty in recording cultivators like *abadkarans, butmars, mundemars* and *latmars* as occupancy tenants who enjoyed somewhat a privileged status during Sikh rule. Besides fixity of tenure these tenants obtained additional privileges which again varied greatly from district to district. Thus in Amritsar *butmars* were not generally called upon to pay any *malikana* though the same was demanded from the *mustakil puranas* of the Jhelum district. In Shahpur also these tenants' dues were determined in such a manner so as to give them a certain amount of profit on the outturn.[21]

But the recognition of tenants' rights did not constitute a new development in the Punjab during the period under review. It was largely a legacy of Sikh rule which the first batch of English settlement officers could not altogether ignore in fixing the records of the different categories of tenants at the outset of British rule.[22] They also faced very little opposition from the proprietors in recording them hereditary in most of the districts of the province. On numerous occasions, reported these officers, the proprietors were more eager to grant than the tenants were to accept, the occupancy title.[23] They frequently allowed these tenants to hold lands at revenue rates; they were often ready to forego their *malikana* with a view to keeping them tied to their lands. These developments were particularly reported from Gujranwala, Montgomery and Dera Ghazi Khan during the early years of the first regular settlements.[24]

This proprietary willingness was again largely due to general fall in the prices shortly after the annexation of the province. During the summary settlements of the early 1850s the prices of agricultural products sank so low that the proprietors found it pretty hard to fulfil their revenue obligations in cash. Later on when the regular settlements were introduced, the dullness in the market persisted and so did the consequences of the summary settlements.[25] Under such circumstances the proprietors were naturally very glad to induce any of their tenants to share this burden of the money demand. During these years the position of these tenants was further strengthened when the Government forbade any alteration of the existing rent rates of cultivators with occupancy rights during the term of settlement and 'a general provision to the same effect was inserted in the Punjab Civil Code'.[26] Here again the proprietors' misgivings about their ability 'to pay a money demand regularly no doubt often led them willingly to acquiesce in these proceedings'.

During the early years of British rule the positions of these tenants were thus comparatively strong vis-a-vis the proprietors.[27] But from the 1860s the tables were turned. Now the abolition of the vexatious customs transit duties coupled with the modern means of communications opened up new markets while the canals not only extended the area under the plough but also brought in their train an increased output per acre. There was a significant rise in the land value of the province. Naturally in the context of rising prices, these tenants were very anxious to maintain the privileged position they had held since the early years of British rule. They often tried to secure money rent rates in order to enjoy some profits to their credit. On the other hand, there was a visible decline in the proprietors' enthusiasm in making these tenants share in the burden of money demand, because they had also become aware of the benefits of grain dues paid by these tenants in recognition of their proprietary rights over lands. Consequently, they were keen on receiving their dues in kind wherever it was possible.[28] Their position was further strengthened with the beginning of a competition for lands among tenants in a number of densely populated districts. Proprietors in such districts even exhibited a marked propensity to keep the entire cultivation of their land to themselves since cultivation of land had become 'the most desired and resorted to of all occupations'.[29]

In this changed background Prinsep (Settlement Commissioner of the Amritsar division) started a revision of settlement (1865) in three districts—Amritsar, Gurdaspur and Sialkot. He carried on a detailed investigation into the position of tenants in these districts and was convinced that a great error had been committed in the matter of recording hereditary cultivators during the period of the first regular settlement in the early 1850s. He pointed out that out of a little over 60,000 cultivators recorded as 'occupancy tenants' in the old records in these districts, only one in four actually enjoyed this status. He concluded that the rest (nearly 45,300) were, 'without doubt, erroneously entered as having right of occupancy' and 'at this settlement they should be rectified'. He accordingly sought official sanction to rectify these tenancy records. While 'rectifying' these errors,[30] Prinsep divided these tenants into five distinct groups. He found that only 15,547 could claim the right of occupancy.[31] Prinsep also drew attention to the fact that out of 60,000 holdings nearly 25,000 were recorded as paying no rent since the days of the first regular settlement. This caused great hardship to the proprietors. He accordingly asked [32] a little over 50,000 tenants to pay rent in cash, 7,320 in grain while only 6,490 were exempted from rent charges.[33]

These changes in the status of non-hereditary tenants have been interpreted by some scholars in terms of 'an aristocratic reaction'[34] or of 'an extensive growth of landlord sentiment'[35] in the Punjab, as in other Indian provinces, in the post-Mutiny years. According to them Prinsep's intended rectifications of the record of right of the first regular settlements in the three districts of the province placed him 'squarely' in the tradition of the 'aristocratic reaction' as thc 'Punjab equivalent of Wingfield' of Awadh. As far as the Punjab was concerned these remarks were based on an inaccurate reading of the contemporary official records. There is little doubt that Prinsep supported the cause of the landlords as against that of their tenants in the Amritsar division. But in this tract the word landlord universally stood for small peasant proprietors with an average of six acres of lands at their disposal and tenants held only four acres of land. Prinsep, unlike Wingfield, can thus hardly be described as the champion of 'landlord sentiment'. He was more truly a supporter of the small peasant proprietors against their non-hereditary small tenants and not of landlords akin to big Awadh *talukdars*.

These intended rectifications of the records of rights of the first regular settlements soon 'galvanised' many experienced officials into action. A group of important officials headed by Colonel Lake (Financial Commissioner) and Melvill (Officiating Commissioner of the Amritsar division) were particularly bitter in denouncing these moves.[36] Soon the Government of India under the Viceroyalty of Lord Lawrence also took note of it. Lawrence openly denounced Prinsep's intended rectifications of the errors of the first regular settlements, of which the main beneficiaries were the actual tillers of the soil with whose cause he had formerly identified himself in the Punjab. He felt that it would be inexpedient to allow thc revenue officers conducting the revised settlements in this province to make any radical change in the status of such tenants as were recorded with right of occupancy at the last settlement.[37] Against this background the Punjab Tenancy Act (Act XVIII of 1868) was passed. Its intention was three-fold. First, to define occupancy right; secondly, to regulate the rate of enhancement of rent; and thirdly, to provide compensation for the eviction of tenants.

According to the provisions of this Act, tenants hitherto recognized as possessing rights of occupancy were 'presumed to possess such rights until contrary was proved by landlords in a regular suit in a court. In this way although aggrieved landlords could regain their lost rights, only few of them challenged the presumption immediately'. The Act further provided that the rent payable by an occupancy tenant could only be enhanced by a decree of the court. But two clauses protected the interests of the zamindars: in the first place, no right of occupancy could be acquired by mere lapse of time and secondly, eviction of occupancy tenants was permitted on payment of compensation.

One immediate effect of the Act was that it nullified the changes in the status of tenants resulting from the measures of officers like Prinsep and others. Steps were accordingly taken to restore the entries of the first regular settlements;[38] it actually reinstated in five districs (namely, Amritsar, Gujranwala, Gurdaspur, Lahore and Sialkot) 63,000 persons to the position of tenants with occupancy rights who had, under the revised settlement proceedings, been reduced to the position of tenants-at-will. While extending occupancy rights to these tenants, the Act also empowered the landlords to enhance their rents on certain specific grounds which they were not slow to utilise. Actually this practice of rent enhancement added a new dimension to the changing form of agrarian relations which may conveniently be studied in the context of the regional variations of the agrarian economy of the province.

To begin with, in the district of Jullundur the holdings were usually so small[39] that proprietors of energetic races like the Jats and Arains often cultivated the lands of others as tenants to supplement their scanty income. At the first regular settlement, rents of the occupancy tenants were generally fixed for the term of the settlement and consisted of a share of the revenue with some extra dues. Similarly the non-hereditary tenants were asked to share the heavy land revenue demand of the state though in many cases their rate of payment often stood below the revenue rates on the cultivated area of the district. But with the rising prices and the competition for lands during these years, their strength was put to severe strain leading to a decided rise in the rent rates. As early as 1872-73 it was estimated that their rent doubled since the passing of the Tenancy Act in 1868. It was then also revealed that this Act brought about a significant change in the landlord-tenant relations. In many cases it 'led to jealous interference on the part of the owners in all proposed improvements by tenants', as it was sure to 'increase the selling value of the tenants' right' and 'diminish their chances of succession' to those holdings.[40] On the other hand, the feeling of the tenants towards the proprietors was that of 'apprehension and distrust'.[41] This was largely an outcome of the persistent attempt of the proprietors to raise the rent rates. Besides demanding half the share of the produce (after deducting the dues of the menials) as rents, they even took a part of the straw.[42] Inability of the tenants to meet the proprietary demands often led to regular rent suits under the Tenancy Act and it was only very rarely that they had their way. Success in legal battles so greatly strengthened the position of the landlords that at the third regular settlement (1918) it was estimated that the rent rates of the tenants were more than double in tahsils like Phillour and Jullundur since the conclusion of the last settlement in the early 1880s.[43]

But the landlord-tenant relations underwent an even more significant change in some of the south-eastern districts of the province. Here also it mainly centered round the problem of enhancement of rent which the tenants tried to fight out by claiming the right of occupancy for themselves. In these districts many of these tenants were descendants of persons who had assisted the proprietary body in the foundation of new villages in the past. They were often closely related to the proprietary body by ties of kinship and were allowed to hold land on condition of sharing the revenue demand of the state. Their relationship with the proprietors was generally cordial and in the recent past they had often assisted one another in repelling the attacks of common foes. But in the 1870s their relation witnessed a gradual change and in this connection Sirsa district[44] deserves our special attention.

During the first quarter of the 19th century Sirsa was almost entirely a waste land with very few permanent villages. But shortly after the establishment of British rule, cultivators from the neighbouring regions started migrating there and brought a considerable amount of waste under the plough. They were generally allowed to hold their lands on condition of sharing the Government dues and the common village expenses. At the first regular settlement (1852-64) proprietary rights were, however, conferred only on those handful of persons who were selected arbitrarily by the settlement officer from among the general body of cultivators and 'all land brought under cultivation before 1852 was declared to be held by the cultivator with right of occupancy'. It was then recorded that 27 per cent of the total cultivated area remained under the proprietors while nearly 66 per cent were held by tenants with occupancy rights.[45]

Another important step taken at the first regular settlement was to confine 'the right to break up new land in the prairie', which had hitherto been opened to all the tenants in most villages to 'the few individuals who were declared to be proprietors of the whole township'. It was then also decided that henceforth no tenant might bring new land under cultivation except with the consent of the proprietors, who might fix any rent they thought proper. And in course of the next ten years, another 2,000,00 acres were brought under cultivation. As the state demand was heavy, the proprietors were at first glad to see the uncultivated land brought under the plough even at a very light rent because this meant an addition to their income and they, therefore, imposed no restriction on the breaking up of the waste by the tenants. But with the expansion of cultivation over the village waste and the rise in the value of lands, the proprietors asserted their right under the Tenancy Act (which forbade the tenants to bring more lands under the plough without the prior consent of the proprietors). They also claimed the right of evicting tenants on their failure to pay the enhanced rent rate over their newly broken up holdings. This significant change in the attitude of the proprietors was sure to cause much hardship to their tenants. In the past they had enjoyed an unrestricted right of breaking the wastes and shared many of the difficulties of colonization. Their past experience convinced them that they would once again be granted occupancy right over the lands they had brought under the plough in the post-regular settlement period. But they were then asked either to pay a higher rate of rent or to face eviction.

Here were the elements of a potential struggle between proprietors and their tenants. At the regular settlement, proprietors remembered that there was nearly a wholesale grant of occupancy rights 'to almost all the tenants in the land they then cultivated'; they also feared its repetition at the revision of settlement. They were, therefore, determined to evict their tenants-at-will, 'thus establishing beyond doubt their true status'. On the other hand, many of these tenants did not hesitate to challenge their right of evicting them from the lands they held since the completion of regular settlement in the early 1850s. They often demanded the right of occupancy over these lands. No one usually thought of ejecting them from the lands they cultivated in the neighbouring Native States of Patiala and Bikaner, from which many of these tenants had come, so long as they paid the requisite amount. Further the general feeling of the countryside, the settlement officer reported, also discouraged the ejection of a tenant 'from the land he cultivated, especially if he or his father had broken it up from the prairie'.[46] Emboldened by all these factors, they contested many of the notices of ejectment served on them by the law courts.[47] These numerous ejectment disputes greatly unsettled the tenants throughout the district[48] and embittered their relations with the landlords. This bad feeling naturally led to many quarrels and prompted some of them to leave their lands which they had brought under the plough. In many cases again, after the ejectment proceedings had been concluded in the proprietors' favour, tenants were allowed to remain in possession of the land at a higher rent,[49] or at a rent in kind instead of in cash, or were given other land in place of that from which they had been ejected.

This struggle over rent between proprietors and their tenants was not only confined to Sirsa. Similar conflicts developed in Gurgaon, Hissar and Hoshiarpur. In Gurgaon, for example, before the revision of the settlement (1872) the great majority of tenants paid their rent at the customary rate (this was often below the revenue rate). But with the revision of assessment in the late 1870s proprietors insisted on a higher rate of rent.[50] They were particularly active in Palwal tahsil where the value of land rose remarkably during these years owing to the opening of the Agra Canal. 'The Deputy Commissioner remarks that the landlords are in consequence attempting to eject as many old tenants paying at customary rents as they can, in order to lease their lands to new tenants at higher rents'.[51] Further there was also evidence that rents in kind were giving place to cash rents in all the five tahsils of the district.

This attempt on the part of the proprietors was naturally disliked by tenants holding lands at privileged customary rents. The tenants were reluctant to admit their demands. In 1875-76 they frequently challenged the ejectment suits instituted by the landlords. In the succeeding years also proprietors continued to stick to this policy and it was only in the late 1870s, that the number of notices of ejectment tended to decline when these tenants agreed to come to terms on conditions of paying a higher rate of rent. In 1883 the settlement officer found that a general increase of average rent had taken place in almost every circle of this district. He also found that much land entered at the settlement as paying rent in kind, was paying rent in cash and that 'much land which then paid rent in varying directly with the land revenue now pays a lump rent or one fixed without much reference to the assessment'. Thus in 274 villages at the settlement (about 1880s), 80,326 acres paid rents aggregating Rs 1,78,289 and averaging Rs 2-4 per acre, and in 1881-82 in the same villages 81,903 acres paid rents aggregating Rs 2,01,042 and averaging Rs. 2.7.[52]

In Hissar also the conflict between proprietors and tenants came out into the open with the revision of settlement in the 1880s. During this period a large number of tenants, who had been in possession of their holdings for long at privileged rates, considered their status to be little inferior to that of tenants with occupancy right. Landlords remembered the somewhat summary creation of occupancy tenures in the settlement of the 1860s. But with the beginning of the revision of the regular settlement, they feared that many of these tenants-at-will might claim occupancy status (because of their length of occupation) and prejudice their own interests. They also feared a considerable enhancement of land revenue demand in this new settlement. The result was that they thought it best to enhance rents wherever they could, and at the same time (by issuing notices of ejectment and thereby procuring an enhanced rent)[53] they sought to prove that the tenants had no occupancy rights. On the other hand, many of these tenants objected to an enhancement of rent. It led to protracted legal battles. These tenants were able successfully to contest the claims of the proprietors only in a limited number of cases. The settlement officer estimated that during these years nearly 75 per cent of the ejectment notices of this period were settled against them and in most cases the ejected tenants were reinstated by their landlords but on a higher rate of rent.[54]

At about the same time Hoshiarpur district witnessed a similar conflict between the landlord and their tenants verging on 'a deep class hostility' so that 'tenancy' became 'a burning question in this district'.[55] Here the size of the proprietary holdings were so small that many small owners and occupancy tenants found it necessary to add to their husbandry by undertaking the cultivation of surplus lands of the big landlords as tenants-at-will. Thus of the area cultivated by tenants-at-will in the tahsils of Hoshiarpur, Garshankar and Dasuya, more than two-thirds was held by tenants who had proprietary or occupancy rights in other lands. Further this district was 'exceptionally situated in respect of the number of holdings with occupancy right and paying rents at revenue rates (with or without the addition of a cash *malikana*)'. There were in this district 47,778 holdings of this kind with an area of 90,000 acres. Reckoning by holding, this was nearly one-seventh of the whole number of occupancy tenancies paying rent in this manner which existed in the Punjab.[56] A fourth of these tenancies paid no rent except the Government's demand, viz., revenue, cesses and local rates on their holdings. The remaining three-fourths only paid a small *malikana*, not usually exceeding two annas per rupee of the Government revenue, and generally only half of this. These tenures included a large portion of the richest lands in the district; their holders generally belonged to the sturdy agricultural communities like the Jats, Arains and Sainis who were 'very tenacious of their rights' over lands.

But with the approaching termination of the regular settlement leading to revised assessment (1879-84), rising value of land and steady competition among tenants to add to their holdings, it was feared that landlords would no longer allow these tenants to hold lands on the existing rates of rents. While explaining it, the settlement officer pointed out:[57]

> The great majority of occupancy tenants all over the district have hitherto paid only nominal rents, *viz.*, at revenue rates plus 10 or 12 per cent on the revenue as malikana. The ruling cash rents in the plain tahsils are now so high that it will be difficult to avoid decreeing the proprietors a rent in which the malikana will amount to 200 to 300 per cent on the Government revenue, and I fear the already strained relations between landlords and tenants will become worse.

Naturally the landlords in general sought to enforce their claims to this higher rate of rent and the existing Tenancy Act also empowered the landlords to raise the rents of the occupancy tenants by about 15 to 50 per cent which the latter did not hesitate to challenge at the earliest possible opportunity. Already their relations with the proprietors had become strained over their respective rights to the trees grown on their lands. Against this background landords' attempt to enforce a general enhancement of rent was expected to lead to further ill-feelings and it often led to legal battles. It was estimated in 1882-83 that already 619 tenancy cases were waiting for disposal while many more were expected to come up very shortly. The Commissioner of Settlement also feared that 'a prolonged litigation would follow' and the 'courts would be flooded with hundreds, not improbably thousands, of these cases'. In many cases, however, an enhancement of more than 66 per cent was already decreed in favour of proprietors and these cases were often settled in the district courts in 'a very perfunctory manner, causing an immense hardship to scores of tenants with valuable occupancy rights' and many of them even left the district for the Native States.[58]

The local revenue officials, being greatly alarmed, drew the attention of the Punjab Government to all these cases. They pointed out that agricultural prosperity of this district largely depended on the 'maintenance of harmony between the several classes composing the agricultural population', whereas these litigations had produced 'a state of uncertainty which prevents things from settling down'. Accordingly they, including the Commissioner of Settlement, wanted the Government to intervenue. The new Tenancy Act (Act XVI of 1887) was soon put into effect and these tenancy cases were settled under the provisions of this new Act. In 1889, for example, 6,408 suits for enhancements of rent were decided out of which decrees of enhancement were given in 6,241 cases.[59] The rent of 14,423 holdings of cultivators with occupancy rights were fixed by these decrees and their rate of enhancement varied from 1 anna to 12 annas per rupee.

This process of enhancement of rent practically continued till the close of the century. One of its striking features was the way in which cash rents were displacing kind rents in many circles, such as the Sirwal and Bakkar circles of the Hoshiarpur and Garshankar tahsils. In the present century the settlement officer estimated that within a period of thirty years (since 1879-84) cash rents were nearly doubled in this district.[60] Almost simultaneously the area under kind rent steadily increased and Prof. Bhalla's Bairampur village enquiry clearly pointed out that good lands were then seldom let on cash rents.[61]

Rent rates also rose steadily in other parts of the province. In Hissar, for example, towards the close of the century there had been a general rise in the rates of cash rents since Anderson's settlement (1887-92). In 1891-92 it was found that in the four tahsils (Hissar, Hansi, Fatehabad and Bhiwani) of this district the average cash rent on irrigated land was Re. 1-1-7 per acre while in 1897-98 it averaged Rs. 2-12-0.[62] In Rohtak both produce and cash rents increased steadily since the settlement of the late 1870s. At that settlement the former varied from one-fourth to one-third according to the class and quality of the land; but at the close of the century one-third to one-half was generally taken, the latter being the rate for *chahi* and *nahri*, the former for *barani*. During the same period cash rents also increased from 4 to 8 annas to 12 annas to Re. 1-2-0 per acre.[63] While reviewing its causes, the Deputy Commissioner reported that owing to decline in recruitment as well as to the disbandment of some of the Jat regiments, the demand for land had greatly increased and this led to a general rise in the rent rates in the district.[64] In most cases, however, the introduction of canal irrigation also hastened the process.[65]

This process was also clearly marked in some of the submontane and central Punjab districts, more particularly towards the close of the century when the grain rent showed definite signs of increase. In Amritsar, for example, famine and scarcity compelled many tenants to pay a produce rent in place of cash in the late 1890s.[66] In Gurdaspur also with the rise in prices landlords tried to exact produce rent in more and more areas and this form of payment was gaining in favour especially on lands irrigated by the Bari Doab Canal.[67] In many cases the proprietors also took a portion of straw from their tenants and compelled them to share canal dues and *kamiana* payment at the post harvest period.[68]

In spite of this general rise in the rent rates there were, however, landlords who had quite a few constraints to face. In some of the south-western and central districts of the province, for example, insecurity of cultivation and scarcity of population often operated as a definite check to the rise of rents. Montgomery district is a case in point. In this district, except where the canal irrigation or the *sailab* was plentiful, tenants (locally known as *rahaks*) constituted the mainstay of cultivation.[69] They were universally of a migratory nature[70] and were always ready to desert their holdings whenever there was a failure of the *sailab* from the Ravi. Consequently, the prosperity of individual estates and proprietors depended largely on their success in attracting and keeping tenants attached to their holdings. Consequently the proprietors had to offer liberal advances almost throughout the year. Again, in many cases, proprietors were also obliged to agree to a lower rate of rent.[71] In some parts of Jhang also the non-hereditary tenants were so strongly placed that the proprietors could hardly think of raising their rents. In this district they were in no way attached to their soil; they were frequently on the move either from the well cultivation to the *sailab* or from bad to fertile lands. They also placed little value to occupancy right and declined to be recorded as such at the regular settlement. Almost all of them were in receipt of *takavi* from their proprietors and generally paid half the produce as their rent. But in reality the proprietors received not more than one-third because the tenants frequently compelled the proprietors to make innumerable concessions from their own share of the produce.[72] Similarly the tenants were favourably circumstanced in the Gujranwala district. Here owing to the large size of the proprietary holdings, the great area of land available for cultivation, and the demand for tenants in the newly opened canal tracts, the competition was not among tenants for lands to cultivate, but among landlords for tenants. All these factors made rents in this district, according to the settlement officer, 'stationary, low and non-competitive. Consequently, the tenants were able to secure good terms from their proprietors and rack-renting was equally very rare. If the proprietors tried to raise their rents, the tenants did not hesitate to throw up their holdings and migrate towards the canal colonies.[73] Similarly in some parts of the Pathankot tahsil (Gurdaspur district) proprietors had to proceed very cautiously in dealing with their tenants who were mostly immigrants from Jammu or Shakargarh tahsil. The Chak Andhar circle of this tahsil was particularly known for its unhealthy climate (often causing malaria) and the improvident habits of the proprietors (who were mostly Rajputs). It was surrounded by the *Bet* Ravi and *Maira Kiran* circles of the Gurdaspur tahsil where lands were more fertile and protected by good well-irrigation. Naturally the lands of Chack Andhar were comparatively in little demand among the tenants. The proprietors, therefore, by way of inducement had to allow them to hold lands at a lower rate of cash rent than it was prevalent in other adjoining circles of the same district.[74]

In some cases again the customary relations between the zamindars and their tenants often tended to check the rise of rents during the period under review. In Rawalpindi and Jhelum, the district officers came across a widespread prevalence of customary rent even towards the close of the century when the rent rate was steadily rising elsewhere in the Punjab. Thus speaking about it, the settlement officer of Jhelum pointed out that the existing rate of cash rent of the district had not reached the pitch which the Tenancy Act permitted in other districts like Hoshiarpur and Jullundur. Competitive kind rent was hardly known in this tract. It was fixed by custom and uniform over large areas. No one even attempted to enhance the existing customary rate of rent and it was always the same for 'all classes of tenants'. Occasionally their relationship became strained, when the landlords tried to enforce on the tenants an appraisement of the value of the produce, which was 'not considered fair' by the latter. Trouble could be avoided in such cases if the landlords gave up the practice of *kankut* and agreed to divide the produce on the threshing floor. Apart from these cases, their relationship was 'fairly good'[75] and this perhaps largely explains the continuation of customary rent rate in Jhelum even at the beginning of the present century.

In Rawalpindi also, in view of closer cooperation and understanding with their tenants at the different levels of rural society, the proprietors could scarcely afford to be 'avaricious and grasping' in their relations with the tenants. They shared alike in their misery and happiness[76] and usually did not try to disturb the existing rate of rent. In some cases, however, 'avaricious' money-lenders were trying to raise the existing customary rent rate and this was particularly evident in Talagang tahsil where they held a considerable tract of land. But this process of change was yet to become the established pattern of agrarian relations in this part of the province.

Finally, the new canal irrigation in the central *bar* also had an important restraining influence on the rise of rent rates in the adjoining tahsils or districts. In Gujranwala, for example, canal irrigation brought in its train a sudden influx of tenants from the adjoining tracts. Towards the close of the century this migration occurred on such a big scale that even in some parts of the densely populated districts like Jullundur or Hoshiarpur, landlords occasionally faced difficulty in procuring sufficient number of tenants to plough their lands. They, as a rule, 'are only too anxious to keep them on, especially in Jullundur and Hoshiarpur, whence large numbers have emigrated to the Chenab canal tracts, tempted by better prospects, and rents are falling in consequence'.[74]

It is, therefore, evident that the rise of rent rate was subject to a number of constraints during the period under review. However, in general, rent rates were steadily increasing in most of the districts of the province in consequence of the high prices and the increased competition for land towards the close of the century. This rise in rents, especially the produce rents, left behind a deep impact on the small tenants' economy. It particularly affected the position of the tenants-at-will who were increasingly subjected to the various forms of kind rents by their landlords. Incidentally the area under their cultivation also steadily increased in the 1890s.[78] All these payments often depleted their small surplus and made their position very much critical over the years. The plight of the tenants had already become alarming in Multan, Muzaffargarh and Dera Ghazi Khan. Here their relations were governed by immemorial custom and in consequence they had no alternative to 'helpless submission'. They lived almost at the mercy of their landlords and scarcely enjoyed any definite rights of their own. They were not unfrequently 'little better than a serf, possessing neither capital nor appliances' of their own, and cultivated land with the landlords' oxen. They were extremely poor, frequently performed *begar* and practically led a hand-to-mouth existence.[79] They carried on their cultivation almost under the strict supervision of their landlords and they were thankful to take what they got in return.[80] They no doubt received advances from their masters to tide over short-term difficulties; but these advances also went a long way towards strengthening the grip of the landlords on them. An enquiry in the late 1870s further revealed that in these districts they often had a running account with the *sahukars* who generally offered them loan on the security of their landowners. These accounts were commonly settled at the time of the harvest. In Dera Ghazi Khan nearly 50 per cent of them were indebted[81] for they had to pay a heavy grain rent to their landlords. In Muzaffargarh also, 40 per cent of the Muhammedan and 20 per cent of the Hindu tenants were in debt.[82] According to the settlement officer, insecurity of harvest caused by irregular supply of canal waters frequently led to borrowing and their yearly debt was equal to 20 per cent of their yearly income.

In other districts of the province too, viz. Amritsar, Firozepore, Ambala and Rohtak, where many of the tenants-at-will were in reality small landlowners supplementing their income by taking extra lands on lease, their condition was not always very satisfactory. Their holdings were carelessly cultivated; manure, unless abundant, was not used and the yield was also below the average.[83] Their small surplus tended to be wiped off by the rise in rent and in consequence they were driven to borrowing. A village enquiry of the Ambala district thus described their condition in the present century:[84]

> Of the twelve small owners . . . owning less than 5 acres cultivated, all paid the land revenue and occupiers' rates from money borrowed for the purpose . . . all of them maintained that, after paying *batai* on the land cultivated by them as non-occupancy tenants, the grain left with them was hardly sufficient for their own consumption. . . . They are, as a rule, obliged to borrow for all purchases made by them requiring ready cash, e.g. agricultural cattle and implements, and clothes and other articles not produced by them. They have also to borrow for paying *neota*, the land revenue and occupiers' rates.

In Amritsar also, a tenant-at-will was a much poorer man than the owner who cultivated his own or another's land.[85] They were 'very shabbily dressed' and sometimes went about 'with only one shoe on the right or on the left foot'. The conditions of their tenures equally discouraged them from making any permanent improvement on their holdings. They also paid a higher rate of rent as well as interest on their debts than the tenants having rights in other lands and it was not easy for them to obtain loans on different occasions throughout the year. But the occupancy tenants had more credit than the mere tenants-at-will since they could offer better security and in consequence were often enmeshed in greater indebtedness.[86] The Tenancy Act of 1887 further raised the credit worthiness of their holdings and frequent cases of land transfers were noticed by the district officers in the late 1890s. Thus in 1888-89 in Jullundur alone, there were 906 cases of alienation of tenants' right involving 1,226 acres.[87] These for the most part consisted of mortgages and were purchased by persons other than the owners, mostly *sahukars*. The owners seldom objected to these alienations because in many cases they themselves were indebted to the same *sahukars*. Similar cases of transfers of tenants' rights were reported from Ambala and Gurdaspur.[88]

NOTES

1. *Sialkot S.R.* 1865, 98-9.
2. These tenants were often known as *boladar harsala* in some of the districts of the province. They held land on agreement renewed or renewable from year to year. Terms with these tenants were generally settled in the month of Cheyt (March-April) when there was a temporary rest from work; they did not, however, take complete possession of their holdings until June when the spring harvest was finished. But the retiring tenant would make no objections if the incoming tenant wanted to plough earlier for cotton. For details, see *Lahore D.G., 1892-93*, 127; *Hissar D.G., 1883-84*, 41.
3. *Jullundur S.R., 1892*, 131; *Lahore S.R., 1894*, 25; *Shahpur S.R., 1918*, 5.
4. *Panipat Tahsil and Karnal Pargana S.R., 1883*, 102.
5. *Sialkot S.R., 1865*, 99.
6. *Shahpur S.R., 1867*, 101-2.
7. Reply from Major Mercer, DC Amritsar, *Parl. Papers, 1870*, LIII, 458.
8. *Amritsar S.R., 1873*, 56.
9. *Jhelum D.G., 1904*, 231; *Jhelum S.R., 1883*, 149; Banga, *op.cit.*, 180.
10. *Dera Ghazi Khan S.R., 1876*, 79.

11. *Amritsar S.R., 1873*, 56; *Rawalpindi S.R., 1865*, 170; *Gujrat D.G., 1883-84*, 58-9.
12. *Ambala S.R., 1893*, 78; Reply from Captain Hawkins, DC Muzaffargarh, *Parl. Papers*, 1870, LIII, 465. In other districts also the rate of *malikana* varied widely. In Gujranwala, *malikana* was 'the exception not the rule', and rarely exceeded 6¼ per cent of land revenue while in Gurdaspur and Kohat it ranged from 15 to 24 per cent and 5 to 10 per cent respectively. But in Shahpur it amounted to only 5 per cent of the land revenue demand and it was no doubt largely due to scarcity of tenants in this part of the province. For details, see *Gujranwala S.R., 1871*, 55; *Shahpur S.R., 1867*, 102-3; *Gurdaspur S.R., 1859*, 88; *Kohat S.R., 1884*, 89.
13. The settlement officer of Multan thus gives a graphic account of *habubat* payment:

    The first of these is *jholi*, which means literally the skirt of the coat. After a partition of the crops, at which the proprietor was present . . . the tenant generally put in 4 or 5 seers. . . . A similar due under the name of *dala*, which means a child's skirt, was sometimes, but very rarely, taken; the *tobrah*, or horse's nose bag, filled with corn, and representing the feed of corn given freely by the tenant, was more common. The *lai gadhah* was a heap or bundle or corn (*gadhah*), representing the wages (*lai*) paid to the labourers at harvest. The *kiraya* was not common, but it was exacted in some villages under the pretence that the tenant was bound to convey the proprietor's share of the produce home for him. Sometimes the proprietor would claim to have his share weighed at 42 seers to the maund; this exaction was called *batalah*, from *betalis*=42. If the proprietor lived near, he sometimes took 2 or 3 *marlahs* of green crop for fodder; this was called *kiarah*, from *kiari*, a flowerbed, a patch of ground. Sometimes *amlanah*, or a contribution to the pay of the proprietors' *amlah* or accountant, and sometimes . . . a charitable contribution, or *bhikh*, was demanded occasionally. The proprietor levied from each well Rs. 2 or 3, or the equivalent in corn, under the head of *malbah*. The above are known under the general name of *habubat*. For details, see *Multan D.G., 1883-84*, 73.
14. *Ambala S.R., 1893*, 78. See also CR Lahore division's review, *Lahore S.R., 1860*, 26.
15. Reply from H. Elphinstone, DC Jullundur, *Parl. Papers*, 1870, LIII, 460.
16. Opinion of C.P. Elliot, Offg. DC, Ludhiana, *Ibid.*, 461.
17. *Lahore S R., 1860*, 8.
18. *Southern Parganas Ambala S.R., 1859*, 72.
19. Dungen, *The Punjab Tradition*, 51-7.
20. This rule sometimes took the form of twelve years' uninterrupted possession of a holding at the same rate of rent before the annexation of the Punjab. It was generally adopted in the districts of Ambala, Lahore and Gurdaspur though in other districts this period was often

lowered or raised. Further, it became usual to draw a distinction between resident tenants and non-resident tenants and 'to accept twelve years' possession as sufficient in the case of the former and twenty years in the case of the latter'. For details, see *Lahore S.R., 1860*, 71; *Southern Parganas Ambala S.R., 1859*, 73; R.N, Cust's report on the Shakargarh Pargana, Gurdaspur district, *Parl. Papers*, 1870, LIII, 486; *S.M.*, 98.

21. *Shahpur S.R., 1867*, 102-3.
22. In this connection the following remarks of the Punjab Famine Commission deserve our special attention: 'They (Occupancy tenants) have not been created by us on abstract grounds of policy; but are the Judicial and Legislative interpretation of the privileges which the older tenants possessed in the times immediately antecedent to our rule; an interpretation ... arrived at by the majority of our Revenue Officers and Judges'. *Punjab Famine Report, 1878-79*, II, 553.
23. *S.M.*, 98.
24. In all these districts, thinness of population coupled with the abundance of wastes often compelled the proprietors 'to give up to all these cultivators the right of possession' while the cultivators to the despair of the proprietors 'strenuously refused to be recorded as hereditary'. For details, see *Gujranwala S.R., 1871*, 55; *Montgomery D.G., 1883-84*, 75; *Dera Ghazi Khan S.R., 1876*, 79.
25. Memoradum by P.S. Melvill, Offg. CR Amritsar division, *Parl. Papers, 1870*, LIII, 524-5.
26. *S.M.*, 99.
27. This will be further evident from the fact that even in the late 1870s nearly 'one-fourth of the total area under this tenancy was held on no further rent than the revenue demand plus a small *malikana* varying from 2 to 3 annas per rupee of the revenue'. *Punjab Famine Report, 1878-79*, II, 553.
28. *Rawalindi S.R., 1865*, 135-6.
29. *RR 1862-63*, 171.
30. Actual classification of tenants (enjoying occupancy rights in Amritsar, Gurdaspur and Sialkot districts by the first regular settlement) as revealed by Prinsep's enquiry.

Classification of tenants	Total number	Area in acres
1	2	3
1. Shareholders in village ownership	8,430	35,381
2. Long resident tenants	14,563	89,264
3. Mere village servants	14,498	68,727
4. Relations of proprietors	1,402	9,389
5. Persons holding mortgages	955	7,714
6. Pahikashts or non-residents	10,555	49,335

7. Jagirdars or revenue free holders	287	1,593
8. Mafidars	8,038	23,161
9. Religious places	1,758	7,644
10. Trustees and Managers	128	620
Total	60,114 [sic 60,614]	2,82,788 [sic 2,92,828]

Source: Report by E.A. Prinsep, SLC Amritsar division, on the tenant right question in three districts of Amritsar division, *Parl. Papers, 1870*, LIII, 532.

31. Changes introduced in the status of these tenants under Prinsep's settlement.

Classification of tenants	Total number	Area in acres
1	2	3
A. Declared to have occupancy rights	15,547	62,094
B. Lease holders and having no occupancy rights	29,558	1,26,609
C. Tenants-at-will	12,592	55,252
D. Tenants made proprietors	1,253	7,228
E. Tenants who have voluntarily thrown up their holdings	1,935	9,515
Total	63,409 [sic 60,885]	2,69,445 [sic 2, 60,698]

Source: *Ibid.*, 533.

32. Changes in the payment of rent under the first regular settlement and revision of settlement.

Details of how many paid rent and how many did not		Number	Area in acres
1		2	3
By former settlement	: Who paid 'rent'	35,407	1,74,872
	: Who paid no *rent*	24,707	1,17,916
		[60,114]	[2,92 788]
By this settlement	: Who pay rent in *cash*	50,209	2,07,754

: Who pay rent in grain	7,320	36,762
Who pay *no* rent	6,490	25,929
	[64,019]	[2,70,445]

Source : *Ibid.*

Note : Here Prinsep somewhat failed to account for the obvious discrepancies in the corresponding total figures of the two settlements. In the revised tenancy records of the 1860s presumably he included many tenants whom he excluded from his calculations for the settlement of the 1850s.

33. It is interesting to note that like Prinsep, Nisbett, the settlement officer, also sought to give effect to the same principle in Gujranwala district. The following table will illustrate this point.

Abstract of enquiry into the rights of hereditary tenants in the Gujranwala district.

Name of Tahsil	Tenants recorded as hereditary at last settlement	Number, whose status has after enquiry been maintained	Number, who have acquired proprietary right	Number declared to have lost the status of hereditary tenants, who can only hold hereafter as inferior tenants without a protective lease for a term of years
1	2	3	4	5
Gujranwala	1,955	271	1	1,683
Wazirabad	1,897	154	8	1,635
Hafizabad	650	30	...	620

Source : *Ibid.*, 594.

34. G.G. Hambly, 'Richard Temple and the Punjab Tenancy Act of 1868', *The English Historical Review*, XXIX, January 1964, 53-4.

35. T.R. Metcalf, *The Aftermath of Revolt 1857-1870* (Princeton University Press, 1964), 202, and also T.R. Metcalf, 'The Struggle over Land Tenure in India, 1860-1868', *The Journal of Asian Studies*, XXI, May 1962, 307.

36. Memorandum by Colonel E. Lake, FC Punjab, on the status of cultivators in the Amritsar division, *Parl. Papers, 1870*, LIII, 435; Memorandum by P.S. Melvill, Offg. CR Amritsar division, *Ibid.*, 525-6.

37. Note by Sir John Lawrence, Viceroy of India, 30 August 1866, *Ibid.*, 426-8.

38. For details, see *F.C. Selections*, New Series, No. 14, No. 40, No. LXVIII, Revision of Tenancy Entries in Mr. E. Prinsep's Settlements subsequent to the passing of Act XXVIII of 1868, 1131.
39. In the early 1890s the settlement officer estimated that the average size of each holding was 4½, 3 and 2½ acres for owners, hereditary tenants and non-hereditary tenants respectively. *Jullundur S.R.*, *1892*, 131.
40. Remarks by A. Brandreth, CR Jullundur division, *ERR 1871-72*, 10.
41. Remarks by Colonel H. Coxe, CR Jullundur division, *Ibid.*, *1872-73*, 7.
42. *Jullundur S.R.*, *1892*, 131.
43. Changes in rent rates between the second (1892) and third regular settlements (1918).

Tahsil	2nd regular settlement			3rd regular settlement		
	Area in acres	Rent in Rs.	Rent per acre	Area in acres	Rent in Rs.	Rent per acre
1	2	3	4	5	6	7
			Rs. As. P.			Rs. As. P.
Jullundur	13,880	1,01,457	7 4 11	23,848	4,23,601	17 12 2
Nakodar	8,955	67,470	7 8 7	17,834	2,31,352	12 5 7
Phillaur	11,988	86,829	7 3 11	14,961	2,31,433	15 7 6
Nawashahr	9,756	1,07,077	10 15 7	13,780	2,65,969	19 4 10
District	44,579	3,62,833	8 2 3	70,423	11,52,355	16 5 10
Increase in per cent				58		10 1

Source : *Ibid.*, *1918*, 34

44. It was subsequently abolished and this tract was included within the districts of Hissar and Ferozepore.
45. *Sirsa S.R.*, *1884*, 330.
46. *Ibid.*, 342.
47. Extent of conflict between proprietors and tenants from 1870-71 to 1880-81 (first quarter) in Sirsa district.

Year	Number of notices of ejectment served	Area from which tenants were ejected in acres	Number of suits to contest liability to ejectment
1	2	3	4
1870-71	43		
1871-72	59		
1872-73	62		
1873-74	288		
1874-75	369		
1875-76	394	6,380	254
1876-77	540	9,928	319

1877-78	417	9,797	275
1878-79	366	7,209	215
1879-80	1,031	18,295	589
1880-81 (First quarter)	1,131	12,922	

Source : Report on the position of tenants in the Sirsa district, 15 October1880, Rew and Agr (R) June 1882, 4A.

48. The following verse clearly expresses their miseries during these years:

'Raiyat malika shah di hoi bahut hairan
Khusgaya hak asamiyan hoiya zulm tamam
Wakif na kanun de ahe eh anjan
Agge kisi na badshah aisa kita kam
Is alake vich sa eh riwaj pachhan
Jo koi vahe zamin kabza usda jan
Hala hissa devanda oh rahe madam
Lakkar sota ghas bhi jo sarkari kam
Dende samidar san varovar tamam
Manji juli devande te sarkar godam
Eh raiyat sarkardi haigi khas ghulam
Itni ranj uthake hon kiti hairan
Kabza kasht khohna haiga bara ziyan.'

'The Queen's subjects are much distressed. The tenant has been deprived of his rights, great injustice has been done. Alas these ignorant people were not aware of the law. Hitherto no king has acted so. In this neighbourhood this was the rule that whoever broke up land should hold it, regularly paying rent in cash or in kind. The tenants gave, each in his turn, wood and grass and whatever was required, sleeping-cots, bedding and supplies. These are Sarkar's subjects and serfs. After enduring such hardship they are now distressed. It is indeed great injustice to take away land from the tenant.' *Sirsa S.R., 1884*, 345.

49. Remarks by Trafford, DC Sirsa, *RR 1881-82*, Appendix A 6.

50. *Gurgaon S.R,, 1884*, 71.

51. *RR 1877-78*, 15.

52. Besides raising their rent rates, proprietors also now ejected a sizable number of non-hereditary tenants who generally held land on condition of sharing in all the profits and losses of cultivation since the first regular settlement. At that time land revenue demand was so heavy that the proprietors were too glad to allow them holding land as partners on these favourable terms. These tenants were then mostly recorded as non-hereditary tenants and they were found in nearly 250 villages of this district. But with the increase in the value of land, proprietors of most of such villages gradually seized the opportunity of the expiry of settlement to get rid of these partners and to assume all the responsibilities of cultivation. They resumed

these lands from their tenants at the revision of assessment (1880s). In 242 out of these villages, reported the settlement officer, 'they have now themselves assumed the whole liabilities and reduced their former partners to the position of tenants only; and in eight the tenants still share the profit and loss'. *Gurgaon D.G., 1883-84*, 60-1.

53. Number of notices of ejectment issued in Hissar from 1878-79 to 1886-87.

Year	Punjab	Hissar	Acres on which notices of ejectment were served
1	2	3	4
1878-79	4,780	606	......
1879-80	5,782	1,347	18,722
1880-81	7,995	3,116	43,166
1881-82	10,659	3,213	45,336
1882-83	9,463	2,872	41,611
1883-84	7,842	1,359	18,249
1884-85	14,364	7,627	1,10,808
1885-86	9,265	2,368	......
1886-87	15,246	6,847	......

Source : *RR 1880-81*, 23; *Ibid., 1884-85*, 27; *Ibid., 1886-87*, 14.

But this does not necessarily mean that tenants were actually evicted from this vast tract of land. In order to ascertain the actual effect of the notices of ejectment, a special enquiry was undertaken in the 1880s in 12 villages of the Hissar district. Its result is given below:

	Acres
(a) Area held by tenants-at-will in 1880	20,162
(b) Area from which tenants were actually ejected by issue of notices up to September 1885	2,601
(c) Area from which tenants were ejected privately at the request of owners, up to September 1885.	6,066
(d) Total area from which tenants were ejected between 1880 and 1885	8,667
(e) Area from which tenants were not ejected in this period, that is the area held for at least five years by the same tenants-at-will	11,495
Total area	20,162

Details of area from which tenants were not ejected (area in 'e'):

(f) Area in regard to which owners made no application for ejectment	2,467
(g) Area in regard to which application was made for ejectment, which on payment of increased rent or otherwise remained in the hands of the former tenants	9,028
Total area	11,495

In other words, the total area in regard to which ejectment notices were served was (2,601+9,028) 11,629 acres while it resulted in actual ejectment from only one-fifth (.22) of the whole. But the landlords took steps, either publicly or privately, to eject tenants from the whole area held by them, except from 2,467 acres i.e., from all except one-eighth. These notices particularly affected the six villages of Hansi and Fatehabad tahsils in which this special enquiry was made. Here 'notices of ejectment were issued in regard to every tenant and every acre of land'. The area held by tenants-at-will in these villages was 11,222 acres and between 1880 and 1885 notices of ejectment were issued in regard to 11,060 acres. This frequent issue of ejectment notices, according to the Deputy Commissioner, 'led to the demoralization of the tenants' and it had again a 'disastrous effect' on all proposed improvement of land by them. For details, see Remarks by A. Anderson, DC Hissar, *ERR* 1886-87, 6-7.

54. The extent of rise of rent (the highest rent compared) during the decade (1874-75 to 1884-85) preceding the revision of settlement in Hissar.

Year	Irrigated	Unirrigated
1	2	3
	Rs. As. P.	Rs. As. P.
1874-75	6 0 9	1 2 0
1884-85	7 8 0	6 0 0

Source : *RR 1874-75* and *1884-85*, Statement No. XXIXA.

55. *Hoshiarpur S.R., 1885*, 155.
56. *Ibid.*
57. Note by Captain J.A.L. Montgomery, SO Hoshiarpur, *RR* 1881-82, Appendix A 4.
58. Remarks by Lieutenant Colonel Gordon Young, CR Jullundur division, *Ibid., 1882-83*, 49.
59. According to another estimate 6,405 suits were decided, out of which in 6,233 cases enhancement was decreed. *Hoshiarpur D.G., 1904*, 125.
60. The increasing popularity of cash rent, according to the settlement officer, was 'a sign of prosperity and of competition among tenants for lands to cultivate as they are paid irrespective of the season and

quality of the crops'. The statement prepared at the time of the second revision of settlement (1910-14) illustrates the extent of change in average rent rate per acre in each circle in the three tahsils of the Hoshiarpur district during the period from 1879-84 to 1910-14. (See table on page 171).

61. Bhalla, *op.cit.*, 82.
62. Remarks by P.D. Agnew, DC Hissar, *ERR 1897-98*, 39.
63. Remarks by Captain P. Burton, DC Rohtak, *Ibid.*
64. Remarks by Lieutenant Colonel Rennick, DC Rohtak, *Ibid.*, *1891-92*, 56.
65. *RR 1901-02*, 13.
66. Increase of the area under produce rent in acres in Amritsar district.

Year	Irrigated area of tenants paying rent in kind	Unirrigated area of tenants paying rent in kind	Total area of tenants paying rent in kind
1	2	3	4
1892-93	80,744	49,243	129,987
1893-94	80,377	50,914	131,291
1894-95	81,910	53,027	134,937
1895-96	87,426	55,284	142,710
1896-97	91,156	57,360	148,516
1897-98	94,346	58,401	152,747
1898-99	98,440	59,650	158,090
1899-1900	101,862	59,826	161,688

Source : Remarks by W. Chevis, DC Amritsar, *ERR 1897-98*, 40; Remarks by W. De. M. Malan, DC Amritsar, *Ibid.*, *1899-1900*, 34.

67. *Gurdaspur S.R.*, *1892*, 9; *Ibid.*, 1912, 4.
68. *Sialkot D.G.*, *1894-95*, 93; *Hoshiarpur S.R.*, *1916*, 26; *Jullundur S.R.*, *1892*, 131; *Ludhiana S.R.*, *1884*, 127; *Amritsar D.G.*, *1914*, 96.
69. Actually cultivation in this district did not afford many attractions to the tenants. At the regular settlement when the proprietors were ready to grant them hereditary status, the tenants universally declined that offer. They insisted on being recorded as non-hereditary tenants. They, as the Commissioner of the Multan division pointed out, 'do not covet the distinction and prefer to keep themselves free, and sometimes put themselves to the highest proprietary bidders for their services'. It was then estimated that occupancy tenants held only 2.65 per cent of the total cultivated area while the tenants-at-will cultivated nearly 68 per cent of the district. 'In a tract like that comprised in this district where laborious well irrigation is an indispensable adjunct to agriculture and population is comparatively sparse, a self-cultivation of proprietor can by himself cultivate only a comparatively small area, the profits of which would scarcely

Name of the circle	Dasuya		Hoshiarpur		Garshankar	
	Rs. As. P.	Rs. As. P.	Rs. As. P.	Rs. As. P.	Rs. As. P.	Rs. As. P.
	a	b	a	b	a	b
1	2	3	4	5	6	7
Sirwal	9 0 9	18 8 0	11 5 5	19 14 9	11 7 4	20 14 3
Rakkar	None	2 15 9	7 15 0	14 9 2	7 8 6	14 14 7
Kandi	None	4 3 0	2 15 0	4 8 7	6 0 10	10 3 4
Maira	3 2 8	6 9 0	......	......	......	......
Bet	3 4 0	10 4 0	......	......	5 13 10	14 8 7
Bit	......	......	......	......	2 15 10	6 8 9

a first revised settlement (1879-84)
b second revised settlement (1910-14)

Source : *Hoshiarpur S.R., 1916*, 26.

suffice to recoup his somewhat heavy initial and recurring annual capital expenditure; he is forced therefore to supplement his income by the rent derived from the cultivation of tenants . . . . Tenant cultivation is thus not so much an accident as a necessary consequence of local conditions . . . . The demand, except in a limited number of estates, is for tenants to cultivate the land and not for land to be cultivated by tenants'. Consequently, they could make almost any terms they liked. They were often allowed to enjoy certain significant privileges which were denied to the other tenants in many of the densely populated districts of the province. For details, see Remarks by Colonel S.F. Graham, CR Multan division, *ERR* 1875-76, 35; Remarks by P.J. Fagan, DC Montgomery, *Ibid.*, 1893-94, 30; Remarks by C.H. Buck, DC Montgomery, *Ibid.*, 1902-03, 2; Remarks by Diwan Narendra Nath, *Ibid.*, *1895-96*, 73-4; *Montgomery S.R.*, *1899*, 28.

70. As early as 1853 the widespread desertion of the tenants became a subject of deep anxiety of the revenue officers of the Montgomery district. It was reported in 1868-69 that nearly two-thirds of the old tenants had already deserted their holdings and many villages were thereby ruined. This process continued even afterwards; it naturally deeply affected the agrarian operations in a number of Ravi villages. For details, see Remarks by A. Brandreth, CR Multan division, *ERR 1868-69*, 63, 69; *Montgomery D.G.*, *1883-84*, 76.

71. FC Punjab's review, *Montgomery S.R.*, *1898*, xviii, 39.

72. Of the innumerable concessions granted to these tenants, at least a few of them may be mentioned here. To begin with, the tenant could cut as much wheat and *jowar* as he liked and he also used to take the whole turnip crop for his cattle. Secondly, 'substantial deductions' were 'made for the wages of the reapers and the fees of the village menials'. Finally, the tenants also expected other allowances from their landlords. As a result the actual share of the produce which the landlords obtained varied from 29 to 36 per cent. For details, see LG Punjab's review, *Jhang S. R.*, *1882*, para 7; *Jhang D.G.*, *1883-84*, 83-8.

73. *Gujranwala S.R.*, *1894*, 56, 96.

74. *Gurdaspur S.R.*, *1912*, 19.

75. *Jhelum S.R.*, *1883*, 151-2; *Jhelum* D.G., *1904*, 233.

79. Kitchin in his settlement report furnishes detailed information on the landlord-tenant relations in this part of the province. He wrote in the late 1890s: 'The cardinal principle of the strong owner is that the tenant is a serf, without rights or privileges, but when this has once been admitted the tenant is not badly treated. In a good year the owner collects half the grain and often half the straw, with several dues, but in a bad year he is always ready with remissions. Dues on marriages and rents from kamins are only exacted when the tenant or kamin shows any reluctance to give. The owner expects to be consulted before his tenants marry, but in return he helps them with

the marriage expenses, and if any disputes arise, sees them settled. When any tenant is subjected to hardship, he may be sure that the owner will take up his quarrel . . . . The straw which has been taken away is never sold, but forms a store upon which tenant can draw in time of need, and loans so given are not collected again. At seed time advances are made, collected, without interest, at harvest time. When in need, grain or money is lent, or the village shopkeeper makes the advances on the owner's security, and collects again with his help, while the owner sees that he does not practice usury. . . . In return for all this, the tenant must do exactly what he is told, and his duty is by no means over when he has ploughed his field and sown the seed. He . . . must not do anything novel without asking for leave, and he must realise that it is not his place to get rich, but that he is entitled only to live and to feed his family, everything more than this belonging to the owner'. For details, see *Attock D.G., 1907*, 229-30.

77. Remarks by Colonel C.F. Massy, CR Jullundur division, *ERR 1895-96*, 73. A similar development was reported from the Charkhri circles of Gujranwala and Sialkot districts. Previously the competition for land among tenants in the more densely populated and highly cultivated villages was so great that it enabled landlords to increase their rents considerably. They claimed rents which were in some cases as high as six maunds of wheat per acre which could only be paid full in good years. Now with this large-scale migration of tenants towards the canal tracts, the rents also 'have shown a tendency to fall'. Remarks by O'Dwyer, DC Gujranwala, *Ibid., 1891-92*, 57.
78. The increasing economic burden of kind rent fell heavily on the tenants-at-will. In 1875-76, 52 per cent of tenants-at-will were paying cash rent while by the close of the century it went down to 21.6 per cent. Simultaneously, the area under kind rent steadily increased during the same period. In 1899-1900 it was estimated that nearly 65.9 per cent of their holdings were under kind rent and they held a little over 80 per cent of the total tenancy cultivation. For details, see *RR 1899-1900*, 29.
79. *Report on the Census of the Punjab, 1881*, I, 382; Darling, *Punjab Peasant*, 99-100; *P.P.B.E.C.*, I, 25.
80. R.K. Seth, Faiz Ilhai, Emerson and Moon, *op. cit.*, 191-6.
81. Reply by Chimman Lal, EAC Dera Ghazi Khan,, *Punjab Famine Report, 1878-79*, II, 533.
82. Reply from E. O' Brien, SO Muzaffargarh, *Ibid.*, 498.
83. Bhalla, *op. cit.*, 82.
84. Sher Singh and H. Fyson, *An Economic Survey of Naggal—a Village in the Ambala District* (The Board of Economic Enquiry, Punjab, Village Surveys No. 5, Publication No. 30, Lahore, 1933), 58.
85. S. Gian Singh and C.M. King, *An Economic Survey of Gaggar Bhana—a Village in the Amritsar District* (The Board of Economic Enquiry,

Punjab, Village Surveys No. 1, Publication No. 16, Lahore, 1928), 70.

86. *Punjab Famine Report, 1878-79*, II, 466, 479-80, 493.
87. Remarks by J.G.M. Rennie, DC Jullundur, *ERR 1888-89*, 47.
88. Remarks by A. Meredith, DC Ambala, *Ibid.*; Remarks by J.B. Hutchinson, DC Gurdaspur, *Ibid.*, 48.

7

The Kamins

The *kamins* were indispensable associates of the zamindars in their agricultural operations all through the year. They have been defined as 'those village servants, the blacksmiths, carpenters, potters, etc., with whom there is a sort of prescriptive contract to do the work of their respective trades for agriculturist, who pays them a certain fixed portion of the produce of his field'.[1] These *kamins* were usually divided into two broad groups, according to the nature of their functions: (1) those whose labour was 'intimately connected with agriculture', generally known as *vadee kamins* or *kamin* proper and (2) those whose services were less regular whom the zamindars called *khangi kamins* or house menials.[2] The former generally included *kamins* like tarkhans (carpenters), lohars (blacksmiths) and chamars (leather workers) while churas (sweepers), dhobis (washerman), nais (barbers), etc. represented the latter. But this demarcation was not strictly observed throughout the province and there were frequent overlappings between the two.[3]

Early British records clearly point out that these *kamins* represented heterogeneous caste groups for they included highly skilled tarkhans as well as socially impure churas who ate carrion and carried the night soil. They also suggest that their concentration varied widely in different parts of the province.[4] Further there was a yawning gap in social status and economic viability among these numerous occupational groups. Besides their traditional caste callings, many of them also worked as agricultural labourers.[5] They helped their masters in ploughing, watering, manuring and weeding their fields. However, even when working as labourers, these menials generally did not constitute 'a distinct class' during the period under review and therefore differed little in social status from the low caste menials like chamars and churas.

These *kamins* had certain customary duties to perform in the rural society of the province. First in order of importance came occupational groups like tarkhans and lohars. Their functions involved comparatively a good deal of technical skill. The former's responsibility was to make and keep in working order all wooden agricultural implements. The materials for this purpose had to be supplied by the husbandmen themselves. They were, therefore, expected to make and repair ploughs, sugarpresses, household furniture, woodworks of the persian wheels, carts and cart wheels.[6] Occasionally they were also asked to dig graves at funerals.[7] Similarly the lohars were to perform certain customary duties, such as making and repairing all the iron implements, zamindars providing iron.[8] These two groups were generally very well distributed over the province, though, like other occupational groups, they were less numerous on the lower frontier than elsewhere. But in certain districts the lohars and tarkhans were not clearly distinguishable, the same men doing both kinds of works.[9]

Kumhars constituted another important group of village *kamins*. They supplied little earthen jars attached to the rims of the persian wheels and large dishes for sugarpresses. They also furnished earthen vessels for domestic ceremonies. For manufacturing all these wares, they procured clay for their oven and fuels for baking pots, free of charge, from village zamindars. They kept donkeys of their own for carrying grain from the threshing floor.[10] As village *kamins*, the importance of kumhars, however, varied from place to place. In the well-irrigated central and submontane districts,[11] they were generally regarded as *vadee kamins*, while in the extreme north-western districts of Kohat and Hazara (where irrigation from wells generally played no such important role in the rural economy) their name did not often occur in the list of village menials.[12]

Another sizable group of *vadee kamins* were the chamars though their social status was far below that of the tarkhans, lohars and kumhars. They were commonly assigned the role of tanners and leather workers and in the more western districts they were called mochis. But in the east of the Punjab they were more than leather workers. They took the hides of all dead cattle and the flesh of all cloven-footed animals; they also made and mended shoes, thongs for the cart and whips and other leather works. They were also the 'field labourers of the village, often performing the *begar* or such works as cutting grass, carrying bundles, acting as watchmen and the like. Sometimes' they plastered the houses with mud.[13]

At the lowest rung of the social ladder of these *kamins* perhaps stood the untouchable churas[14] who were made to work the hardest of all castes.[15] They were to perform all the scavengers' work of the village. 'On them fall', thus wrote the district officer from Amritsar in the present century, 'a large share of the labour of preparing the land for the crop, the whole work of manuring it, and much thankless labour is performed by them in irrigating it during the cold nights. When harvest time comes round most of the reaping and winnowing falls to the lot of the churas, and this is perhaps the hardest in the whole year's round of the field work'. They were really 'very indispensable servants of every zamindar' and performed all the 'most disagreeable work which the zamindar would otherwise have to do himself'.[16]

For all these services, these *kamins* were rewarded with wages which almost invariably took 'the form of a fixed share of the produce'. These payments were commonly known as *sep* in the rural society of the province. At the annexation, they received their wages from the common heap of produce; at the harvest, before any division of produce was made, a small portion of the whole produce was first set apart for their payment. The *kamins* were entitled to these payments as a matter of right and they were therefore 'no less than the agriculturists proper wholly dependent for their support upon the yield of the harvest'. Their wages, however, greatly varied from place to place. Generally, they received a somewhat lower rate in the extreme western districts across the Indus.[18] It was no doubt largely due to the impoverished condition of the zamindars of this region. Here the general standard of cultivation was not also very high; consequently, they could hardly afford to hire *kamins* and had to rely on the help of the members of their families. On the other hand, in the central and submontane districts *kamins* were comparatively well paid which indicated a fair 'standard of comfort and general prosperity of the proprietors'.[19]

It is, however, interesting to note that the remuneration of these different occupational groups of *kamins* again varied widely in different districts of the province, depending on the demand for their labour.[20] Consequently, the tarkhans who rendered manifold services to the village proprietors were generally the most highly paid *kamins* in the province. They were also entitled to the first picking of one day's cotton from the fields at harvest, a privilege usually enjoyed by others only when the tarkhans had done with it. Sometimes there was even a qualitative difference in the crops paid to the tarkhans and other artisans at harvest. Thus when the former received their wages in wheat, others were often remunerated in barley.[21] But the wages of kumhars generally depended on the extent of zamindars' dependence on well-irrigation. In the well-irrigated areas the zamindars constantly looked to them for a regular supply of the water pots for the persian wheels. In such areas, therefore, they were paid in the same rates as the tarkhans. But in the *barani* and *sailab* regions, their services, though required, were not on the same scale; so they had to remain content with a somewhat lower wage rate.[22] Similarly, lohars were paid at one-half the rate of the tarkhans' pay. This was the most common rate enjoyed by them throughout the province.[23] But in some parts of the districts of Karnal, Jullundur and Lyallpur, where tarkhans and lohars often performed similar duties, their rates of remunerations were almost the same.[24] Otherwise the latter could hardly expect to enjoy the benefits usually granted to the former. While explaining this difference in wage rates, the settlement officer of Lahore pointed out that lohars received lower rates of wages than those of the tarkhans because their labour was considered 'much lower'. Similarly the duties and privileges of the chamars were by no means the same in all parts of the province. Apart from their right to the skins of the dead animals, they also got a fixed share of the produce which varied greatly from district to district. While in Gurdaspur they received seven or eight maunds of produce per plough, in Lahore their dues consisted of one maund of grain per well at the spring harvest and half a maund at the autumn harvest. These were 'half the rates' which were paid to potters and carpenters, who performed 'more useful work for the village community'.[25]

Another significant aspect of the *sepidar* payment at the outset of our period was that this was determined by customary rules and there was generally no attempt on the part of the zamindars to interfere with their wages. Although in certain districts they were often called upon to recognize the superior status of the zamindars in the rural society by the payment of a tax,[26] this did not necessarily mean that they 'were a miserable, downtrodden, poverty-stricken people', frequently oppressed by their proprietors.[27] Again one modern scholar in his study of Vilyatpur (a village in the Jullundur district) found that the 'tie between the families of the cultivators and the servants' was often of 'a clearly dependent one from the *sepidars*' point of view'.[28] This, however, is not true of the entire Punjab. Generally the zamindars appreciated the significant role of the *kamins* in the production organization of the village and accepted them as an integral part[29] of the village society. Each was thus equally dependent on the other. This state of affairs, however, did not last long. During the period under review, there was certain significant development in the position of the *kamins* which produced a marked change in their relationship with the village proprietary body.

One of the most striking developments noted by numerous British officials of this period was the gradual change in the wage payment of the *kamins*. The change was recorded by the settlement officer of Rawalpindi district even in the early 1860s[30] while a graphic description was provided by the district officer of Ludhiana in the 1880s:[31]

> Under former rulers when the revenue was realized in kind a small portion of the whole produce was first set apart for the *kamins* and for some servants of the chief, and the remainder was divided between the cultivator and the *Sarkar* in the proportion fixed. With a cash demand this custom disappeared, and the *kamins* now receive their allowances from the cultivating proprietors in a lump at each harvest. There is none of the elaborate division of the produce such

> as is customary in other districts; and even when a tenant pays his rent in kind, no deduction is made from the common heap; but each party gives his *kamins* from his own house a fixed amount of produce and not a share of the whole. This tendency is for the cultivators to alter their agreements with the *kamins* . . . to break up the constitution of the village in regard to these menials, the action being mostly on the part of the proprietors. . . . The result has been that the proprietors attempt to . . . make new terms with the *kamins*. In . . . some villages there are no customary allowances or services at all.

This process of gradual abandonment of the traditional pattern of wage payment, however, assumed innumerable forms in the different districts of the province. These *kamins* were frequently paid in cash[32] and instances of *kamins* having a difficult time with their employers over the recovery of arrears were also not rare. In some cases lohars were paid by tenants alone and separately for each job performed by them.[33] Again in certain regions where well-irrigation had practically no major part to play in the rural economy, kumhars were paid in a similar fashion. Perhaps their position deteriorated[34] with the increasing popularity of canal irrigation during the last quarter of the 19th century.[35] These changes also deeply affected the chamars. With the dying out of the *sep* system, they were sometimes deprived of the skins of the dead cattle which they commonly used to receive in the past.

These changes often led to a general decline in the 'privileges and perquisites' of the *kamins*,[36] at least in some parts of the province. In Ambala this decline was particularly noticeable in the unirrigated tracts of this district[37] where cultivation of land did not require the frequent participation of the *kamins*. In Hoshiarpur the rate of decline was even greater in course of a quarter of a century following the regular settlement in the early 1880s. This was largely due to a steady rise in prices and fragmentation of holdings towards the close of the last century. This often made the employment of the *kamins* unremunerative and the zamindars themselves performed many of the laborious jobs hitherto rendered by these artisans; and when they were remunerated, zamindars paid them at a lower rate.[38]

This steady decline in the *sep* payment, particularly in the context of a general price rise, must have deeply affected the condition of these *kamins*. Besides, zamindars preferred annually contracted rates to customary rates payable year after year. This was particularly noted by the settlement officer of Ludhiana in the early 1880s, while he read through the revenue records. The recurrence of the condition relating to annual contracts in the village records suggests that the practice had been in vogue for sometimes.[39]

The decline was accompanied by a gradual deterioration of their customary relationship with the village zamindars and tension and open hostility made their appearance. In Rohtak, for example, the settlement officer found that in the late 1870s menials were not on good terms as formerly with the zamindars.[40] In Rawalpindi also they were so much on ill terms that they virtually became independent of the village *lambardars*.[41] It was universally admitted that this embittered relationship was largely due to the demand for higher wages by *kamins* which the zamindars in the context of a general price rise often failed to pay. These bitter wrangles and feuds over their respective 'rights and payments' at the time of harvest frequently led to open strike and boycott against zamindars until a satisfactory solution was reached.[42] Actually the higher rates of wages available in the canal districts and elsewhere tended to make them increasingly dissatisfied with the old customary rates. It is, however, interesting to note that the Chenab Colony itself was not completely free from such dissatisfaction.[43]

But it would be wrong to assume that this was a universal phenomenon in the province during the period under review. On the contrary, their attempts to flout the authority of the village proprietary body were often ineffectual. This was particularly so in the case of the chamars who virtually constituted the poorest section of the village artisan groups. They frequently held caste *panchayats* to protest against the high-handedness of the village proprietary body; but the threats of the zamindars to refuse permission to the *kamins* to graze their cattle in the village waste and a fear of starvation soon brought them to terms.[44]

These changes in their customary wage rates, however, had one distinct effect. In many districts their ancestral caste callings often became unremunerative. Kumhars were so hard hit by the introduction of canals and iron buckets of the persian wheels that many of them left their ancestral villages. Of the different village enquiries of this century, at least four clearly indicate that a considerable number of villages which previously had their own potters, later ceased to have even one. In this connection villages like Mahmadpur in Hissar, Kutubpur in Hoshiarpur, Gaggar Bhana in Amritsar, Gajju Chak in Gujranwala could be mentioned. Many of them again started selling their earthen vessels not only in one particular village but in nearby villages. In Muzaffargarh this attempt to extend the area of their trade transactions had been clearly established by the Bhambu Sandila village enquiry of the present century.[45] In Gajju Chak and Gaggar Bhana also the same process had been going on over the years. They also took up the profession of general carriers of different agricultural produce with which they were long associated in the rural society of the province. They had their own donkeys to carry food-grains from the threshing floor to the nearby market centres.[46]

Similarly chamars also found it inconvenient to continue their ancestral vocation in certain districts of the province. Their impoverished condition[47] made them very much vulnerable to the 'competitive principles' of free trade which enabled rural consumers to 'obtain their dressed leather or manufactured leather articles' more cheaply from one of the 'great leather working centres like Kanpur'. Their plight is thus captured in the following remarks of one investigator:[48]

> On the whole the prospects of the leather-worker in the Punjab seem far from bright . . . the old customary system of the 'sep' is fast dying out, and, directly open competition and payment in cash comes in, the crude and imperfect work of the local chamar has no chance in the market. . . . . Under the 'sep' system the leather-worker shared in the fortunes of the agricultural community to which he belonged; now the interests of the two are becoming antagonistic as those of producer and consumer must ordinarily be. The rise in prices and specially in the prices of food has also very injuriously affected these classes. They tell doubly against them, for the zamindars, their best and

> in the agricultural communities practically their only customers, find themselves obliged to economise and haggle over every pice they spend, while the money itself has not the same purchasing power.

Consequently many of them found it convenient to take increasingly to such occupations as weaving blankets and coarse cotton cloth. It offered them a chance of raising their social status; naturally a considerable number of chamars resorted to it during the period under review.[49] A few of them also started trading in cattle.[50] During the same period tarkhans and lohars also faced similar difficulties. In Amritsar and Ludhiana their wages declined by nearly 14.02 per cent and 22.64 per cent respectively between 1873 and 1901.[51] But this was not a universal phenomenon during the period under review and there was a definite rise in their wages in a number of districts of the province. In Gurdaspur, for example, their wage rates strikingly increased during the twenty years following the 1890s[52] while in the canal irrigated areas the rise in their wages was even more remarkable. Thus in Jhang this rise varied from 27.7 per cent to 154.2 per cent during the period from 1889 to 1912.[53] The settlement officer found them placed in a comfortable position and they did not generally receive any harsh treatment from the zamindars. They were 'a far too valuable element in the village community' for the *lambardars* and proprietors 'to oppress them in any extraordinary manner'.

Actually this higher wage rates paid to carpenters and blacksmiths in the colony tracts encouraged many of them to migrate there.[54] Many again flocked to towns where they often worked as independent artisans. In this connection districts like Lahore, Sialkot, Hoshiarpur and Jullundur, with a large-scale building constructions and the manufacture of furniture, etc., afforded a large opening to carpenters.[55] Here they were frequently engaged in carpentry, brick-burning or other forms of labour. They also made carts, all sorts of furniture and boxes and amassed great wealth. Many of them were also in service.[56] Like carpenters many blacksmiths also moved to towns in search of higher wages and better job facilities during the closing years of the last century. Dr. Lucas in his Kutubpur (Hoshiarpur) village enquiry found that many lohars had already emigrated to nearby towns which offered them an opportunity of earning more and thereby improving their economic condition.[57]

This period also witnessed a large-scale participation of these *kamins* in cultivation of village lands. This search for an alternative employment in the form of ownership and direct cultivation of land was also stimulated by the prospect of an elevated social and ritual status which it would confer.[58] But it is extremely difficult to measure accurately the extent of land acquired by these different artisan and menial groups. It is evident from the settlement statistics that many tarkhans and lohars acquired quite a sizable portion of land in Jullundur and Ludhiana.[59] Similarly in Sirsa where a vast tract of land remained practically uncultivated at the commencement of British rule, many Desi-Kumhars were found wholly engaged in agricultural labour rather than in potters' work. 'They are excellent and thrifty cultivators, not inferior to the Bagri Jats from whom they are hardly distinguishable in the physique, dress, habits and language'.[60] In some parts of the Ferozepore district, a few villages were also owned by them who usually surrounded themselves with tenants of their own tribe.[61] This process of acquisition of lands by the *kamins* was also reported in the enquiry conducted by Thorburn towards the close of the last century.[62]

However, the process does not seem to have occurred on a large-scale throughout the province. This was no doubt largely due to the unhappy economic condition of these *kamins*; it generally prevented them from saving even a part of their wages from investment in land purchase. A considerable number of these artisans were again deeply indebted to the village *sahukars*. The Land Alienation Act was also a deterrent. This Act denied the status of agricultural tribe to village artisans and menials and hence they were automatically debarred from acquiring lands. This legal disability imposed by the Act particularly affected the Ramgharias and the Bagri-Kumhars of the south-eastern Punjab districts. They had long been regarded as thrifty and enterprising group of cultivators and had acquired a considerable tract of land in the last century. Exclusion from the land market naturally came to them as a sharp blow. These two groups repeatedly applied to the Punjab Government for including them in the list of notified agricultural tribes. The Government, however, finally agreed to recognize the claims of the Bagri-Kumhars[63] while turning down the same of the Ramgharias.[64]

Besides owning or acquiring land, a considerable number of these *kamins* also worked as agricultural labourers during the period under review. It was the lower caste village menials such as the churas, chamars, nais, dhobis, kumhars, julas and dhanaks who generally offered the largest recruits to this group. These menials when working as agricultural labourers did not constitute 'a distinct class' in the rural society and actually, when they were not employed in field labour, they earned their livelihood by weaving cloth, making shoes, mending harness and selling baskets.[65] This was particularly the case with regard to the chamars and churas who furnished the largest contingent of labourers in all the central and south-eastern districts of the province. Consequently, they not only lived on what they earned by field labour and handicraft but also what they got from the villagers as *sepidars* at the end of each harvest.

These labourers were generally employed by men with more lands than they could themselves look after or by widows or orphans, absentees and others who were unable to till their own lands. They were generally of two types: one worked by the season and the others who did some occasional works at the time of harvest by way of threshing or cutting crops. In the different districts of the province they derived their designations according to the nature of their jobs. Thus the former group was generally known as *kamas*; they were permanent servants of the zamindars and performed all the field operations almost throughout the year. In the central Punjab districts like Amritsar and Lahore they were often recorded as *atris*[66] who were generally sweeper by caste while in Montgomery they were described as *adhjogias*.[67] In the second category of these labourers belonged the *mazdurs*, *lawahs* and *godahs* who rendered certain specific services often at the time of harvest, when the pressure of work was extremely heavy and zamindars required their frequent participation. *Mazdurs* were generally the day labourers who assisted their masters in cutting or threshing crops. But in the Rajput villages of the Jullundur district they were also frequently employed in weeding and reaping. For weeding fields they got two annas a day and also food.[68] In the adjoining Hoshiarpur district these men were often known as *godahs* when employed for hoeing and weeding; and they also received their wages almost at the similar rate, i.e., 2 annas per day or 2 annas and food or 2½ annas without food.[69]

The number of these labourers steadily increased over the years. Curiously enough, the early administration reports of the 1850s as well as first provincial census of 1855 are practically silent about their size. But according to the census of 1868 agricultural labourers and herdsmen engaged in pastoral work constituted nearly 3 per cent of the total population of the province.[70] They were coming in considerable numbers particularly from the districts of Jhang, Multan and Gujranwala which prior to canal construction were the haunt of many nomadic and pastoral tribes. If these men were excluded from this figure, the total size of agricultural labourers would be somewhat less than 3 per cent. If the information furnished by the *Punjab Famine Report* (1878-79) is to be trusted, no major increase in their number was noticeable in the unirrigated regions in the next decade. However, it was then also revealed that in the irrigated tracts their number was slightly higher and this was partly due to the canal excavation work and the increased cultivation of certain valuable crops like sugar-cane and indigo.[71]

But the census of 1891 recorded a major increase[72] in their numbers in most of the central and south-western districts while in 1901 they constituted a little over 8 per cent of the total population of the province. This was largely due to an extraordinary demand for labour in the canal irrigated tracts. Incidentally this period also witnessed a steady decline in the *sep* payment in some of the densely populated districts of the province. This led to a large-scale immigration of labourers which persisted in the 1890s with the opening out of the Chenab Canal Colony. This labour mobility brought in its train a series of changes, one of which was the increasing attempt on the part of the zamindars to pay them in cash instead of in kind which was customary at the time of the annexation. This process of change which had evidently been going on over the years, now gradually affected almost all the districts of the province.

The exact starting point of this change in the form of payment is, however, extremely difficult to trace, for most of the settlement reports of the 1850s and 1860s practically make no mention of it. In the 1870s more detailed information was available and instances of such a change were reported from the districts of Multan and Ambala.[73] Actually at the beginning of the present century it became almost universal in most of the districts of the province. An enquiry in 1909 showed that, in nearly half of 4,278 villages covered in the enquiry, agricultural labourers were paid in cash while in only 3 per cent of them pure grain rate prevailed. The few cases of grain wages that we come across in 1909 in districts like Gujrat, Gurgaon, Hissar, Jhelum, Rawalpindi and Muzaffargarh, nearly disappeared during the next three years. In Gurdaspur also the percentage of villages in which purely grain wages were paid had fallen from 21 to 2 during the same period. The following table shows the change between 1909 and 1912.

Table 1 : Cash, kind and mixed wage paid to agricultural labourers in 1909 and 1912 (percentage of villages)

Year	Purely cash	Cash with grain or other supplement	Purely grain
1	2	3	4
1909	49	48	3
1912	58	40	2

Source : *Report on the First Regular Wages Survey of the Punjab, taken in December 1912*, (Civil and Military Gazette Press, Lahore, 1913) 3.

Thus the purely kind wage rate virtually ceased to exist in many districts by the turn of the last century. Obviously it was an outcome of numerous circumstances which had long been at work in the rural society of the province. To begin with, it was the rise in prices, especially in the prices of food-grains, that compelled zamindars to economise. They found it convenient and profitable to pay their labourers increasingly in cash at the harvest price level, keeping as much crop as they could for themselves. During this period also, cash payment was becoming easier perhaps largely because of the greater availability of money in circulation. Further, the size of the labour market was also fast expanding for there was an additional demand for labour of all kinds to be employed in the extension of cultivation, in various irrigational works, public buildings and communications, etc.[74] In most of these projects, labourers were universally paid in cash; this might have greatly influenced the general trend of wage payment in the villages. Finally, with the growth of modern means of communications and the development of newer job facilities outside the villages, a new mobility was visible amongst these labourers, which again contributed to the collapse of the traditional form of kind wage payment.[75]

It has recently been pointed out that in India as a whole the 'development of commercial crops' was an important factor in the 'increase in the practice of paying cash wages of agricultural labourers'.[76] However, as far as the Punjab was concerned, the cultivation of commercial crops evidently did not lead to an immediate increase in the practice. In the middle of the 19th century, in a number of central Punjab districts, agricultural labourers had the privilege of the first plucking of cotton at harvest. In Gujranwala for instance they were not deprived of this privilege.[77] Similarly in the Chenab Canal Colony, cotton-pickers were almost universally allowed to receive a part of their wages in cotton during the first decade of the present century.

Leaving aside these exceptional cases, the general trend of wage payment was, as noted earlier, from kind to cash. It was commonly believed that as a result of this change in 'rural areas, wages of both agricultural labourers and village artisans' rose 'enormously'. There was also 'a substantial improvement in their material condition—specially of agricultural and general labourers and artisans, who form the majority of the wage earning class'.[78] While explaining this general trend of rise in wages, the Director of Land Records and Agriculture pointed out[79] that at the annexation (1849), agricultural labourers were paid in the equivalent of 1½ annas per day. In 1889 it rose to 2 to 3 annas per day. In 1909 in months in which there was no abnormal demand for labour, agricultural labourers were commonly paid from 2 to 3 annas per day in Gurgaon, 3 annas in Delhi and 3½ annas in Rohtak. These were the only districts in 1909 where the rate of wages per day was under 4 annas. A 4-anna rate was reported in the Salt Range and in Multan, Muzaffargarh, Dera Ghazi Khan, Karnal and Ambala. In Hissar and the submontane districts of Hoshiarpur, Gurdaspur and Sialkot, the rate was 5 annas. In central Punjab districts the common rate was 6 annas per day while in Shahpur, Ferozepore, Lyallpur and Jhang the rate was as high as 8 annas.

But in the light of other official evidence, it is difficult to accept this hypothesis in its entirety; with the rise in prices, wage of agricultural labourers no doubt increased, but the former outstripped the latter. As early as 1869-70 it was admitted officially that the rate of wage was not readily adjusted to the prices of food articles; that was why 'the pressure of scarcity' was 'more severely felt by the labouring classes'. Even in the succeeding years there was any hardly significant change in this situation.[80] This hypothesis receives an additional corroboration from a comparative study of wages paid to agricultural laborers in six major districts of the province. This will lead us to conclude that the rise in real wages of agricultural labourers was far from universal during the last quarter of the 19th century. (See Tables 2 and 3 on pages 190 and 191).

Thus of the six major Punjab districts, a steady rise in their wages occurred at least in Rawalpindi and Multan while districts like Peshawar, Amritsar, Ludhiana and Delhi witnessed a steady decline in real wage rates towards the close of the last century.[81] But in terms of real wage rates, Rawalpindi was again still lagging behind Amritsar where, in spite of a steady fall in real wages since 1873, agricultural labourers continued to enjoy a comparatively better remuneration for their labour. In Rawalpindi even this wage rise did not bring about any significant improvement in their economic condition. It was then found that many of them continued to suffer from a daily insufficiency of food.[82] The situation was even more critical in Delhi. As early as 1879 it was found that their financial condition in the average years was so 'precarious' that they were not commonly trusted by the village *sahukars*.[83] They only received 3 annas as their daily wages at a time when many of the labourers of the central Punjab districts got as much as 6 to 8 annas per day.[84] In Rohtak also their condition was equally miserable

Table 2: Average monthly wages of agricultural labourers in rupees in six districts at the end of each year 1873-1901

Year	Amritsar	Delhi	Peshawar	Rawalpindi	Ludhiana	Multan
1	2	3	4	5	6	7
1873	6.00	5.62	5.62	5.50	5.00	3.25
1874	5.81	5.62	5.00	5.50	5.00	5.5
1875	6.00	5.00	5.00	6.00	5.00	5.37
1876	6.00	5.00	6.00	6.00	5.00	6.31
1877	6.00	5.00	5.00	6.00	5.00	6 00
1878	6.00	5.00	5.00	6.00	5.00	5.37
1879	6.00	5.00	7.00	8.00	5.00	6.37
1880	6.00	5.00	7.00	8.00	5.00	6.44
1881	6.00	5.00	7.00	8.00	5.00	6.75
1882	6.00	5.00	7.00	8.00	5.00	6.75
1883	6.00	5.00	7.00	8.00	5.00	6.75
1884	6.00	5.00	6.00	8.00	5 00	6.75
1885	6.00	5.62	6.00	8.00	5.00	6.75
1886	6.56	6.44	10.00	6.00	5.00	7.50
1887	5.50	5.62	10.00	6.00	6.00	8.00
1888	7.00	5.62	6.00	8.00	5.00	8 00
1889	7.00	5.62	6.00	6.00	6 00	8.00
1890	7.00	5.62	5.50	6.00	6.00	8.00
1891	7.00	5.62	5.50	6.00	6.00	8.00
1892	7.00	5.62	6.50	6.00	7.00	9.00
1893	7.00	5.62	5.50	7.00	5.50	9.00
1894	7.00	7.50	6.00	7.50	5.00	8.00
1895	7.00	5.62	6.50	6.09	5.00	10.00
1896	8.00	5.62	5.50	6.56	7.50	9.00
1897	8.00	7.50	4.50	6.56	6.00	9.00
1898	8.00	5.62	5.50	7.00	7.50	12.00
1899	8.00	7.75	5.50	7.00	5.50	12.00
1900	8.00	7.75	6.50	7.00	7.50	12.00
1901	8.00	7.50	6.50	7.00	7.50	12.00

Source : *Prices and Wages in India, 1902*, 19th Issue, Table 53.

while in Hoshiarpur Dr. Lucas' enquiry clearly revealed that even in average years they had usually very little surplus of their own[85] and they were naturally deeply involved in debt. Similarly in Peshawar many of them were often tied to their creditors in a debt slavery.[86] Even more miserable was the fate of the *halis* of Hazara. Commenting on their condition, the district officer wrote:[87]

Table 3 : Average monthly wages in grain of agricultural labourers in six districts 1873-1901 (in seers of wheat)

Year	Amritsar	Delhi	Peshawar	Rawalpindi	Ludhiana	Multan
1	2	3	4	5	6	7
1873	145.38	106.78	103.69	101.58	125.80	67.67
1874	141.76	108.31	104.30	129.58	127.90	113.96
1875	149.58	107.05	116.45	173.46	131.35	124.80
1876	149.52	123.75	152.10	194.88	129.45	150.37
1877	150.36	92.35	116.55	171.06	125.95	123.42
1878	102.6	70.5	80.80	108.00	88.85	76.85
1879	84.36	70.5	49.42	73.84	76.60	79.31
1880	98.16	87.4	47.32	87.2	88.65	89.90
1881	122.04	96.85	67.76	104.96	99.40	110.30
1882	147.96	92.95	112.21	162.16	128.55	121.97
1883	143.28	94.85	142.59	199.12	120.69	117.70
1884	156.84	100.10	167.70	246.4	127.10	111.64
1885	157.50	126.45	151.74	215.68	139.35	122.04
1886	133.95	122.87	189.6	126.00	110.00	110.62
1887	87.78	82.67	130.00	83.22	99.72	106.93
1888	117.53	82.89	79.50	116.64	90.00	113.68
1889	144.69	97.16	117.00	114.44	131.22	126.98
1890	128.72	91.77	110.31	112.74	114.72	124.00
1891	101.22	78.90	82.06	87.72	93.76	104.00
1892	92.22	81.26	79.10	74.52	102.34	106.83
1893	114.59	93.40	71.72	103.75	98.56	129.78
1894	176.47	153.15	135.24	188.10	127.90	155.86
1895	131.81	97.16	121.61	124.60	100.85	170.40
1896	102.4	66.42	64.29	79.05	98.47	107.46
1897	82.48	74.32	44.73	65.6	66.24	86.58
1898	131.36	80.75	79.31	112.2	132.60	165.48
1899	130.32	113.22	77.6	102.06	92.56	117.96
1900	98.64	87.80	73.90	81.96	92.77	141.00
1901	126.64	99.82	98.28	105.00	118.95	172.20

Source : *Ibid.*

The Halis are generally agriculturists who have had land of their own, and have lost it by debt or poverty. No longer able to keep a plough of their own, they become farm servants of the agriculturists who are well off. The master to whom they engage themselves, commonly pays

> their debts. If a man wants a Hali, he is generally willing to do this to obtain one. The money thus advanced by the master used to vary from Rs. 20 to 60; but now cases are not uncommon, in which a master advances Rs. 200 or even more. . . . If another man wishes to engage the Hali, he generally pays up the debt due to the first master, and the Hali is then transferred to him. Public opinion also holds the heirs of a deceased Hali liable for the debt; and a man who marries the Hali's widow is held similarly liable. These are incidents of the Hali's service, which could not be enforced in our courts, but I mention them because they are commonly acted on by the people concerned.

But some of the central Punjab canal irrigated districts presented a slightly different picture. In these districts canals not only resulted in a large increase in the output per acre but also opened up new opportunities of work for them inside the villages. Consequently, they were usually well paid in the canal irrigated districts like Gujranwala, Shahpur and Jhang and better off than the poorer agriculturists who cultivated their own land or the tenants-at-will paying *batai* rates.[88] There was also 'no fear of their starving' and the proprietors generally tried to keep them in good humour in order to keep them in service. In some cases their wages even rose so strikingly, reported the settlement officer from Jhang, that keeping farm servants had become very expensive and they often did not sympathise with the proprietors' endeavours 'to economise by substituting *china* and other flour for that of wheat'.[89] In these districts, it was a then common thing to hear an agriculturist complaining of the independence exhibited by the plough servants, as compared with their subservience in former days.[90] Even in Amritsar they were often treated 'liberally' in the first quarter of the present century by the zamindars who were on military service.[91]

NOTES

1. *Ferozepore S.R., 1859*, 63.
2. *Rohtak S.R., 1880*, 96; *Jhang S.R., 1882*, 99; Lucas, *op. cit.*, 69.
3. *Ferozepore D.G., 1883-84*, 62; *Lahore D.G., 1883-84*, 78-9.

4. Proportion of four important groups of *kamins* per 1000 of total population in four important districts of the province.

Name of the district	Proportion of menials per 1000 of total population		
	Tarkhan	Lohar	Chamar and Mochi
1	2	3	4
Hissar (South-eastern Punjab)	25	11	98+1
Amritsar (Central Punjab)	39	21	1+27
Sialkot (Submontane Punjab)	41	18	8+15
Bannu (Western Punjab)	17	14	—+12

Source : Ibbetson, *op. cit.*, 298-9, 310-1.

5. *Punjab Famine Report*, *1878-79*, II, 711-24.
6. *Gujrat D.G.*, *1883-84*, 63.
7. Abdur Rahim Khan and Nur Mohammad, *An Economic Survey of Bhambu Sandila—a Village in the Muzaffargarh District* (The Board of Economic Enquiry, Punjab, Village Surveys No. 8, Publication No. 45, Lahore, 1935), 15.
8. *Zira A.R.*, *1888*, 36.
9. Rose, *Tribes*, III, 36.
10. *Panipat Tahsil and Karnal Pargana S.R.*, *1883*, 117.
11. *Pargana Muktsar and Ilaka Mamdot S.R.*, *1878*, 11; *Jullundur S.R.*, *1892*, 87.
12. *Kohat S.R.*, *1884*, 168; *Hazara S,R.*, *1876*, 101-2.
13. *Report on the Census of the Punjab*, *1881*, I, 320.
14. Churas were regarded as untouchables even in the late 1950s. It seems clear from the following remark of an investigator: 'They live on one side of the village. . . . Those high caste Sikhs, especially women, who do not allow Mazhabis [Churas] to enter their houses, usually sit away from the place where Mazhabis are sitting'. For details, see Indera P. Singh, 'A Sikh Village', Milton Singer, ed., *Traditional India* (The American Folklore Society, Philadelphia, 1959), 279-80.
15. *Sialkot D.G.*, *1883-84*, 58.
16. *Ibid.*, *1920*, 110,
17. *Report on the Census of the Punjab*, *1881*, I, 384.
18. Total deductions for the *kamins* in per cent from the gross produce in three important districts of the province.

District	Deductions for the *kamins* in per cent
1	2
Jullundur (Central Punjab)	16
Hoshiarpur (Submontane Punjab)	10
Dera Ismail Khan (Western Punjab)	9.3

Source : *Dera Ismail Khan S.R., 1879*, 371; *Hoshiarpur D.G., 1883-84*, 71; *Jullundur A.R., 1883*, 17.

19. *Hoshiarpur D.G., 1883-84*, 71.
20. *Shahpur D.G., 1883-84*, 56.
21. *Hazara S.R., 1876*, 101.
22. This problem can be better studied with reference to two widely separated districts of the province, viz., Karnal (south-eastern Punjab) and Montgomery (south-western Punjab).

Wages paid to kumhars in two widely separated districts of the province.

Year	District	Wages paid to kumhars
1	2	3
1883	Karnal	The kumhar gets the same as the tarkhan. When he provides earthen jars for the persian wheels, he generally receives 40 to 50 seers per persian wheel and a *gaira* of corn (one *gaira* amounts to 5 seers); otherwise he gets 12 to 20 seers per plough.
1878	Montgomery : villages on the Ravi	During the spring harvest the kumhar receives the same as tarkhan (per well 12 *pais* and 3 bundles of grain). During the autumm harvest, he receives a lower rate of wages in the *sailab* lands (per plough ½ *pai* and 1 bundle of grain).

Source : *Panipat Tahsil and Karnal Pargana S.R., 1883*, 117; *Montgomery S.R., 1878*, 134.

23. *Pargana Muktsar and Ilaka Mamdot S.R., 1878*, 11; *Ferozepore D.G., 1883-84*, 62; *Lahore S.R., 1873*, 62; *Lahore D.G., 1883-84*, 78; *Montgomery S.R , 1878*, 132-3; *Sharakpur A.R., 1893*, 33.
24. *Panipat Tahsil and Karnal Pargana S.R., 1883*, 117; *Jullundur S.R., 1892*, 87; Randhir Singh and Roberts, *op. cit.*, 17-8.
25. J.A. Grant, *Monograph on the Leather Industry in the Punjab, 1891-92* (Civil and Military Gazette Press, Lahore, 1893), 5.
26. *Jhelum, S R., 1883*, 158; *Ibid., 1902*, 50.
27. *Jhang S.R., 1882*, 100-1.
28. Kessinger, *op. cit.*, 57.

29. *Ferozepore S.R., 1859*, 63; *Gujrat S.R., 1916*, 22; *Gurgaon D.G., 1883-84*, 65; *Jhang S.R , 1882*, 100-1.
30. In 1865 Cracroft (settlement officer) found that in the *Chhach* alone kumhars were paid in cash. But in the late 1880s this form of payment became strikingly popular and it is quite evident from the following remarks of Robertson (settlement officer) : 'The *potter* . . . is now very often paid in cash for what he actually supplies . . . . He has in many cases ceased to be in fact a village menial at all'. For details, see *Rawalpindi D.G., 1883-84*, 75; *Rawalpindi S.R., 1893*, 95.
31. *Ludhiana D.G., 1888-89*, 99-101.
32. *Peshawar and Nawshera A.R., 1897*, 70; *Jhelum D.C., 1904*, 124-5; S. Gian Singh and King, *op. cit.*, 21.
33. *Multan D.G., 1901-02*, 187.
34. This decline in the *sep* payment adversely affected the position of the kumhars because it constituted a very important source of their income. The following annual budget estimate of a potter's family will illustrate the point:

Income				Expenditure			
1				2			
	Rs.	A.	P.		Rs.	A.	P.
Cash sale from vessels	3	2	0	Annual expenditure on food	72	0	0
For sowing and cutting grains	50	0	0	Expenditure on clothings	3	9	0
Grain from zamindars	17	4	0				
Earning from donkeys	12	0	0				
Total	82	6	0	Total	75	9	0

Source : Note by J. Maconachie, DC Gurgaon, 17 March 1888, Rev and Agr (F) December 1888, 1-24A.

35. This gradual change in the form of payment of the kumhars was also due to the fact that in some of the central districts greater use of metal utensils, often reduced their scope of employment. Many zamindars found little justification in appointing them as regular *kamins*. For details, see S. Gian Singh and King, *op. cit.*, 23, 149.
36. *Sialkot S.R., 1895*, 6.
37. Decline in *sep* deduction in five tahsils of Ambala district.

Year	*Sep* deduction in per cent in five tahsils				
	Jagadhari	Rupar	Kharar	Ambala	Naraingarh
1	2	3	4	5	6
At the settlement of 1882-87	12-1/2	10	10	10 & 12	10
At the settlement of 1915-20	......	A) 10 B) 8	A) 10 B) 8	8	10

A) Irrigated B) Unirrigated

Source : *Ambala S.R., 1921*, 27.

38. Decline in *sep* deduction in Hoshiarpur district.

Year	*Sep* deduction in per cent
1	2
At the settlement of 1879-84	10
At the settlement of 1910-14	4

Source : *Hoshirpur S.R., 1916*, 25-6.

39. *Ludhiana S.R., 1884*, 130.
40. *Rohtak D.G., 1910*, 143-4.
41. *Rawalpindi S.R., 1893*, 96.
42. Anchal Dass and H. Calvert, *An Economic Survey of Tehong—a Village in the Jullundur District* (The Board of Economic Enquiry, Punjab, Village Surveys No. 3, Publication No. 18, Lahore, 1931), 14-5.
43. *Chenab Colony S.R., 1915*, 82.
44. Raj Narain and Brij Narain, *An Economic Survey of Gijhi—a Village in the Rohtak District* (The Board of Economic Enquiry, Punjab, Village Surveys No. 2, Publication No. 17, Lahore, 1932), 16.
45. Abdur Rahim Khan and Nur Mohammad, *op. cit.*, 15.
46. S. Gian Singh and King, *op. cit.*, 119; Anchal Dass and C.F. Strickland, *An Economic Survey of Gajju Chak—a Village in the Gujranwala District* (The Board of Economic Enquiry, Punjab, Village Surveys No. 6, Publication No. 31, Lahore, 1934), 145-6.
47. A number of village enquiries of the present century clearly indicated that they constituted 'the poorest sections of the village community'. Their income scarcely exceeded 5 annas a day. It often compelled them to borrow from the zamindars whose lands they cultivated as field labourers or from the *sahukars* at an exorbitant rate of interest on the security of their employers. In Gijhi (Rohtak district), for example, it was found that every family was in debt and in each case it was incurred in a year of scarcity for buying food. 'In most cases a part of the interest is paid at harvest time, but the principal and interest have now accumulated to hundreds of rupees in each case'. Their indebtedness was equally widespread in most of the western districts of the province. Here the mochis were generally deeply indebted to the Khojas who advanced credit at a similarly high rate of interest in connection with their trade in leather works. They were often compelled to sell their leather works at a price fixed by their creditors. 'The result, of course, is that the Mochi gets more and more involved in their meshes and finds it utterly impossible to extricate himself from their hands'. For details, see Note by J.A. Maconachie, DC Gurgaon, 17 March 1888, Rev and Agr (F) December 1888, 1-24A; Raj Narain and Brij Narain, *op. cit.*, 10, 16; Lucas, *op. cit.*, 60.
48. Grant, *op. cit.*, 13-4.

49. Ibbetson, *op. cit.*, 296.
50. Anchal Dass and Calvert, *An Economic Survey of Tehong—a Village in the Jullundur District*, 14.
51. *Prices and Wages in India, 1902*, 19th Issue, Table 2,
52. While explaining the causes of this spectacular rise in wages the settlement officer of the Gurdaspur district pointed out : 'The first and main cause of the rise in wages is...to be assigned to the rise in the prices of food-grains. The second main cause is the scarcity of labour produced by (1) depopulation due to plague mortality... (2) increased demand for labour on the canal colonies, on public works, and locally, in factories, coupled with the much greater mobility of labour: the labouring population has at last begun to abandon its former immobility and to take advantage of railways and the improvement in communications. The growing independence of the labouring class, which is a source of complaint from every employer of labour, is the third cause of enhanced wages... . The fourth cause, which is also an outcome of the above, is the general rise in the standard of comfort....' *Gurdaspur D.G., 1914*, 131.
53. *FC Selections*, New Series No. 24, No. 49, No, LXXVII, Memorandum by W.G. Renouf, Director of Agriculture, on the Wages Survey of the Punjab, taken in December 1909 (Civil and Military Gazette Press, Lahore, 1910) Para 10, Table 10; *Report on the First Regular Wages Survey of the Punjab, taken in December 1912*, Table B; *Prices and Wages in India, 1902*, 19th Issue, Table 2; *Ibid., 1913*, 30th Issue, Table 2.
54. *Annual Report for the Chenab, Jhung, Chunian and Sohag Para Colonies, 1902-03*, 11.
55. *Census of India, 1911*, XIV, Part I, 502.
56. *Ludhiana D.G., 1904*, 65.
57. S. Gian Singh and King, *op. cit.*, 13, 22.
58. *Sirsa S. R., 1884*, 184.
59. *Jullundur D.G., 1904*, 104; *Ludhiana D.G., 1904*, 65.
60. *Sirsa S.R., 1884*, 104.
61. *Ferozepore D.G., 1915*, 101.
62. Alienated land held by different artisan groups in four circles of Sialkot, Gujranwala and Shahpur districts in acres.

Name of the circle	Land held by the artisans in acres	Total area held by self-cultivated mortgagees and owners by purchase other than by money-lenders
1	2	3
Charkhri (Sialkot)	131	358
Charkhri (Gujranwala)	417	1,412
Jhelum-Bhera (Shahpur)	2	398
Hill Circle (Shahpur)	315	583

Source : *Agricultural Indebtedness*, General Report, para 74, Rev and Agr (LR) November 1898, 3-22A.

63. *Ferozepore D.G., 1915*, 101; *RR 1937*, 35.
64. The Ramgharias (Sikh tarkhans and lohars) 'had to wait until the mid-fifties of the present century before the Government reclassified them, making it possible for them to buy agricultural land'. It naturally left behind a deep impact on the 'neo-rich' among them. For details, see S. Saberwal, 'Status and Entrepreneurship: The Ramgharia Case', M.N. Srinivas, S. Seshaiah and V.S. Partha-sarathy, eds., *Dimensions af Social Change in India* (Allied Publishers, New Delhi, 1977), 158-67.
65. *Punjab Famine Report, 1878-79*, II, 711.
66. *Amritsar D.G., 1883-84*, 30; *Lahore D.G., 1883-84*, 80.
67. *Montgomery D.G., 1883-84*, 79.
68. *Jullundur S.R., 1892*, 131.
69. *Punjab Famine Report, 1878-79*, II, 714.
70. *Report on the Census of the Punjab, 1868*, Statement IV.
70. *Punjab Famine Report, 1878-79*, II, 710.
72. Agricultural labourers in per cent in four different regions of the province, 1881-1891.

Name of district	Agricultural labourers in per cent of the total population	
	1881	1891
1	2	3
Delhi (South-eastern Punjab)	1.05	4.74
Gurdaspur (Submontane Punjab)	0.87	9.58
Lahore (Central Punjab)	0.57	9.51
Bannu (Western Punjab)	0.10	1.70

Source : *Census Reports* for the respective years.

73. *Punjab Famine Report, 1878-79*, II, 713, 719.
74. *Census of India, 1911*, XIV, Part I, 49.
75. Kessinger, *op. cit.*, 128-9.
76. S.J. Patel, *Agricultural Labourers in Modern India and Pakistan* (Current Book House, Bombay, 1952), 128.
77. *Gujranwala, D.G., 1893-94*, 82.
78. *Report on the Enquiry into the Rise of Prices in India*, I (Calcutta, 1915), 174.
79. *FC Selections*, New Series No. 24, No. 49, No. LXXVII, para 11.
80. *Report of the Indian Famine Commission, 1898*, I (Simla, 1898), 363.
81. In Rawalpindi this rise in wages was said to have been due to 'peculiar causes. Any war on the frontier or big concentration of troops in Rawalpindi at once send up wages'. Actually in the late 1870s, the Kabul campaign, together with the construction of the Punjab Northern State Railways created an extraordinary demand for labour. In the early 1890s the continual tension along the Afghan borders maintained this upward wage movement, though the settlement report of this period indicated a slight fall in their wage rates

since the Kabul campaign 'when all kinds of labour were at famine rates'. Even then the wages of the labourers were higher than what they were thirty years ago and it was also estimated that 'wages have increased by nearly 50 per cent since the Sikh rule'. Similarly in Peshawar, wages rose. Here again the Kabul campaign led to an 'extraordinary demand for labour of all kinds'. In the next decade also there 'has been increasing prosperity from the influx of money and occupation of the district during the Afghan War, the introduction of the railways, the opening of the Swat Canal in Hastanagar and Mardan and the development of peace and security in the Valley'. This period also witnessed a definite rise in the wages of the agricultural labourers in Multan. In the early 1850s and 1860s, Multan was not a very flourishing agricultural tract and zamindars were not rich enough to employ labourers at a rate prevalent in districts like Amritsar. But during the last quarter of the 19th century factors like the opening of the railways connecting Multan with Karachi, commencement of the Sidhnai Canal construction leading to steady extension of cultivation in the arid tracts did not fail to bring about a definite increase in the wages of the labourers.

But in Amritsar and Ludhiana their real wages declined. During the period there was virtually no significant increase of cultivation in these two districts. In Amritsar, for example, already 70 per cent of the total cultivated area was under the plough and the settlement officer clearly pointed out that population was pressing heavily on the cultivable holdings. Similarly Ludhiana was a fairly cultivated region in the early 1880s and the district officer then reported that the scope for new cultivation was extremely limited. Naturally it greatly prevented any significant increase in the size of the labour market in these two districts. In many cases the labourers often migrated to the canal colonies in search of better wages and it became almost an established pattern of the agrarian economy towards the close of the century.

In Delhi also the real wages of the labourers declined. This decline was largely due to three factors. In the first place, recurring famines must be held greatly responsible for it. Here good years were few and bad years many; famines occurred in 1860-61, 1868-69, 1877-78, 1887-88, 1896-97 and 1898-99. They not only crippled the resources of the zamindars but also threw a considerable number of labourers out of employment. Secondly, the Delhi labour market was only marginally affected by the opening of new irrigational projects and the consequent extension of canal irrigation over tracts which often contributed to a rise in the real wages of labourers in districts like Jhang and Multan. Finally, the size of emigration to the canal colonies was also very insignificant in this district. In many cases zamindars often attempted to cut down their wages. For a further discussion on this point, see also the author's unpublished Ph.D. dissertation 'Agrarian Society of the Punjab, 1849-1901', 478-83.

82. Ghulam Ahmed, EAC Rawalpindi's opinion quoted in E.B. Steedman, DLRA Punjab's note on the replies received to the enquiry as to whether the people of India suffer from a daily insufficiency of food, 12 June 1888, Rev and Agr (F) December 1888, 1-24A.

83. *Punjab Famine Report, 1878-79*, II, 711.
84. *Census of India, 1911*, XIV, Part I, 49.
85. Average annual income and expenditure of a field labourer in Kutubpur (Hoshiarpur).

Income				Expenditure			
1				2			
	Rs.	As.	Ps.		Rs.	As.	Ps.
1. Income from profession and other sources	156	14	0	1. Payment of land revenue and other charges	3	12	0
				2. Payment on account of debt by instalments	13	6	0
				3. Payment of interest	1	12	0
				4. Total annual expenditure on the purpose of food	135	8	8
Total income	156	14	0	Total expenditure	154	6	8

Source : Lucas, *op. cit.*, 114-6.

86. *Punjab Famine Report, 1878-79*, II, 721-2.
87. *Hazara S.R., 1876*, 99.
88. *Shahpur D.G.*, 1883-84, 56; *Ibid.*, 1897, 142.
89. *Jhang D.G., 1883-84*, 89.
90. *Punjab Famine Report, 1878-79*, II, 710.
91. *Amritsar D.G., 1914*, 71. For their changed relationship with the zamindars, see also Darling, *Wisdom and Waste*, 273.

8

Conclusions

The rural society of the Punjab experienced some significant changes during the second half of the 19th century. Its prosperous canal colonies in the central *bar* lands, the overwhelming commercial success of wheat cultivation, the predominance of the enterprising Jat zamindars in the land market of the central districts and a general mobility of labour are a few indications of the changes that occurred in the agrarian economy of the province. Simultaneously, water-logging, malaria and *reh* led to a partial contraction of cultivation in some parts of Karnal, Sialkot, Hoshiarpur and Gujranwala while indebtedness and a large-scale expropriation of the zamindars from their holdings, in the opinion of many experienced British officials, constituted a grave political danger threatening the security of the British Empire in India.

Perhaps it was the efficient canal system that largely stimulated the process of change in the different districts of the province. At the annexation, the Punjab could hardly boast of having any major perennial canal. But by the close of the century, one after another nearly all the major Punjab rivers were harnessed for bringing water to their respective *doabs*. This paved the way for the reclamation of many million acres of cultivable wastes and its effects on the agrarian economy were of a permanent nature.

During the period under review, the blessings of irrigation were most evident in the Chenab Colony. With the opening of the canals, there started a general migration of the peasant population from the densely populated, malaria-affected submontane and central Punjab districts like Gurdaspur, Sialkot,

Jullundur and Amritsar towards the *bar* lands leading to the emergence of a healthy colony life the like of which hardly existed in the pre-British Punjab. Prior to it, this virgin prairie was the 'shelter of deer, jackals and rats' and predominantly inhabited by the named Janglis with little inclination to permanent cultivation. But gradually the tract experienced a considerable economic growth and the contemporary ballads amply recorded the nascent confidence of the Punjab peasantry in these canals. There grew up well-planned colony villages with numerous *pakka* houses and spacious courtyards. Their inhabitants were well-dressed and their diet also gained in variety and refinement. There was a general improvement in their standard of living; they now performed 'many a kind of labour which was formerly left entirely to the village sweepers and menials' and paid greater attention to rural sanitation. In the Chenab Canal Colony the peasant grantees carried on their cultivation under certain favourable conditions: they owned large compact holdings and belonged mostly to the sturdy agrarian communities like Jats, Arains and Kambohs, possessing part of the initial capital for the cultivation of the virgin lands and enjoying an assured supply of water almost throughout the year. These canals also resulted in a greater awareness among the peasant grantees about the selection of seeds, rotation of crops and the use of agricultural implements and their cropping pattern was often adjusted to the needs of the external markets.

Many of these developments were scarcely confined to these colonies. There was a general increase in the total cultivated area of the province and it outstripped the rate of population growth during the period under review. In the submontane districts, however, the growth rate was minimum because they were already widely cultivated even before the annexation of the province; here with the increase of population zamindars mostly brought the inferior marginal lands under the plough. But in the south-western districts this increase generally ranged from 20 to 30 per cent. Of all the south-eastern districts, Hissar experienced the most significant development due to the availability of a considerable amount of waste in the Sirsa region while Karnal closely followed it with the realignment of the Western Jumna Canal. In the central part of the province the growth rate varied from district to district. In Jullundur and Amritsar there was no notable increase due to the non-availability of the culturable lands. But other central districts, viz., Gujranwala, Shahpur and Jhang, experienced a radical increase in their cultivated area; in all these districts the cultivated area nearly doubled. Here the soil was extremely fertile, capable of producing all types of valuable crops. The canals also did not fail to increase the per acre yield of crops like wheat, cotton, maize and *toria* which replaced the pre-canal inferior staples like *jowar*, *bajra* and barley. Blyn's study for the period 1891-1947 also pointed out that this process continued even in the present century. His findings further revealed that in the Punjab the increase of food-grains was nearly equal to the average rate of population growth while the non-food crops increased with a faster rate. There was also a definite increase in investment in the construction of numerous masonry wells, and manufacture of Behia mills and modern iron ploughs and carts.

Canals were not an unmixed blessing, however. With the extraction of water from the different rivers, the downstream *sailab* cultivation in the districts of Gujranwala, Jhang and Montgomery was largely disrupted. It reduced a considerable number of peasant population to such an abject poverty that the Government had to reduce its land revenue demand toward the close of the century. The Ravi *bet* villages were so strikingly affected in the 1890s that 'not even a bark of a dog was to be heard'. Besides over-irrigation, bad alignment of canals frequently led to water-logging and *reh* in different districts of the province and threw much fertile land out of cultivation. The process continued even beyond our period and an enquiry in the present century estimated that the area rendered unfit for use by water-logging and *reh* was about 0.25 per cent of the total irrigated area of the province. *Reh* was first detected around the 1840s in nearly one-tenth of the total number of canal villages watered by the Western Jumna Canal. In Sialkot also, at places the rise of the sub-soil water-table damaged the very foundations of houses while in Amritsar it was responsible for an epidemic of malaria in the present century. Actually the water-logged land provided ideal conditions for the outbreak of malaria which became an annual occurrence towards the close of the century. It brought about a large-scale loss of human life; it also greatly devitalised the rural folk and made them too weak to reap their ripe crop. Cultivation tended to decline in Gurdaspur, Sialkot, Ambala, Delhi, Rohtak and Hoshiarpur. Even the Chenab Colony suffered from malaria, *reh* and water-logging. 'Here water-logging', thus reported the settlement officer in the present century, 'has reached the acute stage, and irrigation is not only unnecessary, but positively injurious. . . . The curtailment of irrigation is only one of the unfortunate effects to be apprehended. The physique of the agricultural classes is also gravely endangered, for a malaria-ridden peasantry cannot hope for other than weak offspring. That is a reflexion which must give pause to the ardour of the keenest enthusiast for the spread of irrigation'.

A major development in the second half of the century was a steady commercialization of agriculture in the province. Apart from the growth of a market outside India and also of the one within, a significant factor in this was a general improvement in the means of communication facilitating a quicker movement of agricultural produce from one part of the province to another. This process was further stimulated by the general improvement in the means of water supply which led to a significant change in the crop pattern. The Punjab wheat was now the most important staple of the province and it found ready markets across the English Channel and its commercial success did bring economic prosperity to a considerable number of big landlords of the province. They enjoyed a considerable amount of independence and autonomy in their credit relationship as well as on commercial resources. Relative profitability of certain commercial crops often played a decisive part in their cropping pattern and in their cases at least commercialization of agriculture was not a forced and artificial one. Many of them did successfully maintain their hold over their harvested crops and sell them directly in the market, thus securing a comfortable profit. These developments were often reported from Montgomery, Karnal and Amritsar towards the close of the century. Kessinger's findings on Vilyatpur clearly indicated that market orientation often played a decisive role in the economic life of the villages of the Jullundur district. Similarly in Ferozepore and Ludhiana, the enterprising Jats were the beneficiaries of the growing commercialization of agriculture. They chiefly controlled the trade in agricultural produce and their frugal habits enabled them to save a part of their income which they later transferred to land purchases.

This growing commercialization of agriculture in conjunction with other developments brought about a significant change in the rural credit relations. Prior to British rule, moneylenders generally extended credit to the zamindars throughout the year and charged a moderate rate of interest for the loans. During British rule, the brisk trade in agricultural produce resulted in a gradual change in their mode of operations. Many of them were petty dealers in grain who advanced credit to the producers with the ulterior motive of getting hold of their debtors' crops after the harvest. It was now frequently seen that as soon as the harvesting was over, *sahukars* went to the threshing floor of the zamindars and virtually took away the bulk of the produce in repayment of their debts. Actually zamindars of smaller means, after satisfying their various needs throughout the year, practically had no surplus stock of their own left with them to be sold independently of the *sahukars*. They were even so much in their clutches that they were often compelled to sell their produce at a price arbitrarily fixed by their creditors. This evidently led to a general increase in their indebtedness and by the close of the century it became nearly universal in the province. Numerous village enquiries of the present century further revealed that zamindars were so weighed down by indebtedness that they had 'little or no imagination, their minds had become dull and blank'. The problem of growing rural indebtedness was further aggravated by the 'fixed, rigid and inelastic' land revenue administration of this period. The Punjab Government, however, refused to share this view and introduced fluctuating land revenue demand in the dry tracts of the province. Thorburn's detailed inquiry in the Rawalpindi division and Prof. Bhalla's findings about Bairampur (Hoshiarpur) clearly revealed that 'dates of payment of land revenue and the harvest time often coincided' which frequently compelled zamindars to ask for loans from the *sahukars*. In Montgomery *bet* also, many villages were found to have been indebted due to harsh and rigid land revenue administration.

Rural indebtedness led to a large-scale transfer of lands, however, by no means a new development during British rule. During Sikh rule, alienations of lands did occur. However, two major constraints on them were the low prices of land and the limited land market. In the second half of the century, with the improvements in canal irrigation and the consequent commercialization of agriculture, prices steadily rose and land became a marketable commodity. Transfers of lands thus steadily increased over the years. In 1876-77, nearly 309,000 acres of lands changed hands through sale and mortgage which further rose to 1,200,000 acres in 1886-87. This large-scale alienation of lands naturally meant a considerable expropriation of the Punjabi zamindars from their ancestral holdings. In a number of districts of the province, lands passed into the hands of professional money-lenders who scarcely had any interest in the improvement of the techniques of cultivation. Being predominantly traders, they generally allowed the expropriated zamindars to remain in possession of their alienated holdings on condition of paying a higher rate of rent. Sometimes they were even asked to render free labour to their new 'masters'. Numerous district officers also frequently referred to different forms of debt slavery resulting from this large-scale alienation of lands.

This was, however, scarcely true of the whole of the Punjab. At least in some cases, lands were transferred from unenterprising proprietors to thrifty ones; they invested their labour and capital in their newly acquired holdings and contributed to the emergence of healthier units of cultivation in different districts of the province. The Malis of Ambala, the Jats of Ferozepore and the *sahukars* of Multan are a case in point. In the Pipli tahsil (Ambala), the Malis acquired a considerable amount of lands from the 'broken-down zamindars' or from the non-resident proprietors like the money-lenders and the bankers of the towns. They also did their best towards a better tillage of their newly purchased lands. Similarly in Multan the Hindu *sahukars* were not always parasitic landholders, they undertook a series of improvements. In

Ferozepore also transfers of land from the thriftless Rajputs and Dogars to the enterprising and frugal Jats created conditions for a stable peasant economy.

Towards the close of the century, these widespread transfers of lands, however, greatly worried a number of British officials. A feeling gradually gained ground that these zamindars were being unjustly deprived of their lands by the *sahukars* who were not at all keen on holding them under their direct cultivation. In the early 1890s when approximately 9 lakhs of acres of lands were annually alienated by sale and mortgage by the zamindars to their creditors, these officers were convinced that something must be done to put a stop to this process. Or else the Punjabi zamindars would be completely enslaved by the *sahukars*. The problem was further complicated by communal antagonism in as much as the majority of the zamindars of western Punjab were of Muslim extraction while the *sahukars* came mainly from among the Hindus. The zamindars often retaliated by brutally attacking their creditors. This widespread rioting and general agrarian unrest led to serious apprehensions of a corresponding mutiny in the Indian army largely recruited from among the warlike communities of western Punjab districts. Equally disturbing to the official mind was the political implications of this problem affecting the loyalty of the entire Punjab peasantry.

With a view to coping with these evils, the Land Alienation Act was passed prohibiting transfers of lands of the zamindars to the professinal money-lenders. They were virtually debarred from occupying the lands of those notified as agricultural tribes under this Act. However, the Act failed miserably to stop the process of expropriation of the weaker zamindars; there was simply 'a change in the direction of land transfers'. The condition of the Rajputs and the Dogars is an exampte. Instead of being absorbed by the *sahukars,* they were now made helpless victims of the stronger agricultural tribes. In the present century also they continued to be displaced by the thrifty Jats and Arains in a number of central, submontane and south-eastern districts of the province. Similarly the Act could hardly offer any effective solution to the problem of growing rural indebtedness of the Punjabi zamindars. Its volume continued to increase over the years and the Punjab Banking Enquiry Committee estimated that the total debt in the province increased from Rs. 90 crores in 1921 to Rs. 135 crores in 1929.

This period also witnessed a gradual change in the landlord-tenant relationship and it largely centred round the problem of rent. Prior to British rule land was abundant and population scarce and almost everybody was allowed to hold land on condition of sharing the heavy land revenue demand of the Sikhs. The proprietors were fortunate if they could manage to secure some *malikana* from their tenants, in recognition of their rights over lands. Even during the first few years following the establishment of British rule, the situation remained almost unchanged because of the low prices of grain and a general glut in the market. Proprietors then faced extreme hardship in paying the heavy land revenue demand in cash. They were then willing to concede to their tenants even the right of occupancy on condition of sharing this heavy burden. Such cases were particularly reported from Shahpur, Jhelum, Montgomery, Sirsa and Gurgaon. However from the 1860s when with the rise in prices, land became a worthwhile investment, zamindars tried to assert their rights and frequently demanded a higher rate of rent. Their position was further strengthened by the enforcement of the Tenancy Act of 1868. It greatly empowered them to enhance the rents of their tenants on certain specific grounds and they frequently utilised them.

These developments naturally affected the position of these tenants who were long accustomed to a favourable treatment from their proprietors. Many of them reacted sharply and frequently contested the notices of ejectment served on them by their landlords. It led to bitter wrangles and disputes and added a new dimension to the changing form of agrarian relations in the last quarter of the 19th century. During these years, in the opinion of many officials, rent problem became a 'burning question' and the landlord-tenant relations became extremely strained over this issue. In Sirsa, Gurgaon and Hoshiarpur districts law courts were flooded with rent suits and it was only very rarely that the tenants had their way.

Consequently, they had to agree on a higher rate of rent; sometimes they were even called upon to pay in kind in place of cash rent; occasionally they were also denied their customary right of enjoying the produce of the trees grown on their lands. These changes greatly upset the tenants of the province and the second Tenancy Act was a significant attempt to place the landlord-tenant relations on a sounder footing. But it could hardly offer an effective answer to the problem of enhancement of rent. Except in a few districts, viz., Montgomery, Gujranwala and Jhang, rent rate steadily rose over the years and it deprived the tenants of the benefits of price rise. In the submontane and south-western districts they were so deeply affected by it that they had virtually no surplus of their own and borrowing became an established pattern of their economy.

But this increased rental income of the zamindars was scarcely invested in the cultivation of village lands. There is the example of the 'capitalist' grantees of the Chenab Colony. As early as 1895 the colonization officer reported that these absentee landholders 'came to regard their colony holdings as nothing more than a source of profit, upon which as little as possible was to be expended' and their relations with their tenants were 'equally marked by endless dissensions and ill-feeling'. Under such circumstances, they could hardly play the role of enterprising landlords which the Government expected from them. The *sahukars* of the submontane and central districts had no better performance to their credit as landlords. Similarly the Rajput zamindars who often 'cultivated through the agency of servants, or leased out their land to tenants', did not enjoy the full benefits of this rent rise, for they had to give away a sizable portion of the outturn of their fields in payment of various expenses incurred throughout the year. But the enterprising proprietary communities like the Jats and Arains of the central districts were not always parasitic groups. In many cases they often showed a decided preference in taking up the lands of others on lease and managed 'to reap the profits of both the landlord and cultivator'. They also invested a considerable part of their additional income in the purchase of land or in making improvement in the cultivation of their ancestral holdings. This difference in the utilisation of their additional income from rent was largely due to the fact that the professional money-lenders were usually busy in trade while the Jats of central Punjab considered cultivation to be their sole occupation.

The relations between the landholders and their village servants also changed during our period. At the annexation, they were universally paid in kind at customary rates out of the common heap of produce. But towards the close of the century this traditional form of wage payment was generally replaced by annual contracts and their wages were often determined by the utility of their service. In many cases they were even paid in cash for each job performed by them.

This was largely an outcome of the steady price rise which compelled the zamindars to cut down their cost of cultivation by reducing the wages of their *kamins*. Now they also performed different odd jobs which in the past were exclusively kept in reserve for their artisans and menials. This economic reorientation in the attitudes of the zamindars deeply affected the position of the *kamins*. In a number of densely populated submontane and central districts their wages declined so strikingly that their relations were no longer marked by a spirit of mutual co-operation and understanding. They became extremely critical and hostile. These changes in the traditional form of wage payment also led to a general mobility of labour in the province. With a declining wage rate, many of them left their villages, abandoned their ancestral caste callings and migrated elsewhere in search of higher wages and better livelihood. Many of them flocked to towns which offered various avenues of employment. The opening of the different canal irrigated tracts, particularly the Chenab Colony in the *bar* lands, stimulated this process. Here an extraordinary demand for labour for cultivating the virgin soil as well as various other forms of new job opportunities encouraged them to migrate and settle in this tract. In the Chenab Colony tract, higher wages of labour made them very much independent of the zamindars and their relations with them were 'both less fixed and less friendly'.

But it would be wrong to assume that this was a universal phenomenon by the close of the century. In the non-canal regions, particularly in the extremely northern and south-western districts, their position was not generally a very happy one. Here they suffered miserably and 'the fear of ejection from the village' was 'a yoke' which kept their head down. They had very little surplus of their own and frequently suffered from a daily insufficiency of food. They were deeply indebted to their employers and remained almost in a state of debt slavery. In the south-eastern districts their condition was equally miserable; they were frequently called upon to render *begar* and they practically constituted the poorest section of the village social order.

What emerges from this study is the picture of an immense complexity of the agrarian changes occurring in the Punjab during this crucial phase of British rule in the province. These changes were far from uniform in type and nature. The old agrarian structure was considerably modified in some places though nowhere in the province do we find evidence of any fundamental structural change, particularly from the point of view of organization of the peasant economy. It would be misleading to apply either of the labels—economic growth or economic decline, to the complex changes occurring in the province as a whole. Though it is difficult to estimate the changes in the per capita output over the years, it would be a legitimate inference that conditions for any increased agricultural production were present in very many parts of the province. However, the economy did decline in some other regions though this was not entirely attributable to the innovations during British rule.

Glossary

abadkaran	a tenant who acquired occupancy right by bringing the waste under cultivation
adhjogia	an agricultural labourer who worked for one harvesting season
adnamalik	an inferior proprietor
alamalik	a superior proprietor
asami	a tenant (in the old settlement literature sometimes confined to a resident tenant)
atri	an agricultural labourer, often sweeper by caste, who worked for a season
bahi	account book
bajra	spiked millet
bangar	upland tract
banjarshigafan	tenant who brought the waste under cultivation
bar	table land lying between two rivers
barani	dependent on rain
batai	division of produce; the system of taking land revenue or rent in kind
begar	forced labour generally taken from chamars and other untouchables
behia	new sugar-cane mill
belna	indigenous sugar-cane press
benami	transfer in the name of a fictitious person
bet	low-lying riverain country
bhaewal	relative or intimate associated as co-partner to cultivate lands; they enjoyed no right in the village common waste
biswi	literally 1/20th, signified 5 per cent of the revenues paid to superior proprietors
butmar	a tenant whose right was based on having cleared the jungle

chahi	irrigated from a well
chakdar	owner of a *chak* or well, as opposed to the land attached to the well, acquiring certain rights over the produce of the land irrigated from his well
chari	great millet
charyat	a tenant who was put in, with or without a term being fixed by the proprietor, to cultivate land already cleared and fit for crops
china	a kind of millet
choh	an intermittent hill stream
dam dupat	a common rate of interest according to which the interest of a loan accumulated only to the extent of the capital
dhak	a tree (*Butia frondosa*)
dhaula	a variety of sugar-cane
diwali	a popular festival of lights in Northern India held in October-November
doab	tract of land between two rivers
gaira	one *gaira* amounts to 5 seers
godah	a labourer employed for hoeing and weeding
gur	unrefined sugar
habubat	different types of extra dues paid by tenants to proprietors
hak-i-kamini	customary dues paid to village servants and labourers at the end of harvest
hakk zamindari	a fee paid to superior proprietors in cash or kind in the south-western districts of the province
hali	agricultural labourer
hissachuk	a resident tenant who shares the payment of land revenue
ilaqa	a region, an area of several villages connected historically or by kinship ties
inam	a cash allowance paid out of land revenue generally in return for specific duties
ismi	a proprietary fee
jagir	an assignment of land revenue, usually applied to those assignments which have been

	given for political reasons to men of local influence or ex-rulers or to men who have served Government well
jagirdar	the holder of a *jagir*
jamabandi	register of holdings of owners and tenants showing land held by each and amounts payable as rent and land revenue
jhil	a marsh
jhuriband	a tenant cultivating after the payment of the *jhuri* (an instalation fee) to the proprietor who marks out the plot given by tying down the bushes and grass in knots
jinswar	relating to crops, also the crop statement for any particular harvest
jowar	a kind of millet
kachcha	not lined with masonry (of a well)
kalar	barren land, also applied to *reh* efflorescence
kama	agricultural labourer who works for a season
kamiana	a cess generally paid by artisans to proprietors
kamin	a general term referring to village artisans and menials who earned their livelihood by supplying landowners with goods and services
kangi	a kind of millet
kankut	division of the standing crops by appraisement
kardar	Sikh revenue official
khadir	low lying land near a river
khalsa	Sikh army
khangi kamin	a village servant who renders household functions of the agriculturists
kharif	autumn harvest, sown in April-May and reaped in October-November
khatri	a caste to which most of the Hindu revenue officials belonged in the Punjab; a trader, shopkeeper and money-lender

killa	one-twenty-fifth of a square and one square was equivalent to 27.7 acres
kirar	contemptuous term for Hindu money-lender
kuhmar	a tenant who earned his title by sinking a well (*kuh*)
lambardar	village headman
landa	written character used by the shopkeepers
latmar	a tenant who acquired right in land by embanking fields
lawa	a reaper
lekhamukhi	a kind of usufructuary mortgage in use in the south-western and frontier districts of the province
maddul	a coarse grain used for bread
mahajan	trader and shopkeeper
maina	a weed (*Medicago denticulata*); abundantly grown and generally gathered for fodder, being considered good for milk
maira	sandy loam
malba	fund out of which common village expenses were defrayed
malik	owner, also a leading man in a section of a tribe
malikana	a fee paid by the tenants to their proprietors in recognition of their rights over lands they cultivated
malik kabza	a man who owned the land actually in his possession, but had no share in the common village waste
malrab	a kind of preparation from sugar-cane
manjah	the portion of land between the Beas and Ravi rivers and includes the tahsils of Amritsar, Tarn Taran, Kasur and parts of Lahore and Chunian
mandi	market
maund	a unit of weight, about 80 pounds
mazdur	a day labourer
milan khasra	an area statement abstracted from the *khasra* (field register) annual area statement

mundemar	a man who acquired occupancy right in land by clearing it of jungle
muqaddam	superior proprietor, also a leading man or headman in a village
muzarain mustakil	occupancy tenant
muzarain-i-ghair-mustakil	tenant-at-will
mori	stake planted at the founding of a village
morigad	planter of *mori* tree
nahari	irrigated from a canal
naksra intikal	statement of land transfers
nazrana	tribute paid by an official on a regular basis or on special occasions
neota	a contribution given by the guests at a wedding to defray the expenses of the festival
pahikasht	a tenant who did not live in the village in which he cultivated land
pai	a measure of capacity equal in weight from 16 to 25 seers
pakka	permanent, lined with masonry (of a well)
panchayat	council of village elders
povindah	a mixed Pathan confederacy of travelling merchants, half traders and half soldiers
patwari	a village accountant, a Government official who maintained the records and statistics of the village
rab	concentrated cane juice
rabi	spring crop generally sown in October-November and reaped in April-May
rabia	a manufacturer of molasses
rahak	a tenant
ras	capital
reh	saline efflorescence, crystallized in the dry season on the surface and in the upper strata of salt-affected soils
sahukar	a small-scale dealer, trader and money-lender

sailab	flooded or kept permanently moist by river
sam	literally meaning one-fourth of the produce earned by a plough, it often suggests debt slavery
seer	a measure of weight equivalent to 2.2 pounds
sep	customary grain dues paid to village artisans and menials
sepidar	one who rendered the service called *sep* and received customary remuneration at the end of the harvest
shakkar	sugar in a coarse and unrefined state
sildar	the holder of a proprietary right acquired over the bricks (*sil*) of a well, sunk by him and also over the land commanded by that well
takavi	loans advanced by Government for agricultural purposes
taraddadkar	inferior proprietor of the Jhang district
tumandar	Baluchi tribal chief
vadee kamin	village servant whose labour was directly connected with the agrarian operations in the village
varyoon	a tenant who had cultivated land for several years
vasee	a resident tenant
waris	proprietor of the frontier districts, also descendant of warlike tribe
zabti	fixed cash rent per acre for a particular crop which cannot be conveniently divided

Bibliography

PRIMARY SOURCES

UNPUBLISHED

1. Records of the Government of India: National Archives, New Delhi.
   Foreign (Secret, Political and Miscellaneous) Department Consultations, 1847-1850.
   Home (Public) Department Consultations, 1855-1860.
   Home (Judicial) Department Proceedings, 1890-1900.
   Revenue, Agriculture and Commerce (after 1879 Revenue and Agriculture) Department Proceedings, 1871-1904.
   Legislative Department Proceedings, 1887-1900 (including papers ralating to Act XII of 1900).
2. Records of the Government of the Punjab: Punjab State Archives, Patiala.
   Revenue and Agriculture Department Proceedings, 1891-1902 (only a limited number of files are available).

PUBLISHED

1. Parliamentary Papers: House of Commons

1854, LXIX, *General Report on the Administration of the Punjab Proper 1849-50 and 1850-51.*

1859, XVIII, *General Report on the Administration of the Punjab Territories Comprising the Cis and Trans-Sutlej States for the Years 1856-57 to 1857-58.*

1870, LIII, *Punjab Tenancy Act.*

1884, LIX, *Statement of the Trade of British India with British Possessions and Foreign Countries for the five years, 1878-79 to 1882-83.*

1885, LVIII, *Statement of the Trade of British India with British Possessions and Foreign Countries for the five years, 1879-80 to 1883-84.*

1893, LXVI, *Statement of the Trade of British India with British Possessions and Foreign Countries for the five years, 1887-88 to 1891-92.*

2. Official Reports and Publications

Abstracts of the Proceedings of the Council of the Governor-General of India Assembled for the Purpose of Making Laws and Regulations, 1899-1900 (Calcutta, 1901).

Administration Report on the Railways of India for the Calendar Year 1900 (London, 1901).

Annual Report for the Chenab, Jhang, Jhelum, Chunian and Sohag Para Colonies, 1901-02 to 1909-10 (Lahore, 1903-11).

Annnal Report on the Punjab Alienation of Land Act XII of 1900, 1901-02 to 1907-08 (Lahore, 1902-09).

Annual Report on the Revenue (or *Land Revenue*) *Administration of the Punjab, 1861-62 to 1912-13, 1927 and 1937* (Lahore, 1861-1914, 1928, 1938).

Area and Yield of Rice, Wheat, Oilseeds, Jute, Indigo, Sugar-cane for various periods from 1891-92 to 1901-02 (Calcutta, 1902).

Census of India, 1891, XIX-XX.

Census of India, 1901, XVII-XVIIA.

Census of India, 1911, XIV.

Census of India, 1931, XVII.

Note on the Trade Statistics of the Punjab, 1869-70 to 1877-78 (Lahore, 1871-79).

Prices and Wages in India, 19th and 30th Issues (Calcutta, 1902 and 1913).

Punjab District Gazetteers: First Series (1883-1889); Second Series (1892-1896); Third Series (1912-1925).

Punjab Report in Reply to Inquiries issued by the Famine Commission, I-II (Lahore, 1878-79).

Punjab Wheat: Its Varieties, Distribution and Husbandry (Lahore, 1884).

Report of the Department of Land Records and Agriculture, 1893-94 to 1904-05 (Lahore, 1895-1905).

Report of the Famine of 1860-61 (Calcutta, 1861).
Report of the Indian Famine Commission, 1898, I (Simla, 1898).
Report of the Indian Cotton Committee, I-IV (Calcutta, 1920).
Report of the Indian Irrigation Commission, 1901-03, II and Appendix (Calcutta, 1903).
Report of the Indian Sugar Committee (Simla, 1921).
Report of the Punjab Provincial Banking Enquiry Committee, 1929-30, I-II (Lahore, 1930).
Report on the Administration of the Punjab, 1860 to 1902 (Lahore, 1861 to 1902).
Report on the Census of the Punjab, 1868.
Report on the Census of the Punjab, 1881, I-III.
Report on the Cotton Cultivation of the Punjab, 1870-71 to 1882-83.
Report on the Enquiry into the Rise of Prices in India, I, (Calcutta, 1915).
Report on the Famine in the Punjab during 1869-70 (Lahore, 1870).
Report on the Famine in the Punjab in 1896-97 (Lahore, 1898).
Report on the First Regular Wages Survey in the Punjab, taken in December 1912 (Lahore, 1913).
Report on the Internal Trade (and Manufactures) of the Punjab, 1879-80 to 1901 (Lahore, 1880-1902).
Report on Plague in the Punjab, 1901-02 (Lahore, 1904).
Report on the Season and Crops of the Punjab, 1901-02 to 1909-10 (Lahore, 1902-1910).
Revenue Report of the Irrigation Department, Punjab, 1874-75 to 1894-95 (Lahore, 1876-96).
Royal Commission on Agriculture in India, VIII, *Evidence taken in the Punjab* (Calcutta, 1927).
Sarhind Canal opened by H.E. The Marquis of Ripon (Lahore, 1882).

3. Selections from Official Records

Circular Orders issued by the Board of Administration in the Revenue Department during the years 1849 to 1853, I (Calcutta, 1856).
Punjab Government Records, I, *Records of the Delhi Residency and Agency, 1807-1857* (Lahore, 1911).

Punjab Government Records, II, *Records of the Ludhiana Agency, 1808-1815* (Lahore, 1911).

Punjab Government Records, III, *Lahore Political Diaries, 1847-1848, Political Diaries of the Agent to the Governor-General, North-West Frontier and Resident at Lahore* (Allahabad, 1909).

Punjab Government Records, IV, *Lahore Political Diaries, 1846-1849, Journals and Diaries of the Assistants to the Agent, Governor-General North-West Frontier and Resident at Lahore* (Allahabad, 1911).

Punjab Government Records, V, *Lahore Political Diaries, 1847-1849, Political Diaries of Lieut. H.B. Edwardes, Assistant to the Resident at Lahore* (Allahabad, 1911).

Punjab Government Records, VI, *Lahore Political Diaries, 1847-1849, Political Diaries of Lieutenant Reynell G. Taylor, Mr. P.S. Melvill, Pandil Kunahya Lal, Mr. P.A. Vans Agnew, Lieutenant J. Nicholson, Mr. L. Bowring and A.H. Cocks* (Allahabad, n.d.).

Selections from the Public Correspondence of the Punjab Administration, I-II (Lahore, 1852-55).

Seleetions from Punjab Native Papers, 1898-1902.

Selections from the Records of the Government of India, No. VI, (Foreign Department) General Report on the Administration of the Punjab Territories comprising the Punjab Proper and Cis and Trans-Sutlej States, for the years 1851-52 and 1852-53 (Calcutta, 1854).

Selections from the Records of the Government of India, No. XI, (Foreign Department) Report on the Census taken on the 1st January 1855 of the Population of the Punjab Territories (Calcutta, 1856).

Selections from the Records of the Government of India, No. XVIII, (Foreign Department) General Report on the Administration of the Punjab Teritories from 1854-55 to 1855-56 (Calcutta, 1856).

Selections from the Records of the Government of India, No. XLII, Public Works Department Correspondence Relating to the Deterioration of Lands from the Presence in the Soil of Reh (Calcutta, 1864).

Selections from the Records of the Government of India, No. XLVI, (Foreign Department) Report on the Settlement of the Peshawar District (Calcutta, 1865).

Selections from the Records of the Government of the Punjab and its Dependencies, New Series, No. III, Memorandum on the Beloch Tribes in Dera Ghazi Khan District (Lahore, 1869).

Selections from the Records of the Government of the Punjab and its Dependencies, New Series, No. VI, Sanitary Surveys of Villages Watered by the Western Jumna Canal (Lahore, 1870).

Selections from the Records of the Government of the Punjab and its Dependencies, New Series, No. IX, Notes on the Dera Ghazi Khan District, North-West Frontier and its Border Tribes (Lahore, 1871).

Selections from the Records of the Government of the Punjab and its Dependencies, New Series, No. XII, Report on Current Rates of Interest on Loan Transactions in the Punjab (Lahore, 1876).

Selections from the Records of the Government of the Punjab and its Dependencies, New Series, No. XIII Report on Papers Regarding Alienation of Estates of Insolvent Proprietors to the Money-lending Class (Lahore, 1876).

Selections from the Records of the Government of the Punjab and its Dependencies, New Series, No. XV, The Chohs of Hoshiarpur (Lahore, 1879).

Selections from the Records of the Government of the Punjab and its Dependencies, New Series, No. XVI, Note on the Revenue and Resources of the Punjab (Lahore, 1880).

Selections from the Records of the Government of the Punjab and its Dependencies, New Series, No. XVII, Notes on the System of Fluctuating Assessments in the Punjab (Lahore, 1880).

Selections from the Records of the Office of the Financial Commissioner, Punjab, New Series No. 8, No. 34, No. LXII, Papers Relating to Canals (Lahore, 1887).

Selections from the Records of the Office of the Financial Commissioner, Punjab, New Series, No. 11, No. 37, No. LXV, Papers on Indebtedness of Agriculturists in the Punjab and Foreclosure of Mortgages (Lahore, 1887).

Selections from the Records of the Office of the Financial Commissioner, Punjab, New Series No. 14, No. 40, No. LXVIII, Revision of Tenancy Entries in Mr. E. Prinsep's Settlements subsequent to the passing of Act XXVIII of 1868 (Lahore, 1889).

Selections from the Records of the Office of the Financial Commissioner, Punjab, New Series No. 24, No. 49, No. LXXVII, Memorandum by W.C. Renouf, Director of Agriculture, on the Wages Survey of the Punjab, taken in December 1909 (Lahore, 1910).

4. Settlement Reports (of a district or a part of district, years indicating their date of publications)

Ambala (*1859*, *1893* and *1921*).

Amritsar (*1873*, *1893* and *191*

Attock (*1905* and *1909*).

Bannu (*1879*).

Chenab Colony (*1915*).

Delhi (*1846*, *1882* and *1910*).

Dera Ghazi Khan (*1876* and *1898*).

Dera Ismail Khan (*1879*).

Ferozepore (*1859*, *1878*, *1884*, *1891*, *1892* and *1915*).

Gujranwala (*1871*, *1874*, *1894*, *1908*, *1914* and *1927*).

Gujrat (*1874*, *1893*, *1916* and *1929*).

Gurdaspur (*1859*, *1876*, *1892* and *1912*).

Gurgaon (*1884* and *1909*).

Hazara (*1876*).

Hissar (*1875*, *1892* and *1912*).

Hoshiarpur (*1852*, *1876*, *1885*, *1915* and *1916*).

Jhang (*1882* and *1907*).

Jhelum (*1883* and *1902*).

Jullundur (*1892* and *1918*).

Karnal (*1883* and *1912*).

Karnal-Ambala (*1891*).

Kohat (*1884*, *1889* and *1896*),

Lahore (*1860*, *1873*, *1894* and *1916*).

Ludhiana (*1859*, *1884* and *1912*).

Mianwali (*1908*).

Montgomery (*1878*, *1899* and *1925*).

Multan (*1901* and *1921*).
Muzaffargarh (*1882* and *1904*).
Peshawar (*1878* and *1898*).
Rawalpindi (*1865*, *1893* and *1909*).
Rohtak (*1880 and 1910*).
Shahpur (*1867*, *1894* and *1918*).
Sialkot (*1865*, *1895* and *1918*).
Sirsa (*1884* and *1905*).

5. Assessment Reports (of tahsils, years indicating their date of publications)

Amritsar (*1892*).
Charsadda (*1894*).
Dasuya (*1883*).
Dera Ghazi Khan (*1896*).
Dipalpur (*1897*).
Garshankar (*1884*).
Gohana (*1878*).
Gugera (*1894*).
Gurgaon (*1883*).
Gurdaspur (*1890*).
Gujrat (*1890*).
Hafizabad (*1893*).
Hansi, Hissar, Barnala and Fatehabad (*1890*).
Ilaka Mamdot (*1875*).
Jajjar (*1879*).
Jampur (*1896*).
Jullundur (*1883*).
Kaithal (*1888*).
Kasur (*1891*).
Kharian (*1892*).
Kushab (*1892*).
Lahore (*1893*).
Lodhran and Mailsi (*1900*).
Moga (*1887*)
Muktsar (*1890*).
Nakodar 1883).
Nawashahr (*1883*).
Pakpattan (*1897*).
Palwal (*1876*).
Pathankot (*1890*).

Pasrur (1893).
Peshawar and Nawshera (1897)
Phalia (1891).
Phillour (1883).
Rajanpur (1896).
Rohtak (1878).
Sampala (1879).
Shakargarh (1890).
Sharakpur (1893).
Tarn Taran (1891).
Zafarwal (1892)
Zira (1888).

6. Official and Semi-official Monographs

Arora, F.C., *Commerce by River in the Punjab or a Survey of the Activites of the Marine Department of the Government of the Punjab, 1861-62 to 1871-72* (Punjab Government Record Office Publications, Monograph No. 9, Lahore, 1930).

Bhalla, R.L., *An Economic Survey of Bairampur in the Hoshiarpur District* (The Board of Economic Enquiry, Punjab, Publication No. 1, Lahore, 1922).

Calvert, H.H., *The Size and Distribution of Agricultural Holdings in the Punjab* (The Board of Economic *Enquiry*, Punjab, Publication No. 4, Lahore, 1925).

Dass, Anchal & Calvert, H., *An Economic Survey of Tehong—a Village in the Jullundur District* (The Board of Economic Enquiry, Punjab, Village Surveys No. 3, Publication No. 18, Lahore, 1931).

Dass, Anchal & Strickland, C.F., *An Economic Survey of Gajju Chak—a Village in the Gujranwala District* (The Board of Economic Enquiry, Punjab, Village Surveys No. 6, Publication No. 31, Lahore, 1934).

Dayal, Shiv & Brayne, F.L., *An Economic Survey of Bhadas—a Village in the Gurgaon District* (The Board of Economic Enquiry, Punjab, Village Surveys No. 7, Publication No. 43, Lahore, 1936).

Fazal, Cyril P.K., *A Note on Sales of Land between the Notified Agricultural Tribes in the Punjab during the Quinquennium 1922-23 to 1926-27* (The Board of Economic Enquiry, Punjab, Publication No. 32, Lahore, 1931)

Hoey, William, *A Monograph on Trade and Manufactures in Northern India* (American Methodist Press, Lucknow, 1880).

Garrett, H.L.O. (tr. & ed.) *The Punjab—A Hundred Years Ago, as described by V. Jacquemont* (*1831*) & *A. Soltykoff 1842*) (Languages Department, Punjab, Patiala, 1971).

Grant, A.J., *Monograph on the Leather Industry in the Punjab, 1891-92* (Civil and Military Gazette Press, Lahore, 1893).

Khan, Abdur Rahim & Mohammad, Nur, *An Economic Survey of Bhambu Sandila—a Village in the Muzaffargarh District* (The Board of Economic Enquiry, Punjab, Village Surveys No. 8, Publication No. 45, Lahore, 1935).

Lucas, E.D., *The Economic Life of a Punjab Village* (Civil and Military Gazette Press, Lahore, n.d.).

Mahendru, I.D., *Some Factors Affecting the Price of Wheat in the Punjab* (The Board of Economic Enquiry, Punjab, Publication No. 49, Lahore, 1937).

Narain, Brij, *Eighty Years of Punjab Food Prices, 1841-1920* (The Board of Economic Enquiry, Punjab, Publication No. 13, Lahore, 1926).

Narain, Raj & Narain, Brij, *An Economic Survey of Gijhi—a Village in the Rohtak District* (The Board of Economic Enquiry, Punjab, Village Surveys No. 2, Publication No. 17, Lahore, 1932).

Rai, Gulshan, *Agricultural Statistics of the Punjab, 1901-2 to 1935-6* (The Board of Economic Enquiry, Punjab, Publication No. 49, Lahore, 1937).

Sarkar, K.M., *The Grand Trunk Road in the Punjab* (Languages Department, Punjab, Patiala, 19/1).

Seth, R.K., Ilahi, F., Emerson, H.W., & Moon, E.P., *An Economic Survey of Durrana Langana—a Village in the Multan District* (The Board of Economic Enquiry, Punjab, Village Surveys No. 11, Publication No. 54, Lahore, 1938).

Shah, F.A. & Dawar, L R., *Finance aud Marketing of Cultivators' Wheat—Being a Report of Investigation in the Lyallpur, Forezepore and Attock District of the Punjab during 1930-31* (The Board of Economic Enquiry, Punjab, Publication No. 38, Lahore, 1934).

Singh, Deva, *Colonization of the Rechna Doab* (Punjab Government Record Office Publications, Monograph No. 7, Lahore, n.d.).

Singh, S. Gian & King, C.M., *An Economic Survey of Gaggar Bhana—a Village in the Amritsar District* (The Board of Economic Enquiry, Punjab, Village Surveys No. 1, Publication No. 16, Lahore, 1928).

Singh, Randhir & Roberts, W., *An Economic Survey of Kala Gaddi Thamman (Chak 73 G.B.)—a Village in the Lyallpur District* (The Board of Economic Enquiry, Punjab, Village Surveys No. 4, Publication No. 27, Lahore, 1932).

Singh, Sher & Fyson, H., *An Economic Survey of Naggal—a Village in the Ambala District* (The Board of Economic Enquiry, Punjab, Village Surveys No. 5, Publication No. 30, Lahore, 1933).

SECONDARY SOURCES

1. Works by the British and Indian Officials

Ali, Sahamat, *The Sikhs and Afghans* (Languages Department, Punjab, Patiala, 1970).

Baden-Powell, B.H., *The Indian Village Community* (Cosmo Publications, Delhi, 1972).

——*The Land Systems of British India*, II (Clarendon Press, Oxford, 1892).

——*Hand Book of the Economic Products of the Punjab*, I (T.C.E. College Press, Roorkee, 1869).

Bingley, A.H., *Sikhs* (Languages Department, Punjab, Patiala, 1970).

Buckley, Robert B., *The Irrigation Works of India and their Financial Results* (W.H. Allen & Co., London, 1880).

Burkely, D.G., (ed.) *The Non-Regulation Laws of the Punjab* (Punjab Printing Company, Lahore, 1871).

Calvert, H.H., *The Wealth and Welfare of the Punjab: Being Some Studies in Punjab Rural Economics* (Civil and Military Gazette Press, Lahore, 1922).

Campbell, Sir George, *Memoirs of My Indian Career*, I-II (Macmillan & Co., London, 1893).

Cunningham, Joseph D., *A History of the Sikhs* (S. Chand & Co., Delhi, 1966),

Darling, Malcolm Lyall, *Rusticus Loquitor or The Old Light and the New in the Punjab Village* (Oxford University Press, London, 1930).

——*Wisdom and Waste in the Punjab Village* (Oxford University Press, London, 1934).

——*The Punjab Peasant in Prosperity and Debt* (Manohar Book Service, New Delhi, 1977).

Douie, Sir James, *Punjab Setttlement Manual* (Superintendent, Government Printing, Lahore, 1930).

——*Punjab Land Administration Manual* (Superintendent, Government Printing, Lahore, 1931).

Edwardes, Major Herbert B., *A Year on the Punjab Frontier in 1848-49*, I-II (Languages Department, Punjab, Patiala, 1971).

Elphinstone, Mountstuart, *An Account of the Kingdom of Caubul*, I (Oxford University Press, Karachi, 1972).

Grey, C., *European Adventurers of Northern India, 1785 to 1849* (Languages Department, Punjab, Patiala, 1970)

Griffin, Lepel H., *Ranjit Singh* (Kitab Mahal, Allahabad, 1967).

——*The Rajas of the Punjab* (Languages Department, Punjab, Patiala, 1970).

Ibbetson, Sir Denzil, *Panjab Castes: Being a reprint of the Chapter on the 'Races, Castes and Tribes of the People' in the Report on the Census of the Panjab published in 1883 by the Late Sir Denzil Ibbetson, K.C.S.I.* (Languages Department, Punjab, Patiala, 1970).

Lal, Mohan, *Travels in the Punjab Afghanistan and Turkistan* (Languages Department, Punjab, Patiala, 1971).

Lawrence, H.M.L., *Adventures of an Officer in the Punjab*, I-II (Languages Department, Punjab, Patiala, 1970).

Leitner, G.W., *History of Indigenous Education in the Punjab* (Languages Department Punjab, Patiala, 1971).

O'Dwyer, Sir, M., *India As I Knew it 1885-1925* (Constable & Co., London, 1925).

Prinsep, Henry T., *Origin of the Sikh Power in the Punjab and Political Life of Maharaja Ranjit Singh* (Languages Department, Punjab, Patiala, 1970).

Roberts, W. & Faulkner, O.T., *A Text Book of Punjab Agriculture* (Civil and Military Gazettee Press, Lahore, 1921).

Rose, H.A., *A Glossary of the Tribes and Castes of the Punjab and North Western Frontier Province of India*, I-III (Languages Department, Punjab, Patiala, 1970).

Ross, David, *The Land of the Five Rivers and Sind* (Languages Department, Punjab, Patiala, 1970).

Royle, J. Forbes, *Review of the Measures which have been adopted in India for the Improved Culture of Cotton* (Smith, Elder & Co., London, 1857).

Lieut.-Colonel Steinbach, *The Punjaub* (Languages Department, Punjab, Patiala, 1970).

Temple, Sir Richard, *James Thomason* (Oxford University Press, 1893).

Thorburn, S.S., *Musalmans and Money-lenders in the Punjab* (William Blackwood & Sons, Edinburg, 1886).

——*The Punjab in Peace and War* (Languages Department, Punjab, Patiala, 1970).

Trevaskis, Hugh Kennedy, *The Land of the Five Rivers : An Economic History of the Punjab From the Earliest Times to the Year of Grace, 1890* (Oxford University Press, 1928).

Tupper, C. L., *Punjab Customary Laws*, I-III (Superintendent of Government Printing, Calcutta, 1881).

2. Other Works: Books

Bailey, F.G., *Caste and the Economic Frontier* (Manchester University Press, 1957).

Banga, Indu, *Agrarian System of the Sikhs* (Manohar Book Service, New Delhi, 1978).

Barrier, Norman G., *The Punjab Alienation of Land Bill of 1900* (Duke University, Durham, N.C., 1966).

Blyn, George, *Agricultural Trends in India, 1891-1947: Output Availability and Productivity* (University of Pennsylvania Press, Philadelphia, 1966).

Chaudhuri, B.B., *Growth of Commercial Agriculture, 1757-1900*, I (Indian Studies, Calcutta, 1964).

Chaudhuri, K.N. & Dewy, Clive J., (eds.) *Economy and Society: Essays in Indian Economic and Social History* (Oxford University Press, New Delhi, 1979).

Chhabra, G.S., *Social and Economic History of the Punjab, 1849-1901* (S. Nagin & Co., Jullundur, 1962).

Dungen, P.H.M. van den, *The Punjab Tradition: Influence and Authority in Nineteenth Century India* (George Allen & Unwin, London, 1972).

Epstein, T.S., *Economic Development and Social Change in South India* (Manchester University Press, 1972).

Grewal, J.S., (tr. & ed.) *In the By-Lanes of History: Some Persian Documents from a Punjab Town* (Indian Institute of Advanced Study, Simla, 1969).

Grewal, J.S. and Banga, Indu, (trs. & eds.), *Early Nineteenth Century Panjab* (Guru Nanak Dev University, Amritsar, 1975).

Gupta, Hari Ram, (ed.) *Punjab on the Eve of the First Sikh War: A Documentary Study of the Political, Social and Economic Conditions of the Panjab as depicted in the daily letters written chiefly from Lahore by British Intelligencers during the period from 30 December 1843 to 31 October 1844* (Punjab University, Chandigarh, 1975).

Gupta, Sulekh C., *Agrarian Relations and Early British Rule in India* (Asia Publishing House, Bombay, 1963).

Gustafson, W. Eric & Jones, Kenneth W., (eds.) *Sources on Punjab History* (Manohar Book Service, New Delhi, 1975).

Habib, I., *The Agrarian System of Mughal India.* (Asia Publishing House, Bombay, 1963.)

Hamilton, W., *A Geographical, Statsitical and Historical Description of the Hindostan and the Adjacent Countries,* I-II (John Murray & Co., London, 1820).

Kessinger, Tom G., *Vilyatpur 1848-1968: Social and Economic Change in a North Indian Village* (University of California Press, 1974).

Kumar, Dharma, *Land and Caste in South India* (Cambridge University Press, 1965).

Kumar, Ravinder, *Western India in the Nineteenth Century: A Study in the Social History of Maharashtra* (Routledge and Kegan Paul, London, 1968).

Leaf, Marry J., *Information and Behaviour in a Sikh Village: A Social Organization Reconstructed* (University of California Press, 1972).

Low, D.A., (ed.) *Soundings in Modern South Asian History* (Weidenfeld and Nicholson, London, 1968).

Metcalf, Thomas R., *The Aftermath of Revolt, 1857-1870* (Princeton University Press, 1964).

——*Land, Landlords and the British Raj* (Oxford University Press, New Delhi, 1979).

Neale, Walter C., *Economic Change in Rural India: Land Tenure and Reform in Uttar Pradesh, 1800-1955* (Yale University Press, New Haven, 1962).

Patel, Surendra J., *Agricultural Labourers in Modern India and Pakistan* (Current Book House, Bombay, 1952).

Paustian, Paul W., *Canal Irrigation in the Punjab* (Columbia University Press, New York, 1930).

Raj, Jagdish, *The Mutiny and British Land Policy in North India, 1856-1868* (Asia Publishing House, Bombay, 1965).

Sen, Sunil, *Agrarian Relations in India, 1793-1947* (People's Publishing House, New Delhi, 1979).

Siddiqi, M.H., *Agrarian Unrest in North India: The United Provinces, 1918-22* (Vikas, New Delhi, 1978).

Singh, Harbans & N. Gerald Barrier, (eds.) *Essays in Honour of Dr Ganda Singh* (Punjabi University, Patiala, 1976).

Singh, Teja & Singh, Ganda, (eds.) *Maharaja Ranjit Singh First Death Centenary Memorial* (Languages Department, Punjab, Patiala, 1970).

Sinha, N.K., *Ranjit Singh* (A. Mukherjee & Co., Calcutta, 1968).

Smith, R. Bosworth, *Life of Lord Lawrence*, I-II (Elder & Co., London, 1883).

Spate, O.H.K. & Learmonth, A.T.A., *India and Pakistan* (Methuen & Co., London, 1967).

Spear, Percival, *Twilights of the Mughals* (Cambridge University Press, 1951).

Stokes, Eric, *The Peasant and The Raj* (Vikas, New Delhi, 1978).

Tandon, Prakash, *Panjabi Century, 1857-1957* (Orient Paperback, New Delhi, 1961).

Thorner, Daniel & Alice, *Land and Labour in India* (Asia Publishing House, London, 1962).

Whitcombe, E., *Agrarian Conditions in Northern India*, I, *The United Provinces under British Rule, 1860-1900* (Thompson Press, New Delhi, 1971).

4. Articles

Barnes, Alexander, 'Political, Geographical and Commercial Report sand Papers [1835-37]', *The Panjab Past and Present*, XII, Part I, April 1978, 29-102.

Barrier, Norman G., 'The Formulation and Enactment of the Punjab Alienation of Land Bill', *The Indian Economic and Social History Review*, II, No. 2, April 1965, 145-65.

——'The Arya Samaj and Congress Politics in the Punjab, 1894-1908', *The Journal of Asian Studies*, XXVI, No. 3, May 1967, 363-79.

——'The Punjab Disturbances of 1907: the response of the British Government in India to Agrarian Unrest', *The Panjab Past and Present*, VIII, Part II, October 1974, 444-76.

——'The Punjab Government and Communal Politics, 1870-1908', *The Journal of Asian Studies*, XXVII, No. 3, May 1968, 523-39.

Chandra, Bipan, 'Reinterpretation of Nineteenth Century Indian Economic History', *The Indian Economic and Social History Review*, V, No. 1, March 1968, 35-75.

Chaudhuri, B.B., 'Rural Credit Relations in Bengal, 1858-1885', *The Indian Economic and Social History Review*, VI, No. 3, Septemder 1969, 203-57.

Dewey, Clive J., 'Annals of Rural Punjab', *Modern Asian Studies*, X, Part I, June 1976, 131-8.

Gopal, Jai, 'The Tenants and The Punjab Tenancy Act of 1887', *Proceedings of the Punjab History Conference*, Ninth Session, April 1975, 157-67.

Habib, Irfan, 'Evidence for Sixteenth-Century Agrarian Conditions in the Guru Granth Sahib', *The Indian Economic and Social History Review*, I, No. 3, March 1964, 64-72.

Hambly, G.R.G., 'Richard Temple and the Punjab Tenancy Act of 1868', *The English Historical Review*, LXXIX, No. CCCX, January 1964, 47-66.

Kohli, Sita Ram, 'Land Revenue Administration under Maharaja Ranjit Singh', *The Panjab Past and Present*, V, Part II, October 1971, 435-53.

Mathur, Y.B., Revenue and Financial Administration of the Punjab, 1849-1875', *Journal of Indian History*, XLV, Part III, December 1967, 696-726.

Matsui, Toru, 'On the Nineteenth-Century Indian Economic History—A Review of a "Reinterpretation" ', *The Indian Economic and Social Review*, V, No. 1, March 1968, 17-33.

McLane, John R., 'Peasants, Money-lenders and Nationalists at the end of the Nineteenth Century', *The Indian Economic and Social History Review*, I, No. 1, July 1963, 66-73.

Metcalf, Thomas R., 'The Struggle Over Land Tenure in India 1860-1868', *The Journal of Asian Studies*, XXI, No. 3, May 1962, 295-307.

Morris, Morris D., 'Towards a Reinterpretation of Nineteenth-Century Indian Economic History', *The Indian Economic and Social History Review*, V, No. 1, March 1968, 1-15.

——Trends and Tendencies in Indian Economic History', *The Indian Economic and Social History Review*, V, No. 4, December 1968, 319-88.

——'Economic Change and Agriculture in Nineteenth Century India', *The Indian Economic and Social History Review*, III, No. 2, June 1966, 191-206.

Mukherjee, K., 'Land Prices in the Punjab', M.K. Chaudhuri (ed.) *Trends of Socio-Economic Change in India, 1871-1961* (Indian Institute of Advanced Study, Simla, 1969), 529-44.

Naidis, M., 'John Lawrence and the Origins of the Punjab System, 1849-57', *Bengal Past and Present*, LXXX, No. 1, 1961, 38-46.

Prabha, Chander, 'District-wise Rates of Growth of Agricultural Output in East and West Punjab during the Pre-Partition and Post-Partition Periods', *The Indian Economic and Social History Review*, VI, No. 4, December 1969, 333-50.

Raychaudhuri, T., 'A Re-interpretation of Nineteenth Century Indian Economic History?', *The Indian Economic and Social Hisotry Review*, V, No. 1, March 1968, 77-100.

Saberwal, S., 'Status and Entrepreneurship: The Ramgharia Case', M.N. Srinivas, S. Seshaiah and V.S. Parthasarathy, (eds)., *Dimensions of Social Change in India* (Allied Publishers, New Delhi, 1977), 158-67.

Singh, Indera P., 'A Sikh Village', Milton Singer, (ed.), *Traditional India* (The American Folklore Society, Philadelphia, 1959), 273-97.

Index